David McKittrick and Eamonn Mallie, two of the most respected writers on Irish affairs, have been granted unique access to the research undertaken for the television series *Endgame in Ireland*. This book, as in the television series, tells more vividly than ever before the inside story of the Irish peace process from 1981 through the words of the key people involved – many of whom have never talked 'on the record'. Those interviewed include both British and Irish prime ministers and their most senior aides, including former cabinet secretaries. They also include former leaders of both the IRA and loyalist terrorist groups.

'In common with all the best history, *Endgame in Ireland* alternates anecdote with revelation.'
Guardian

'Intelligent, gripping . . . chock full of anecdotal, human detail and insights into the operations of power, it's utterly fascinating.'
Time Out

'The most intimate examination yet of the extraordinary tortuous quest for peace in Northern Ireland.'
Daily Telegraph

'You feel as if you're eavesdropping on history as it's being made – wholly absorbing.'
Irish Independent

'A fine example of contemporary history.'
Economist

The television series *Endgame in Ireland* is a Brook Lapping Production for the BBC, RTE and PBS.

*Eamonn Mallie and
David McKittrick*

Endgame in Ireland

CORONET BOOKS
LIR
Hodder & Stoughton

Copyright © 2001 by Eamonn Mallie, David McKittrick,
and Brook Lapping Productions Limited
Preface copyright © 2001 Norma Percy

First published in Great Britain in 2001
by Hodder and Stoughton
A division of Hodder Headline
First published as a Coronet Lir paperback in 2002

The right of Eamonn Mallie and David McKittrick to be identified
as the Authors of the Work has been asserted by them in
accordance with the Copyright, Designs and Patents Act 1988.

A Coronet Lir paperback

1 3 5 7 9 10 8 6 4 2

A CIP catalogue record for this title
is available from the British Library

ISBN 0 340 82169 8

Typeset in Monotype Sabon by
Rowland Phototypesetting Ltd,
Bury St Edmunds, Suffolk
Printed and bound in Great Britain by
Mackays of Chatham plc, Chatham, Kent

Hodder and Stoughton
A division of Hodder Headline
338 Euston Road
London NW1 3BH

Contents

Putting History on Television
Norma Percy, Series Producer

The series *Endgame in Ireland*, first broadcast in Britain and Ireland in July 2001, arose from a guilty feeling that having done *The Death of Yugoslavia*, *The Second Russian Revolution*, *Watergate*, *The 50 Years War: Israel and the Arabs* – that is, having dissected the politics of other people's conflicts – it was time to examine our own.

Since 1988 when Brian Lapping left Granada television to set up an independent company, all the history series we made together set out to make viewers feel what it was like to be *there* when certain big political decisions were made. These decisions are taken by a few people – in private. We would never be allowed to film them being made. By their nature such meetings are secret and their very existence often only known to those present. What we do is ask the people who made the decisions – as far as possible *all* the people involved in making them – to tell us afterwards what they said and did.

But it is a method with a problem. If the key decision makers are too busy to talk, or won't talk because they are afraid it will upset delicate negotiations, or are just plain frightened to speak – we are stuck.

We have found that the main participants are most likely to speak freely just after the story has reached an end point. Then they can be coaxed to reminisce about their own role in the completed jigsaw puzzle.

So 1998 seemed the right time to tackle Ireland. When

Mark Thompson, then controller of BBC2, commissioned the series in the wake of the Good Friday Agreement, it looked as though Northern Ireland's troubles were finally over.

That August we planned our first trip to Belfast to consult, as any sensible seeker of the inside story of Northern Ireland's politics must, David McKittrick and Eamonn Mallie. We had learned the basics from David's lucid pieces in the *Independent* and seen Eamonn and his omnipresent microphone in there at every big news event. What's more, they were the authors of the *The Fight for Peace,* the book that first lifted the veil of the peace negotiations. (While we never put journalists or commentators on camera, we always begin with tutorials from the acknowledged experts.)

However, the weekend before our visit, a bomb planted by the Real IRA killed twenty-nine people in the market town of Omagh. And each of our subsequent visits seemed to coincide with a fresh crisis. The main research trip to Belfast in February 2000 began during the frantic weeks of negotiation that led up to Peter Mandelson's suspension of the new Northern Ireland executive.

The team had no choice but to plough on. Producer/directors Mark Anderson and Mick Gold and I tackled the great and the good; the associate producers, David Alter and Nava Mizrahi, immersed themselves in the intricacies of the loyalist paramilitaries and republican movement. But all the main players, high and low, were preoccupied with making politics.

It was a real problem. Our programmes recreate particular events with unique witnesses. For us, only Ulster Unionist leader David Trimble could tell us why his meeting with Martin McGuinness – called to save the Northern

Ireland executive – went so badly wrong. And why, immediately afterwards, he told Mandelson that he must honour his promise to suspend the executive – or else. But the story wasn't over yet.

Only Prime Minister John Major and Taoiseach Albert Reynolds could express the exasperation that each felt at their tête-à-tête in Dublin Castle in December 1993. Their Joint Declaration negotiations were on the rocks – and each blamed the other. We needed to be able to film them both to show how their mutual affection got them around the impasse.

Most difficult of all: we needed Prime Minister Tony Blair and Taoiseach Bertie Ahern to describe their management of the all-night sessions which created the Good Friday Agreement – and the decommissioning crises that followed. With both still in office, and still struggling with Northern Ireland, they didn't manage to schedule their interviews until three days after our 'absolutely final' deadline.

It wasn't just politicians we had to coax in front of the cameras. Although there were many witnesses to the carnage as Michael Stone tried to assassinate Gerry Adams and Martin McGuinness at Milltown cemetery in March 1988, only Stone himself could tell why and how he did it.

We have some advantages. A television history has a wider audience than a scholarly book, so politicians are more willing to find us some time. Our sort of television, which relies as far as possible on the participants' on-screen accounts, gives witnesses more protection against misquotation than a briefing to a print journalist.

But our biggest advantage is time. With two years to research and film, to immerse ourselves in the details of the story, we can refine our questions, build up a relationship with the material – and with the main participants. The extra months which the broadcasters give us allow me time to write the sixth or seventh letter to a reluctant participant – and for the persuasive team: David, Nava, and researcher Daniel Edge to make dozens more phone calls.

Our relationship with the republican movement was a case in point. On 21 January 1999 Brian Lapping, David Alter and I were summoned to the border town of Dundalk in the Irish Republic. In a bare hotel function room we put our case before Sinn Fein's publicity committee. (We understand they were not impressed.) It was not until we had gone through a further twenty-three months of letters, phone calls and inquisitions, that our first interview with a Sinn Fein witness, the party leader Gerry Adams, took place. That was just before Christmas 2000. Our first three-hour session with Martin McGuinness was in January 2001; we didn't get the third and final session with the busy minister until April.

The best interviewees don't just rely on fading memories. The Irish prime ministers and their officials really did their homework. The British star was John Major, who at our first meeting pointed to a large table in the corner of his Commons office: 'Last night I had it entirely covered with notes and official documents. It took me four hours to go through them and I only got through half your questions – you will have to come back.' And so, in five sessions stretching over six months, come back we did.

So, did we discover much that was new? Well, it depends on how you look at things. What we did is present the evidence – from the horse's mouth. And many of those mouths have never been opened on television before.

For example, Father Alex Reid from Clonard monastery. Many thought of him as the unseen 'Holy Ghost', the go-between who helped the peace process to happen. But since discretion was his stock in trade, no one knew quite what he did. In his first detailed interview – a coup for David Alter and Nava Mizrahi on their last day on the project – Father Reid told us how he had got the peace process going when he asked SDLP leader John Hume to take on the job of bringing the republican movement in from the cold.

Or the story of the secret 'back-channel' between John Major's government and the IRA, the group they denounced as terrorists. Eamonn Mallie revealed this secret link on the front page of the *Observer* on 28 November 1993. But no one knew quite how it worked, and only three people knew the truth about the message, one of the most important in Irish history, which emerged from that channel: 'The conflict is over but we need your help to bring it to an end.'

The British insisted that their contacts with the IRA only began when they received this message from Martin McGuinness. Sinn Fein insisted he never sent it. Each accused the other side of lying – and continue to do so until today.

But Denis Bradley, and his two colleagues in 'the link', solved the mystery – and also revealed another unsung hero of the peace process, an MI5 agent known as Fred. (For the whole story see Chapters 5 and 6.) We have one regret – we never found him.

We are asked what it's like to do the interviews. Well,

there was only one so singular that Dan and I felt we had
to write it down.

* * *

Our BBC executive producer, Alex Holmes, said firmly,
'It won't be definitive without him'. But after nine
months of trying, we were beginning to despair. On the
Friday before our deadline, the call finally came: 'It's
the office of William Jefferson Clinton: we've found forty
minutes. Can you be at his home in Chappaqua on
Tuesday?'

A frantic few days followed: first, exactly where were
we going? Until the Harlem premises were ready, his staff
were working out of his Washington DC house, and they
weren't too certain about the geography of New York's
Westchester suburbs.

Somehow all was arranged, and three days later we were
handing over our passports at the gate. All our twenty-one
pieces of equipment were searched by a burly man with
– of course – regulation blue blazer, aviator shades,
walkie-talkie and gun bulge. Six others, more or less
identical, stood by. None of them smiled. The neighbour-
hood was silent and still – you wondered if the CIA had
bought all the properties within rifle range.

Through the open study door we saw a pair of massive,
shabby tennis shoes resting on a desk; attached to them
were some loose denim jeans and a turquoise golf shirt,
topped by a very familiar face.

Over his desk hung stars and stripes, and delightfully
tacky embroidery with the legend 'Hillary'. The in-
tellectual content of the study was impressive: serious
books didn't just line the walls but were piled everywhere
and many were in the middle of being read. An opened
and marked copy of Anthony Giddens' *The Third*

Way peeked out from that week's *New York Review of Books*.

Clinton paid us no heed and made call after call. Even if he was just arranging rounds of golf, he *seemed* to be solving a succession of international crises. The quiet was only punctuated by his booming laugh. Hillary was away on senatorial duties.

Now the President was expounding to someone on the telephone about how 'the IRA lost it for us'. Now this was news: *EX-PRESIDENT BLAMES IRA FOR ELECTION LOSS*. But as we bustled about pretending not to listen, it soon became clear he meant the NRA. The National Rifle Association.

As we set up lights, Clinton disappeared to change. He reappeared pristine in dark blue suit, switched on to the task at hand, eyes darting around, taking each of us in. The camera rolled, and the interview started with Bernadette Devlin's 1969 by-election victory. Was it this that turned him on to the Irish question?

'Sure, I remember Bernadette. It was my second term at Oxford. I thought she was really something – that maiden speech! The fact that a twenty-one-year-old woman got herself elected to Parliament . . .' I mentioned that I too had been an American student in London then. There was no reaction, but talking after the interview he suddenly turned to me: 'You mean you came to England when I did – back then – and you have been there all this time?' A politician who listens!

Usually before filming we cover the ground first with a long research interview to prime the subject's memory – no such luxury with the President. And our fifteen-page brief had not reached him. So when we asked about the White House meeting to decide whether to grant a US visa to Gerry Adams, we braced ourselves for the reply we most dread: 'Oh, there were so many meetings . . .'

I began: 'Remember, it was a Saturday afternoon, and you just had lunch with Helmut Kohl. . . .' Clinton took the ball and ran with it: 'Yeah. Kohl loves to eat – and so do I – so we'd had a big time; and I thought: "Now . . . indigestion. . . ." The State Department was dead against the visa, the career people thought it would be devastating to our special relationship with Great Britain and we needed their help in Bosnia . . .' It was impressive. Here he was dealing with Ireland as an afterthought to the problems of reunifying Germany and he could remember the intricacies of every move.

With Clinton in full flow, the cameraman signalled it was time to change tapes. This is always an awkward moment: you don't want to talk about the substance of the interview in case he says his best stuff off camera, and small talk always dries up. We asked about the handwritten line of Seamus Heaney's poetry framed in his study: 'It was a fortunate wind that blew you here.'

And he was off again. We were treated to a spectacular digression on the Greek myth of Philoctetes on which Heaney's poem is based:

Philoctetes is a member of the Greek expedition to rescue Helen from Troy. But on the journey, his foot is horribly wounded and he drives his comrades crazy with his festering sores and cries of pain. So Odysseus abandons him on a deserted island. But – he has this magic bow, okay? (Clinton paused dramatically.)

So – the war against the Trojans goes badly for ten long years. Then the Gods pronounce that Troy will only be taken with the help of Philoctetes' bow. Well, Odysseus is afraid to approach him so he sends Achilles' son. But Philoctetes works out that this kid's running a scam. So Odysseus has to confront the guy himself, tell him: 'Look, I'm sorry I left you, we can't win the war without you, *please* come back,' – and he says: 'Yes.'

As Philoctetes is riding off, there are these wonderful lines on hope and history rhyming, and he looks back at this piece of rock he's been stuck on for ten years and says, 'It was a fortunate wind that blew me here.'

Dan, only two years past an Oxford classics degree, was open mouthed. Not only did Clinton tell it as if it had happened to him, he was word perfect in every detail. It's not clear whether the President sees it as an allegory for his life or for Northern Ireland. Or both.

'The lines are stunning,' he enthused, 'Seamus Heaney wrote them out and sent them to me on my first trip to Ireland.'

'About that trip,' I said, realising we were well past our forty minutes, and hadn't even reached the negotiations for the Good Friday Agreement.

Our problem about the President's pilgrimage to Northern Ireland was that the news film of masses of people out on the streets was spectacular but everyone we asked about it had just come up with platitudes. Could he say something surprising? 'They all came out together, both Protestants and Catholics, to light the Christmas tree and hear me speak – but you see, it was *dark* – and nobody really knew who was there.' Northern Ireland's tentative peace process in a nutshell.

But what he was best at was describing each of the Northern Ireland adversaries' bottom lines – and more persuasively than they could themselves. That's what

9

made him such a good negotiator. (For his unorthodox argument to Gerry Adams in favour of the principle of consent, see Chapter 15, pages 276–7.)

An hour and a half later, as the crew packed up, he showed us round the study – clutching a Diet Coke and fiddling with his eclectic CD collection. Still researching my last series but one, I asked about President Assad of Syria. 'One of the cleverest. I kick myself that I didn't start negotiating with him earlier. By the time we got down to it he knew he was dying – he was afraid to upset the Baathists and ruin his son's succession.' Arafat? 'What a deal he had! Abba Eban said it: "The Palestinians never miss an opportunity to miss an opportunity".' Clinton sighed. Clearly he still wakes up in the middle of the night reliving his attempt to broker a peace deal at Camp David. He called himself 'a complete failure' for not having pulled it off.

It seems certain that Bill Clinton's international peace-making days are not over. But for the moment he cheer-fully accepted his role as Hillary's 'First Man' – that night he was going into the City to stand in for her at, as it happens, an Irish fundraising dinner.

As we flew back to London we puzzled over what had motivated the leader of the Western world to spend so much of his time trying to settle the problems of one small province with a population of 1.5 million.

And Clinton was not the only head of government to do so. Irish Prime Ministers Garret FitzGerald and Albert Reynolds could have left it to their foreign ministers. John Major's Home Secretary, Kenneth Clarke, advised him to think twice before getting involved with an unorthodox route to a Northern Ireland peace. Major thought again – but went ahead anyway. Tony Blair and Bertie Ahern spent much of the week before the summer recess closeted in a Shropshire country house trying to save the Northern Ireland's Executive again. Of course they would get a lot of credit if they pulled off a really final peace settlement. But it's something more than that. Whatever it is, it makes quite a story.

Norma Percy
London, 7 September 2001

Introduction

Although we are the authors of this book, both the inspiration and a great deal of the perspiration behind it came from Norma Percy, Brian Lapping and their team at Brook Lapping Productions. They first conceived the idea of a television series on the Northern Ireland troubles, made to the highest production values, with key players each telling their own stories of how the troubles came to enter their endgame. This resulted in the *Endgame in Ireland* series, which was broadcast, to widespread acclaim, by both BBC and RTE in June and July 2001. In 1998 Norma had approached us, and others, to discuss the project and we had had some input into it.

We were aware of Brook Lapping's international reputation, but as the months passed we watched with amazement as Norma and her team achieved the seemingly impossible by gaining access to the highest in the land, and indeed some of the lowest also. They conducted lengthy interviews with more than 70 key players, distilling their comments and revelations into the best TV series on Northern Ireland we have ever seen.

The material was of such high quality that we felt strongly that it should be used in a book. We knew from experience that in television a great deal is inevitably left on the cutting-room floor, and it was agreed with Brook Lapping that we should sift through their raw material. We knew their researches and interviews were exhaustive, but we had not realised just how much they had amassed. The team did the deepest research into the troubles and the part played in key events by individuals. These were then grilled for hours in exhaustive television interviews, which took well over a year to film. Next, the interviews were carefully transcribed for the programme-makers to pore over and isolate key quotations.

When this material was transmitted to us it choked up our e-mail systems and seized up our computers with its sheer volume. We found, for example, that the interviews with David Trimble produced 25,000 transcribed words, John Hume 23,000, Albert Reynolds 35,000, John Major 30,000 and Gerry Adams 46,000. In all, the material amounted to around one million words, a staggering amount. On reflection, it helped explain the sheer quality of the series, given that so much thought, time and trouble had gone into the project. Only a fraction of all that could be used in the television series. We have been able to use more in this book.

At times the sheer volume threatened to overwhelm us. The fact that it did not is due in large part to the skills of our friend David McVea, author and researcher, who applied to this project his formidable abilities to collate and organise, sort out the computers and generally impart a sense of calm and competence. We are much in his debt.

In putting together this text we have included as many as possible of the nuggets uncovered by Brook Lapping. In maintaining the narrative we have also drawn on our own material, in particular our previous work, *The Fight for Peace*. We wish to thank Heinemann for their kind permission to draw on its text.

Due to its origins, the structure of the book is episodic rather than in the form of a continuous detailed narrative, with various episodes touched on only sketchily. Fuller versions of many incidents and developments are to be found in *The Fight for Peace*, in *Making Sense of the Troubles* by David McVea and David McKittrick, and in *Lost Lives* by Seamus Kelters, Chris Thornton, Brian Feeney, David McVea and David McKittrick.

Particular thanks to the team who conducted the interviews: series producer Norma Percy, producer-directors Mark Anderson and Mick Gold, associate producer Nava Mizrahi, researcher Dan Edge and, most particularly, associate producer David Alter, who built up a mastery of the intricacies of Irish politics.

Our thanks must also go to Pacemaker Press of Belfast for the photographs used in this book. Many of them are the work of the agency's owner, Marty Wright, who died at a tragically young age in July 2001. We are grateful too for the secretarial skills of Kathryn Bell. Most of all, we thank our families for their forbearance.

Eamonn Mallie and David McKittrick

Belfast,
2001

I
The Brighton bomb
———

'The air was full of cement, cement and dust. You know, it was grit in your teeth,' Margaret Thatcher remembers of the immediate aftermath of the explosion which the IRA hoped would assassinate her and most of her cabinet in 1984. 'But I have remained forever grateful that the lights were on, on our floor and as we went down,' she adds.

The bomb which sent the cement and dust flying killed five people and wrecked much of Brighton's Grand Hotel. It represented a lethal republican strike against the heart of the British establishment. Yet within a few years the Thatcher government would be secretly in contact with the IRA (Irish Republican Army) as part of Ireland's extra-ordinary peace process. And less than two decades later, the man who planted the bomb would argue that it was a necessary episode in that process. But in the wake of the explosion on 12 October 1984 there was no thought of the future: all thoughts were focused on who had died and who had survived, and who might be injured and trapped beneath the mounds of rubble that had generated the cement and dust.

When the bomb went off at 2.54 a.m. most of the hotel's occupants were asleep, but Thatcher was working in the sitting room of her first-floor suite. She and her staff and advisers had just finished the speech she was to deliver to the Conservative party conference later that day, and the final version was being typed in the next room. She was joined by her private secretary, Robin Butler, who years later as Cabinet Secretary was to play an important part in the Irish peace process. Despite the late hour, he had brought her a memo, which, for some reason, Number 10 felt required urgent attention: it was a paper from Michael Heseltine about what would happen to the Liverpool Garden site after the Garden Festival.

Butler takes up the story:

Actually, by past standards it was quite an early hour for her to have finished. I said to her, 'Could you look at this overnight, and give me an answer at breakfast?' And she said, 'Well if you wouldn't mind I'd much rather do it now, and then I can forget about it and concentrate on the speech.' So we were sitting in her sitting room in the Grand Hotel; she was reading this minute; and I wasn't doing anything except thinking how nice it would be to be in bed in about five minutes' time, and I was woozy. And there was suddenly this great explosion.

As Thatcher recalls events, 'I looked at the papers very quickly and decided, and just as I handed them back to him there was this loud blast.' At the time no one knew it in the confusion, but the IRA bomb had blown out the front wall of the hotel, causing some floors to cascade down, destroying the roof and bringing down a large chimney-stack. The rubble fell to the basement, filling it and the two floors above.

The device that did such damage had been planted almost a month earlier by Belfast IRA member Patrick Magee and another republican. They had stayed in room 629, checking in on 15 September and leaving on the 18th. He signed the register as Roy Walsh, giving a false address in London. During their stay the pair carefully concealed a bomb containing up to 30 lb of explosives in room 629's bathroom. The device had a long-term timer which set it off at 2.54 a.m., the intention clearly being to kill as many as possible of the hotel residents, many of whom were attending the annual Tory conference in the seaside town.

As the initial shock wave subsided, Butler and Thatcher looked at each other. He recalls:

My first thought was that it was a car bomb outside the hotel, and so I said to her, 'You'd better come away from the windows,' and we moved across the room. And then, before I could restrain her, she said, 'I must see if Denis is all right.' She opened the door to the bedroom and she plunged into the darkness, through which one could hear the sounds of falling masonry and water. That was the bathroom collapsing, as we afterwards discovered. You could hear falling masonry and dripping water through it.

Butler was momentarily transfixed as the prime minister of Britain left the apparent safety of the sitting room to plunge into a dust-filled room in search of her husband. He remembers: 'I was left in the doorway wondering how I was going to explain to the tribunal of inquiry that I'd let the prime minister go into this maelstrom, perhaps never to be seen again. Fortunately, within a few seconds she and Denis emerged, Denis pulling a pair of flannels over his pyjamas and clutching some shirts.'

Cabinet ministers and others gathered in the corridor, but debate on what to do ended with Thatcher announcing: 'I'm not leaving Brighton.' Then a fireman appeared, and led them through the hotel. As they made their way out, Thatcher's detectives tried as best they could to ensure her immediate security, fearful that a second device had been planted. The thick cement dust covered the prime minister's clothes and went into her mouth as, in her words, 'I clambered over discarded belongings and broken furniture towards the back entrance of the hotel.'

While she was being driven to a local police college, Butler went back upstairs, picking up important papers and clothes for both Thatchers. He commented: 'If I'd known the hotel was hanging by a thread above my head I wouldn't have done it.' Thatcher recalls that no one spoke as she was driven to the police college. When she arrived, with her personal assistant, Cynthia 'Crawfie' Crawford, she recalled: 'I could only think of one thing to do. Crawfie and I knelt by the side of our beds and prayed for some time in silence.'

A few hours later, millions watched on television as rescue workers gingerly brought injured minister Norman Tebbit out of the shattered hotel. There were heroics among the rubble. One consultant surgeon who rushed to the scene worked with masonry falling around him, jolted by electric shocks caused by water cascading on to live cables. It quickly became obvious that the bomb had claimed lives. A fireman who saw a hand sticking out of the debris felt for a pulse but found no sign of life: it was a Tory MP, one of two men and three women killed in the attack. Dozens more were injured.

As the toll of death and injury mounted, Butler was astonished to hear Thatcher declare: 'Well, of course we must get to the conference on time.' He related:

I couldn't believe it. I said to her, 'You're not reckoning to continue the conference when you've got your colleagues, some dead, some still being dug out of the wreckage?' And she said immediately: 'We cannot let terrorism obstruct democracy – it's what those people would want. We must start on time.' And I was appalled – but she was right. I spent the morning helping to rewrite the conference speech, which clearly had to have its tone completely changed. It was now a very sombre occasion and all the jokes, indeed all the political jibes, had to be taken out.

Thatcher radiated defiance and contempt for the IRA in her conference speech, and never lost her strong instinct that the Northern Ireland problem was essentially one of security rather than a political matter. Her attitude to republicans was that they had to be faced down and defeated. She would say of her decision to go ahead with the conference: 'It was a very British reaction. We were British, that's what it was.'

Sir Patrick Mayhew, later one of her Northern Ireland Secretaries, would recall: 'She very frequently came up with the view that the task was to defeat the IRA – this was fundamental to her thinking. It became more so, not unnaturally, after the IRA tried to blow her up in Brighton. She constantly asked the military and security people to look at the options for dealing with security, and she honestly had rather less interest in trying to resolve the political aspects of the problem.'

The IRA at the time concurred with her view that the Northern Ireland problem was essentially military rather than political. In a statement addressed to Thatcher after Brighton, the organisation chillingly declared: 'Today we were unlucky, but remember we only have to be lucky once. You will have to be lucky always. Give Ireland peace and there will be no war.'

The bombing had its effects on the prime minister on a personal level: she was always grateful that the lights in the Grand Hotel had stayed on, and was haunted by the idea of being left in the dark in the event of another attack. For months afterwards she kept a torch by her bed when staying in a strange house. She was adamant, however, that the Brighton attack would not deflect her one millimetre from her course of action. She was, at the time, in the course of a series of conversations and contacts with the Irish prime minister of the day, Garret FitzGerald. He condemned the bombing, both publicly and in a private letter to her. She continued the contacts, and at their next meeting insisted it would not change her views.

Recalling the meeting, Dermot Nally, the Irish Cabinet Secretary, said: 'She was very vehement about a number of issues. You see, the Brighton bomb had just gone off and so the first thing she said was, "Anything I say here and now is not influenced by the bomb, I am not going to be influenced by that sort of stuff. Anything I do, I will do it because I am convinced it should be done, not because people throw violence at me." '

Yet she was sometimes prepared, under pressure, to turn from security to explore other avenues, two of which would prove to be vital episodes in the development of the peace process. Less than a year later she would sign a historic accord with the Irish Republic, which laid more emphasis on politics than on security. A little later still, she did not prevent the intelligence agency, MI5, from contacting the IRA, the people who almost killed her in Brighton.

Meanwhile, fingerprint experts went to work on the Grand Hotel's registration cards. On the card signed by 'Roy Walsh' no marks were visible to the naked eye. A laser test revealed one mark, which initially did not provide sufficient detail. The card was then subjected to the chemical ninhydrin, which reacts to the amino acids contained in human sweat. This test produced four marks, one of which was a palm mark at the bottom edge of the card. Four more marks developed when the card was subjected to a further treatment known as chemical physical developer, which reacts to the fat and waxy content of the sweat. One of these was a fingerprint.

This led police to Patrick Magee, who was already known as an IRA member and had been involved in republican activity in Belfast, England and Holland. The fingerprint evidence helped convict him at the Old Bailey in 1986. Giving Magee eight life sentences, the judge told him: 'You intended to wipe out a large part of the government and very nearly did. These are crimes of an exceptional gravity. Members of the public must be given the maximum protection I can provide.' He recommended Magee should be kept behind bars for a minimum of 35 years. The Brighton bomber did serve 14 years, during which he gained a first-class honours degree and a doctorate in politics and literature. In an interview later with a Dublin newspaper, he said he frequently thought of his victims: 'I regret the deaths at Brighton. I deeply regret that anybody had to lose their lives, but at the time did the Tory ruling class expect to remain immune from what their front-line troops were doing to us? I have argued that the military campaign was necessary, and equally now I would argue that it is no longer necessary. It's as simple as that.'

Magee sought to trace a continuity between the Brighton bomb and the peace process which led to his early release after fourteen years behind bars rather than 35. He said he did not regret failing in his aim of assassinating the prime minister, declaring: 'The awareness that it could have been worse actually gave the IRA more leverage than if they had killed her. In fact, if half of the British government had been killed it might have been impossible for a generation for the British establishment to come to terms with us.'

In the event, Britain and Irish republicanism were to come to terms, of a sort, during the 1990s, as key figures on each side came to believe that each should lower its sights from absolute victory to a negotiated settlement. But it would be a long and difficult road, with many deaths and much political turbulence along the way.

The roots of the Irish problem lie deep in history, involving Protestants, Catholics and Britain. Most of the Protestants were descendants of settlers who emigrated from England and Scotland to various parts of Ireland, with the encouragement of English governments, mainly in the sixteenth and seventeenth centuries. A major aim of the settlements was to plant a loyal British garrison community to establish control in the face of periodic Irish uprisings, which at times threatened English security by linking up with England's traditional Catholic enemies, France and Spain. The issue of whether and how that British interest had changed was to be a key question in the peace process of the late twentieth century.

Although there was some intermarriage between the Catholic natives and Protestant settlers, the two communities, especially in the north, continued down the years to regard themselves as separate entities. They were differentiated primarily on the basis of conflicting national identities, but there were other important points of difference – religious, territorial, economic and social. The existence of these kept communal divisions fresh and raw.

Protestantism was by no means synonymous with Unionism, by which is meant allegiance to the Union with Britain. There have been many prominent examples of Protestants who became Irish nationalists: in 1798, for example, many northern Presbyterians themselves unsuccessfully rose against the British. In the decades that followed, however, the Presbyterians and the Anglicans made common cause, becoming a solid phalanx for the Union with Britain.

In the nineteenth century, Catholic Ireland produced a series of movements seeking to cut or lessen the ties with Britain, led by nationalist heroes such as Daniel O'Connell, Thomas Davis and Charles Stewart Parnell. But most of the Protestants, who were largely concentrated in the north-eastern corner of the island, were hostile to such movements. While most of the island was rural, the northeast had been built into the British economy and had become heavily industrialised, resembling Liverpool and Glasgow more than Limerick and Galway. Protestants tended to have the better jobs.

The Protestants wished to keep their advantages and to stay part of the British economy. They also regarded themselves as British and were fiercely proud of the British Empire, and wanted no part of any new independent or semi-independent state. Another strong factor was that they feared, in their potent slogan, that Home Rule would mean Rome Rule, picturing a nightmare state in which their Protestant heritage would be actively attacked. By the early twentieth century they had created formidable organisations such as the Ulster Unionist Council, the forerunner of today's Ulster Unionist party, and the Orange Order to oppose any weakening of the link with Britain. All this was in direct opposition to the nationalist Home

Rule movement, which pressed for a measure of autonomy for Ireland. The tide of history seemed to favour the nationalists, for various British administrations were inclined to favour Home Rule. The Unionist response to what they saw as a threat to their British citizenship, religious traditions and economic well-being was to pledge their determination to oppose Home Rule by 'all means which may be found necessary.'

In the spring of 1914, the Unionist establishment smuggled 25,000 rifles and three million rounds of ammunition into the north of Ireland from Germany. They proclaimed their readiness to act outside the law and a major military confrontation seemed inevitable, but the outbreak of the First World War intervened and the Home Rule issue was put on ice for its duration.

1916 saw the Easter Rising in Dublin, with a small number of republicans staging an armed rebellion. The rising itself was quickly put down, but the action of the British government of the day in executing many of its leaders rebounded: London was deemed to have over-reacted and a wave of sympathy for the republicans ensued. Within a few years, faced with a wave of strong republican sentiment and violence from the newly formed IRA, London was ready to give Ireland a large measure of autonomy. But the determination of the northern Protestants to stay British was recognised, and the six north-eastern counties were allowed to remain under British rule. Thus was the state of Northern Ireland born.

Its creation did not bring security for the Protestants who made up two-thirds of its population of a million and a half, for it was clear that London was not as committed to the Union as they were. They constantly feared a 'sell-out' – a switch of British policy in favour of a united

Ireland. They also remained deeply suspicious of the half-million Catholics who found themselves within the boundaries of the new Northern Ireland state. Those Catholics considered themselves trapped in this new state, denied their Irish identity, cut off from their co-religionists in the south and politically powerless. Their plight was worsened by their belief that the Unionist establishment, which was to run the state on the basis of strict majority rule for the following half-century, actively discriminated against them in terms of jobs, housing and political rights.

Today, northern nationalists have formidable political leaders in John Hume and Gerry Adams, as well as considerable influence in Dublin, Europe and Washington. But between 1921 and the early 1970s, the Catholic community was politically isolated. The system was then based on Protestant rule, to the virtual exclusion of Catholic and nationalist influence. The Stormont parliament had a built-in Protestant majority, as had most local councils. In many places Protestant and Unionist control was artificially contrived, or reinforced by devices such as distortions of electoral boundaries. Thus 32,000 Catholics elected seven members of Fermanagh county council, while 25,000 Protestants elected 13 and hence took power.

The government, the judiciary and the security forces, the Royal Ulster Constabulary (RUC) and Ulster Special Constabulary, were either exclusively or overwhelmingly Protestant. The system survived for so long because of Unionism's monolithic strength, aided by divisions within nationalism, Westminster indifference and the impotence of the south. It may not have been a fair arrangement, but in London's terms it worked: the system placated the Protestants, who kept the Catholics in line, and a potentially vexatious state remained reasonably quiet. In effect, Britain considered the Irish question closed.

The Catholic community's fortunes did not materially improve until the late 1960s, when, inspired by Martin Luther King's civil rights movement in the United States and by student agitation in Paris, northern nationalists adopted the civil rights idiom. Some of their leaders were merely trying to wrong-foot Unionism, but many others were motivated by an urge to participate in the business of the state. The civil rights campaign was thus a major departure from old-style nationalist politics which was characterised by boycott and doleful complaint. But the Unionist system could not cope with demands which were by most standards modest. Unionism split into moderates, who were prepared to consider concessions to the nationalists, and those – such as the fundamentalist preacher and politician, the Reverend Ian Paisley – to whom the idea of any compromise was anathema. Civil rights demonstrations produced counter-demonstrations; some marches degenerated into violence; and it was not long before street disruptions were common. Widespread rioting in the cities of Belfast and Londonderry overwhelmed the police force, the largely Protestant RUC, and in August 1969 the British Army had to be sent in to restore order.

They failed, and the quarter-century that followed was one of the most remorselessly violent in centuries of Irish history. Protestant attacks on Catholic ghettos in Belfast led to the re-emergence of the IRA: at first it professed to be a defensive organisation, but it quickly became a terrorist organisation of fearsome force. By 1972 large Protestant paramilitary organisations had emerged, with tens of thousands of men marching around the streets of Belfast. A violent hard core of these groups was not content to remain as defensive vigilantes, and in the summer of 1972 began killing substantial numbers of Catholics.

Political crisis followed political crisis; terrorist outrage followed terrorist outrage. In 1972 the British government dismantled the Unionist system, and then spent two decades attempting to replace it with a new arrangement, in which Unionists and constitutional nationalists could work together. In the early days, the general view was that the issue was reasonably straightforward: the problem was defined as one of helping the Catholics who had suffered for decades under a discriminatory Protestant regime.

The question became much more complicated, however, as violence steadily increased, reaching its peak with a death toll of almost 500 in 1972. The fact that many of the deaths were caused by the IRA reduced British and international sympathy for the Irish nationalist point of view, leading many observers to redefine the problem as one of terrorism rather than civil rights. The authorities found themselves attempting to deal with two major factions on the Catholic side, one prepared to participate in politics, the other intent on overthrowing the state by violent means. Hume was prominent in the former, while Adams was active in the latter.

London remained focused on ways of securing Catholic participation in government. This appeared to have been achieved when, early in 1974, Hume's nationalist Social Democratic and Labour party came together in a power-sharing devolved administration in partnership with moderate Unionists. Within months, however, extreme loyalists organised a Protestant general strike which brought down the new arrangement. That element of Unionism which had been prepared to share power with nationalists disappeared virtually overnight. Thereafter, the British government policy that Catholics must be allowed into government was matched by the reality that Protestants would not have them. Much hope had been vested in the power-sharing initiative, and its collapse meant that disillusion developed in many quarters.

The IRA was clearly not interested in any such settlement, and was intent only on forcing the British out through a military victory. Similarly the Reverend Ian Paisley and a strong body of Protestant ultras were implacably opposed to sharing power with Catholics. The British government was not about to give in to the IRA and withdraw from Northern Ireland; nor was it going to buckle to the loyalist demands and reinstate another version of majority rule. It seemed obvious that the way ahead was to bring Catholics to identify fully with the state, and that this could only be done by offering them participation in government; yet the bulk of the Protestant community consistently made clear its determination, and its ability, to frustrate any attempt to do so.

At this stage, most British politicians concluded that nothing could be done, dismissing the problem as intractable. The decline in sympathy for the Catholics continued, largely because the IRA kept up its campaign, while loyalist killings, which had always received less publicity and attention than republican violence, decreased sharply after 1977. The upshot was a stalemate which lasted for many years. The death toll dropped from an average of 275 deaths per year to 85 per year. IRA violence significantly decreased in the face of a tough new security policy adopted by Britain's then Labour government.

This approach included the abandonment of internment without trial, which had gained the republicans considerable domestic and international sympathy, and a concentration instead on extracting confessions from IRA suspects in specially designed interrogation centres, principally at Castlereagh in Belfast. The confessions were usually enough to secure convictions in court, and steady streams of republicans and loyalists were imprisoned. Another facet of the policy was the increased use of the SAS (Special Air Services), who killed a number of IRA members in a series of carefully laid ambushes.

Little political progress was made, while recurring security crises buffeted Northern Ireland and occasionally Britain and the Republic: one incident among many was the IRA assassination of Lord Mountbatten as he relaxed on his boat off the Sligo coast in 1979. By the early 1980s a form of surly stalemate had been established: a large security apparatus was holding the violence down to lower levels than previously, but was unable to eradicate it completely.

2
Hunger strike

The 1981 hunger strike brought the republicans perhaps as close as they ever came to their aim of destabilising both parts of Ireland. A long-running dispute at the Maze prison (as Long Kesh had been renamed) over the status of paramilitary prisoners led to months of protests: the inmates wanted what was, in effect, political status, to differentiate themselves from non-paramilitary prisoners. The authorities refused to give way.

The Brighton bombing had its origins three years earlier in the hunger strike, an event which not only led to many deaths but also plunged Northern Ireland into some of the worst convulsions it ever experienced. The Unionist and nationalist communities plumbed new depths of polarisation and division, reaching new levels of bitterness. The IRA and Sinn Fein were revitalised, laying the basis for a new cycle of violence, combined with political intervention.

In the year of the hunger strike, Margaret Thatcher had been prime minister for only two years. She had not quite solidified her reputation as the Iron Lady, though this dispute would help do so. To her mind, the issue was stark and straightforward. IRA and other republican prisoners had for years been protesting that they were different from 'ordinary criminals' and demanded to be treated differently. In the course of the dispute they had disrupted prison life, while on the outside the IRA had killed a number of prison officers in support of the campaign.

They then escalated the campaign by turning to a traditional republican weapon, the hunger strike. For Thatcher, the idea of conceding on this point amounted to giving in to blackmail by convicted terrorists. Just as three years later at Brighton she would insist on the Conservative conference going ahead, so in the hunger strike her keynotes were defiance and determination. She saw the prison confrontation as one between good and evil, democracy and terrorism. She spelt out her position at the time, declaring: 'I want this to be utterly clear. The government will never concede political status to the hunger strikers or to any others convicted of criminal offences.' British Cabinet Secretary Robert Armstrong described her approach: 'Mrs Thatcher was certainly very much against any concessions. She did not want to start a process whereby there would be successive hunger strikes, during which she or the British government would be asked or begged to give further ground. That was always her clear position on the hunger strike.'

Republican prisoners listed five demands, including the right to wear their own clothes and free association with each other. But everyone believed their demands as a whole amounted to political status, in other words an unmistakable acknowledgement that they had a legitimate cause and were not criminals.

Inside the Maze prison an extraordinary pressure-cooker atmosphere had built up. A description of this has been given by Laurence McKeown, a Belfast IRA man who at the time of the hunger strike was aged 24 and serving a life sentence. He was part of a close-knit community behind bars, some of whom had been on protests of various types for up to five years. He signed up as a hunger striker, he said, because he had no wife or children and was totally committed to the protest. A hundred others volunteered with him. During an inconclusive earlier hunger strike, he said, the prisoners thought there was a good chance someone would die; in a hunger strike led by IRA prisoners' leader Bobby Sands, however, they thought: 'They're definitely going to let someone die this time.'

The IRA leadership had been opposed to the whole hunger strike, which was launched very much as an initiative from the prisoners themselves. Adams recalled: 'When Bobby began to argue that they needed to go on a hunger strike we argued, and I actually wrote to him, saying that we were morally and strategically and tactically and physically opposed to it.' One of Adams's closest lieutenants, Danny Morrison, who was to demonstrate a flair for publicity and propaganda, recollected Sands in the prison: 'I said, "Bobby, we don't want another hunger strike. We want this resolved." In actual fact, it took up so much of our resources and time over a four- or five-year period that we could do nothing, because everything was jail-orientated.'

But as the hunger strike went on, the republicans were presented with an extraordinary opportunity to demonstrate that, whatever Thatcher's stance, they had a political status. This arose from the unexpected death of an independent nationalist who was Westminster MP for the Fermanagh–South Tyrone constituency. The resulting by-election led to a fierce debate within the IRA and Sinn Fein: should the leading IRA hunger striker, Bobby Sands, be put up to run for the seat?

There were voices for and against. The IRA had always been wary of what they condemned as 'electoralism', believing that even flirtations with conventional politics could blunt the cutting edge of the IRA and pollute what they proudly saw as its revolutionary clarity. In pragmatic terms, however, Fermanagh–South Tyrone had a nationalist majority, and victory for a convicted republican prisoner would be a huge coup both for the prison campaign and for the republican cause in general.

Gerry Adams of Sinn Fein, who would later become President of the party and had a reputation as its most astute political thinker, recalled:

A number of people came up with the same idea independently and we discussed it. It was decided that we should get the views of people in the constituency first, because there were differences of opinion about it. I attended a meeting with Fermanagh people, and people in the constituency were very difficult to persuade. I think they were afraid that if a prisoner stood and lost then it would have a big effect, and you were almost putting the whole prison struggle on the line.

A meeting called to decide the issue reached the conclusion that Sands should not run, Ruairí Ó Brádaigh, then President of Sinn Fein, reporting: 'When this was put to the delegates they were very critical, and they opposed it and they turned it down.' Martin McGuinness, then an important young republican figure based in Derry, remembered: 'The big concern was the prospect that a hunger striker would stand in the election and not win, not be elected. That could then be used by the British government around the world as portraying that there was little support for republicanism or for the hunger strikers.'

At this time, however, the balance of power within republicanism was starting to shift, with the movement's centre of gravity moving away from Ó Brádaigh and the more conservative southern and rural elements who had tended to dominate. Instead, the lead was increasingly taken by a younger and brasher northern element, more open to innovative risk-taking. At this point some of the traditionalists and most of the more adventurous northerners were in favour of putting Sands forward. After the meeting which had decided not to run Sands, Morrison's telephone rang: 'I got a call from Gerry Adams, around quarter to twelve that night of the meeting, telling me that it wasn't passed, they didn't agree to run Bobby Sands. I said to Gerry, "That's madness – Bobby has to run." It was because the movement was so suspicious of politics – politics equalled compromise, equalled constitutionalism.'

Ó Brádaigh was to reflect: 'What has to be done in these cases is to calculate the risk. There's nothing dead certain, there's nothing sure in revolutionary business.' With influential figures from various sections of the movement of the same mind, behind-the-scenes moves began. Ó Brádaigh wryly recalled: 'Another convention was arranged and on more mature consideration it was carried.'

McGuinness remembered: 'I said to Gerry Adams that I thought that this was a risk worth taking. The repercussions of a hunger striker winning a seat, being the MP for Fermanagh–South Tyrone, in terms of the international focus that it would give to the hunger strike itself, all of that was absolutely huge.' Crucially for the Sands campaign, the republicans persuaded – some say pressurised – any other nationalists to stand clear so as to give Sands a clear run against the Unionist candidate, an old-fashioned politician closely associated with the old system of Unionist majority rule.

The republicans could tell their campaign was going well, Ó Brádaigh remembering: 'There was a church-gate collection held the Sunday before the election and this was a tremendous success. People were throwing in notes, and it was so successful that I was really elated. I knew from my experience that when you can get money voluntarily like that in such quantities, there are going to be votes to back that up.'

So it was that on 9 April 1981 the air at the election count was rent by Danny Morrison's delighted, if vulgar, war whoop as the returning officer intoned that, while the Unionist candidate had amassed 29,046 votes, Sands had won 30,492. No fewer than 87 per cent of the electorate had turned out to vote.

Gerry Adams heard the result while driving in his car: 'The news came through on the radio that Bobby Sands had been elected. I was on this long country road and I remember nearly bouncing the car off the hedges and pounding the steering wheel. It was a huge thing to know that against all the odds that we'd pulled it off and the prisoners had been vindicated. That the people – who were always the arbiters of whether one was a terrorist, a criminal or a freedom fighter – that the people had decided.'

The news of Sands's election victory reached republican prisoners via a secret radio set. According to McKeown: 'The place just erupted. Everybody simultaneously just shouted, roared, probably unintelligible sort of screams. I think that just went on for about ten, 15 minutes. There were people dancing around their cells. We just were all shouting, banging off the walls, cups rocking, pipes banging, doors – whole place just went mad.'

Although the republicans were ecstatic at what they saw

as a famous victory, they were mistaken in thinking it would change Thatcher's mind. Instead, she stuck to her position, holding firmly to the view that making concessions to prisoners amounted to being soft on terrorism. 'There can be no question of political status for someone who is serving a sentence for crime,' she declared. 'Crime is crime is crime. It is not political, it is crime.' One problem with this stance was that practically no one equated republican inmates with other prisoners. Those who supported them regarded them as heroic prisoners of war. Those who condemned them, which included most of the Unionist and Protestant community, thought they were much, much worse than what prison staff sarcastically referred to as ODCs – 'ordinary decent criminals'. No one thought they were the same.

Tensions mounted to an extraordinary degree as the strike went on amid a major propaganda battle, with extreme polarisation between ordinary Protestants and Catholics. For many nationalists the issue left no room for ambiguity, and many who did not support the IRA nonetheless reacted against what they saw as British inflexibility.

One of those who was most keenly aware of this was SDLP leader John Hume, whose policy was one of working towards an agreed Ireland by peaceful means. He pressed for a compromise settlement which would defuse the confrontation: 'One of the things about the hunger strikes that worried us most,' he would say, 'was the tensions that they were creating and the danger of creating greater support for the IRA, particularly among [the] young. Therefore it was central that they be resolved. We knew, living in the community that we live in, that was the danger of the whole hunger-strike situation, which is why we wanted it dealt with urgently, more urgently than it was dealt with.'

Many of those who turned out to vote for Sands were, in normal circumstances, natural supporters of Hume's party. Later they would revert to the SDLP, but in the Sands election they felt they had to lend their votes to the republicans. It did not mean they supported violence: they were protesting against what they viewed as Thatcherite intransigence. They knew well enough the damage the IRA had done, but, if only momentarily, they came to view Sands as worthy of support.

After the initial republican jubilation, the realisation slowly spread that in Thatcher's mind nothing had changed. Behind the scenes, intensive efforts were made to mediate or find a compromise resolution of the dispute, but it all came to nothing. Marcella Sands visited her weakening brother after he had been on hunger strike for more than two months. She recalled: 'He said he'd always love us and pray for us, although he was blind and couldn't see us. The next day we expected him to be sitting up and ready to talk, but when we walked in he was in a coma.'

Adams summed up Sands's approach: 'While Bobby Sands didn't want to die in the hunger strike, the way he constructed the hunger strike and the way he controlled the mechanisms within the prison show clearly that he believed that he would have to die. He was trying to make sure that his will prevailed, and that it became a battle between him and the British.'

On 5 May, less than a month after his election to the Commons, the emaciated Sands died at 1.17 a.m. on the 66th day of hunger strike. He instantly entered republican mythology as one of its most revered martyrs: his portrait, annually repainted, remains one of the most prominent of the many republican murals on Belfast's Falls Road. Nearly two decades later, when Sinn Fein delegates moved into government offices to negotiate what would become the Good Friday Agreement, one of the first things they did was to hang a portrait of Bobby Sands on the wall. At the time of his death, Thatcher described Sands as 'a convicted criminal who chose to take his own life'. Some years later, however, she would admit to a grudging respect: 'It was possible to admire the courage of Sands and the other hunger strikers who died, but not to sympathise with their murderous cause.'

Within the Maze, a Catholic priest broke the news of Sands's death to one of the leaders of the republican prisoners. He shouted to the others: 'Bobby's dead.' Laurence McKeown related: 'The wing had been very quiet because we didn't know what was happening. But when the news came through the wing just in general died, I think for the rest of the day.'

The IRA may have been responsible for around half of all troubles deaths, and many of its members have the hardest of hearts. But those involved in the hunger strike still become visibly emotional when turning their minds to events which took place two decades ago. Adams would say years later: 'I cannot yet think with any intensity of the death of Bobby Sands and the circumstances of his passing without crying.' Morrison choked as he said in an interview: 'The next time I saw him was in his coffin when he was just failed away. His hair had been shaved and he looked like somebody from Belsen.' The hunger striker's funeral then turned into a huge political statement, as 100,000 or more people attended. Both Adams and Morrison took turns at carrying the coffin.

The months that followed saw widespread disturbances

and a mounting death toll. The confrontation continued, with neither the government nor the hunger strikers prepared to give way. With hindsight, it is clear that each deeply misunderstood the other: Thatcher never came close to grasping the IRA's psychology, while many republicans persisted in believing that she was bound to give in eventually.

The deaths continued both on the streets and in the prison. Four hunger strikers were dead and buried when Laurence McKeown was told in mid-June that he would be joining the protest later that month. He knew this would probably mean death. He was to recall: 'At that time I got a comm [communication], a very brief comm, from the [IRA] Army Council. It was written on one cigarette paper. It says, "Comrade, you have agreed or decided to join the hunger strike. Do you know what this means – you will be dead within two months, re-think your decision – Army Council." It was very blunt and probably meant to be very blunt to make you think about it.'

When he went ahead with his decision McKeown was brought to meet other hunger strikers. He remembered: 'The only person who was missing from the room at that early stage was Joe McDonnell, and if I hadn't known that Joe was absent I wouldn't have recognised the person that come through the door. This person was wheeled in in a wheelchair. His head was lying off on to his shoulder, his eyes were really sunken, his lips were all hacked and there was saliva running out. I wouldn't have recognised this person at all. And the first thing he said was, "Do people get cigarettes in here?"'

On another occasion, a group of hunger strikers was joined by Gerry Adams, who told them that no negotiations were going on with the British government, and there were no indications of any movement to meet the prisoners' demands. McKeown recalled what Adams conveyed to them:

That if we were to give up the hunger strike there and then, no one would have anything but respect for us. That people respected what had taken place, and the struggle that the prisoners had made. There'd be no shame or embarrassment or whatever else. But that if we continued with the hunger strike, what we could be sure of was that everybody round the table would be dead within two months – carry on with this and you're dead in two months. So it was a very stark picture, a very honest picture of what was happening. After that the whole conversation became a sort of light-hearted banter, but by the time we all went to our cells the reality of what Gerry had said came back to us.

The days passed: the test of will continued. McKeown, weak and emaciated after 60 days without food, overheard a prison official saying he could die within 48 hours. He had already turned down an emotional plea from his father to abandon his hunger strike. His family was allowed into his room in the prison hospital. He recalled:

My mother came in, sister, brother, my father and different uncles. And I think all of them, except my mother, asked me to come off the hunger strike. I was still lucid at that time. There was a lot of crying and a lot of silences.

I can remember the morning of the 69th day, when I got some time with my mother. I was probably just dozing off, sleeping and waking up, and when I was waking up I was lucid. My mother had been a bit religious, not in a big way but she had a sort of quiet faith, I suppose you would say. I remember her saying to me, 'You know what you've to do and I know what I've to do.' That was the way it was left between us. I think what my mother meant was that it was God's will and if it ended up in a situation where I was in a coma, then she would act to save my life. I didn't pursue it any further, as I thought I would just die instantly.

Apparently, on the evening of the 69th day I was talking to people who weren't there, and calling people by the wrong names. On the morning of the 70th day the doctors were looking for certain reflexes and I wasn't responding in any way. And I think about noon, my mother authorised medical intervention. There had already been several people this had happened to: I was the last one that it happened to because the hunger strike ended a few weeks afterwards. I had a whole mixture of emotions. I can't say I was happy to be alive, but I certainly couldn't say I was sad to be alive. I was alive, I wasn't even thinking about what was going to happen in the future.

While such deadly drama was being played out in the prison, the continuing protest was having important implications internationally. This was particularly the case in the United States, where many of the millions of Irish-Americans were descendants of people who had left Ireland in painful and traumatic circumstances during and after the famine years of the mid-nineteenth century. Many of their descendants saw Britain as the villain of the piece. When the troubles broke out, the IRA were seen by large numbers of Irish-Americans as anti-colonial freedom fighters intent on driving out the British army of occupation. In the early 1970s, this translated into large donations of dollars sent openly to republicans, as well as a surreptitious flow of arms shipments.

The picture had changed by the late 1970s, largely as a result of an initiative headed by John Hume and Irish diplomats. One of these, Michael Lillis, who was later to play a major part in putting together the Anglo–Irish Agreement, encouraged prominent Irish-American politicians to organise themselves as an alternative focal point, to draw support away from the violent republicans and towards peaceful nationalism. But the hunger strike reversed this trend, helping the IRA hugely. This process has been described by Peter King, a Republican member of Congress, who, unusually for one in his party, strongly supported Irish republicanism. He recalled: 'Nothing had more of an impact on the United States than the hunger strikes. This issue appealed to young college graduates, professionals. These were Irish-Americans who had basically thought the Irish issue was one for their parents or grandparents, and who probably in their own mind thought they had outgrown their Irishness. Suddenly they were radicalised by hunger strikes, and the reaction of the British government.' To many, the IRA suddenly stopped looking like the aggressors, and assumed the mantle of victims.

The Irish Ambassador to the US at that time, Seán Donlon, recalled his problems in Washington:

It was a particularly difficult time, because we'd come a long way in terms of educating the American public and particularly the Irish-American public. We had, in particular, educated them to the view that Britain was not the cause of all these problems, that it was slightly more complicated than that. But the hunger strike set us back, because it suddenly became quite a stark Anglophobic point of view in the Irish-American community. They were seeing the harrowing funerals of the hunger strikers, they were reading newspaper articles which tore at the hearts of Irish-Americans, even those who had for years been opposed to the violence of the IRA.

Essentially, we were doing two things. First of all we were trying to recruit President Reagan and the White House in support of what I would call an Irish nationalist position – please talk to Mrs Thatcher, explain to her the damage that she is doing, she's building up support for the IRA, she's not confronting it in a constructive way. The second thing was to try to hold the tide back, prevent the deeper greening of Irish-America. It had taken years to move Irish-America from that IRA position to the non-violent position: we were just about there, but with the hunger strike the stone began to roll back down the hill again.

After the deaths of ten hunger strikers, the end came in the autumn of 1981, largely through the efforts of families and particularly mothers, who, encouraged by prison chaplain Father Denis Faul, sanctioned medical intervention when their sons lapsed into a coma. Once the strike was called off, the prisoners were quickly allowed to wear their own clothes, but they had no sense of triumph: the initial reaction was that Britain, and in particular Thatcher, had faced them down.

McKeown recalls that in the prison the prevailing sense was one of relief, coupled with determination that their campaign would continue in other forms: 'We didn't even realise the strength that we had in our numbers. We were able to capitalise on five years of protest, and the hunger strike that had built up a bond of solidarity. It built a trust, it had built an awareness of one another, it had built communications systems, it had instilled politics.' All of those things would be redirected in a new way.

Father Faul, who was reviled by the IRA for his role in ending the hunger strikes, sensed that a sea-change had taken place. He recalled:

As these men died, there was a colossal revulsion of feeling among the Catholic people, the nationalist people against the British, and against the Unionist people and the Protestant people, and this was very regrettable. A friend of mine said to the British – 'You think you're winning this thing? You've held out, these men are dead. The men won by dying and that's the way it is in Ireland.' It was a very deep thing. They were all united by Sinn Fein, they had the emaciated body in the bed, just like the kind of relic you'd see in one of the churches in Rome or in Milan or relics of an ancient saint, quite emaciated.

And then the Irish tricolour flag and the hooded men standing around, and then you see the miles of queues – people and particularly young people, youngsters, young boys coming in to see this, and it could make an indelible impression on them. The IRA could recruit all they liked on the basis of that element of sacrifice. The British were in a no-win situation, but they couldn't see it. They were in offices in Belfast, they weren't down the lane-ways and the by-ways of West Belfast or South Derry or South Armagh, where these prisoners were buried.

The sense of self-sacrifice, the Anglophobia highlighted by Donlon and the new rawness across Northern Ireland society all worked to the IRA's advantage. The wave of anti-British rage, the huge crowds at the funerals of Sands and the others, and his victory in the Fermanagh–South Tyrone by-election meant that the despised 'electoralism' suddenly offered republicans new avenues to pursue their campaign.

Mitchel McLaughlin, then a young Sinn Fein activist from Derry who would become party chairman, recalled: 'Within one year of the hunger strikes ending, the party was contesting elections. Martin McGuinness was the Sinn Fein candidate from Derry and I was his election agent – neither of the two of us had ever voted in our lives before.' McGuinness remembers: 'Someone stood up and proposed me – it probably was Mitchel – and that was seconded. On the day of the election we had such an amount of workers all over the city – people knocking on doors and asking people to come out and vote – that I realised then that we could actually do this. We had arrived big-time on the political scene.'

For the rest of the 1980s Sinn Fein would win around 11 per cent of the vote in Northern Ireland elections, with party President Gerry Adams taking a Westminster seat in 1983. The politics went hand in hand with the violence in what became known as the strategy of 'the Armalite [rifle] and the ballot box.' This arose from a speech by Danny Morrison when he encapsulated the approach with a ringing declaration: 'Who here really believes we can win the war through the ballot box? But will anyone here object if, with a ballot box in one hand and the Armalite in the other, we take power in Ireland?'

Morrison would recall: 'As I was waiting in the queue to speak, an image came to me. It wasn't planned, wasn't discussed, and in a sense I was of course playing to the gallery. Some said, "Oh my God, what have you done now?" But by and large it was an assurance to people who were politically orientated, and to people who were militaristically orientated, that it was possible to simultaneously wage an armed and a political struggle.' Republicans gained international sympathy, a voting base, recruits and a new sense of energy and commitment. It was the opening of a new era for them.

3
Anglo–Irish Agreement

In London, Thatcher and most of the establishment believed that with the failure of the hunger strike a crushing blow had been dealt against terrorism. Things looked less rosy in Belfast, however, where a new Northern Ireland Secretary, James Prior, arrived to find 'an embittered and totally polarised society.' They looked even worse in Dublin, where the Taoiseach (Prime Minister), Dr Garret FitzGerald, surveyed the northern scene with real alarm. Watching the rise of Sinn Fein as a political force, he concluded that the British and Irish governments needed to act, as a matter of urgency, to avoid the risk of a complete breakdown of order throughout Ireland.

At their annual summit at Chequers in November 1983 he broached the subject: 'I said to Margaret Thatcher that the problem as we saw it was that support had grown substantially for Sinn Fein, representing the IRA, after the hunger strike. It was still growing, and it looked as if they could come to replace the SDLP as the major nationalist party. That could be very destabilising, and they might then take a chance on raising the level of violence to civil war level. For all of us it was vital that we do something to prevent this happening.'

Irish Cabinet Secretary Dermot Nally amplified the argument: 'We are not talking about a normal situation, we are talking about a situation where people are totally alienated from the institutions of government. Because if you do not provide an alternative, violence will grow and we could not foretell what the consequence will be.' The FitzGerald plan was for London and Dublin to work together to develop new levels of political cooperation, largely aimed at combating the increasing republican menace.

David Goodall, a senior British civil servant who came from a Catholic family with Irish connections, described Thatcher's general approach to Ireland. He remembered:

There was a dinner in 1982 and the guests left, and Mrs Thatcher said to me to come and have a drink. So we went and sat down with her private secretary, just the three of us. The conversation turned to Ireland, and it turned out that she had read quite a lot about the Irish problem. People said she didn't know anything about it, but actually she did know quite a lot about it.

I said that one of the complicating factors in the relationship was that so many British people were of Irish descent, and indeed, though they don't like to admit it, a very high proportion of the population of the Republic is actually of British descent. Mrs Thatcher said: 'I am completely English.' But it was clear from the conversation that she felt that most things had been tried and nothing seemed to work. She didn't have a clear idea of what she wanted to do but she wanted to have another go at the problem.

Another senior official said privately: 'Perhaps Mrs Thatcher had a less than comprehensive grasp of Irish history, but she's an intensely pragmatic politician. She was conscious of the need to do something – not to solve the situation, but to move it forward from the impasse which it had reached. It was logical to explore the possibilities of the Anglo–Irish dimension.'

Although Thatcher listened carefully to FitzGerald, it turned out that she was on a very different wavelength. While FitzGerald proposed a political approach, she viewed the problem as essentially one of security. She took particular exception to his use of the word 'alienation' in relation to northern Catholics. Seán Donlon recalled: 'It had reverberations for her which were simply not acceptable, because it brought us into the Left–Right Communist type thing. She reacted quite badly to the word.' Goodall confirmed this: 'She roundly rejected the idea of alienation. She never liked the term, I think because she thought it had Marxist overtones. And of course Garret would always go on about alienation, so there was an argument about words which wasn't at all helpful.'

The difference in approach between the two prime ministers went beyond mere vocabulary. FitzGerald's recipe for reducing what he saw as the dangerous levels of alienation lay in tackling the problem on a political level, by giving northern nationalists a sense of belonging which they conspicuously lacked. This, he believed, could be achieved by building nationalism into key institutions such as the police and the courts. At best, he hoped for Thatcher's agreement to a new form of administration amounting to joint authority, to be exercised by both London and Dublin. To his mind, in other words, alienation was a political phenomenon to be addressed by political means.

But Thatcher, as her senior aide Charles Powell was to explain, was wedded to tackling the problem through security methods:

The issues of alienation of the minority, which Dr FitzGerald used to talk about so much, would disappear if terrorism could be eliminated. Her thinking was based crucially on getting rid of terrorism, and that meant all aspects of security. And many different ideas came out early in her thinking, such as having a security zone on either side of the border, or a zone of hot pursuit on the Irish side of the border. These were all steps which, in her mind, would make it easier to deal with the problem of terrorism.

The Thatcher preoccupation with security led her to toy with ideas much more radical even than hot-pursuit zones. One of these, had it been widely known when she was in office, would have astounded and appalled the Unionist population of Northern Ireland, for it involved repartition and the redrawing of the border between the two parts of the island. This sprang not from any lack of attachment to the Union, for she regarded herself as a strong and deeply committed Unionist; rather, it came from purely military considerations, of how best the territory of Northern Ireland could be defended.

As Powell explains it:

For Mrs Thatcher security was paramount, and this led her to focus particularly on the issue of security at the border with the Republic. She many times came back to this both with me and with other officials, and I'm sure at times with the Irish government. She said, 'Couldn't we redraw the border to at least make it more defensible?' Indeed, at various times she even speculated on the possibility of population movement, though it very quickly became apparent this was not a politically feasible task. Would it help if we could somehow change the population balance a bit more, so that there were fewer nationalists in the north and the terrorist problem would be diminished, and it would be easier for the armed forces to defend that border?

Now and again she got the Ministry of Defence to do various studies of this, but it never worked out. She thought that if we had a straight-line border, not one with all those kinks and wiggles in it, it would be easier to defend. But the military always came back and said No, it would simply be too difficult. It's so reflective of her approach to the whole issue – it was security first, second and third.

Robert Armstrong recited the arguments against population movement: 'It wasn't as simple as that, because the nationalist communities were not all in one place, not all in Fermanagh and Tyrone and South Armagh and so on. There were many in Belfast, and the idea of a partition in Belfast or moving large numbers of population didn't seem to be very attractive.'

After one session involving the two prime ministers at Chequers, Thatcher called her officials in for a whisky. Goodall recalls: 'We had a fair knockabout. Her way of teasing out a problem was to throw out various outrageous suggestions. She said, "The Irish are quite used to movements of population. If the northern population want to be in the south, why don't they move over there? After all, there was a big movement of population in Ireland, wasn't there?" And nobody could think what it was. So finally I said, "Are you talking about Cromwell, Prime Minister?" She said, "That's right, Cromwell."' Goodall and the other officials with a grasp of history felt the Irish would not react well to any such reference, given Cromwell's reputation in Ireland for massacres.

FitzGerald clearly faced a daunting task in attempting to have Thatcher consider a more politically orientated path, but she did not close the door to a channel of communication which was being established between her civil servants and his. Armstrong and Nally, the two Cabinet Secretaries, were in close contact, and so were Goodall and Michael Lillis. These were to be key relationships. Goodall was to emphasise the importance of personal relations:

The Armstrong–Nally group was a very interesting exercise in negotiation. I think the key to it was that Robert Armstrong and Dermot Nally had got to know one another and they trusted one another. They're not much alike, and yet there was a strong bond of sympathy between them. I would also say that Michael Lillis and I are not much alike either, actually, but we took to one another. It was a small group and it developed – critics of diplomacy would say this is the danger with this kind of negotiation, it develops a kind of esprit de corps of its own. That's a danger, but then that's what ministers are for, really – they're there to say well, this is going too far, or this is you know premature or whatever. But if you're trying to negotiate a really tricky agreement it's vital to have that kind of mutual confidence.

Goodall also touched on the combination of diplomacy and gastronomy:

Of course we had a lot of fun because we did quite a lot of business over dinner. I remember a dinner in Dublin in a grand dining room there, and Michael Lillis had procured the wine for this feast and he gave up alcohol always for Lent. With great levity he told us at great length how he procured this really, really very good wine and it was a tremendous sacrifice on his part because he wasn't going to be able to drink any of it, and so on. Another Irish diplomat, Noel Dorr, wittily said in a quiet voice: 'How true it is that it's the martyrs who have to live with the saints!'

In one respect, Dublin often had an edge over London in Anglo–Irish relations, in that many of the best and the brightest Irish officials tended to specialise in London–Dublin relations, while in the British system as a rule they did not. The result was a high quality of Irish representation, which for once, in the case of the Armstrong–Nally committee, was matched on the British side of the table. One British Foreign Secretary, Douglas Hurd, remarked: 'One had to reckon all the time in negotiating with the Irish you were up against absolutely first-class calibre.' Another Foreign Secretary, Sir Geoffrey Howe, referred to the committee as 'this galaxy of skill.'

Thatcher imposed strict limits to the discussions, Goodall recalling: 'She said to Robert and me, "You can go on talking but you've got to make it absolutely clear that joint authority is out, joint sovereignty is not even in question."' Powell added: 'As far as Mrs Thatcher was concerned, from the beginning joint authority of any sort was simply out. When it was first mentioned to her by Garret FitzGerald, she used the word "burglary" to describe the whole concept.'

The Prime Minister thus instructed her officials to draw up a proposal which ignored all FitzGerald's ideas about joint authority and concentrated on border security. When the British officials presented the proposal to their counterparts in Dublin, Nally recalls conveying it to FitzGerald: 'I ran up the stairs to tell the Taoiseach. His reaction was immediate and fairly fierce. He said, "Go back and tell them immediately that there is no question of the security zone, that is ridiculous, the whole idea is ridiculous."'

Armstrong was not particularly taken aback by this brisk rejection: 'It wasn't warmly received. I was not surprised, because it would clearly have involved the possibility of British troops being involved in action on the Republic's territory.' Goodall had a similar response, thinking there was 'too much emphasis on security, with no political compensation – it was just not possible for them.'

At that point, the whole idea of a serious Anglo–Irish negotiation looked distinctly unpromising. FitzGerald's idea of joint authority and Thatcher's notion of a joint security zone had both been briskly rebuffed. The two prime ministers simply did not see eye to eye, either on the solution to the problem or indeed on their basic analysis of it. Yet they did not walk away from each other, partly because, in the words of Seán Donlon, 'happily, they liked one another.' As he characterised their relationship: 'So many of these meetings between Garret FitzGerald and Margaret Thatcher were by nature of being educational. It was slow, it was painful, from an Irish point of view it was exasperating at times – but it had to be done. One has to deal with the person elected to deal with the issues, and we simply had to accommodate to her personality.'

The next summit at Chequers in November 1984 did not go well. FitzGerald, arguing the case for easing the alienation of northern nationalists, presented his arguments: 'I said that she was naturally proud of being British, but in Northern Ireland there was a big minority who were proud of being Irish and their identity had to be taken into account.' Thatcher asked, as Charles Powell remembered, 'Why could the minority in the north not be satisfied with effective policing, the rule of law – why did they have to have their own signs and symbols? They had after all seats on local authorities, they had votes; if they wished to put their view there were democratically elected bodies in which to put it.'

FitzGerald remembered: 'She said the Sikhs in Southall didn't want to fly their own flag and I said, "Well, there's no law preventing them from flying their own flag; in Northern Ireland there is a law preventing nationalists flying the flag to which they gave loyalty."'

Although she liked FitzGerald, Thatcher had no sympathy for the culture he represented. According to Powell: 'Mrs Thatcher had little understanding of Irish nationalist aspirations – she tended to identify them almost instantly with terrorism. For her, many of the justifications for nationalism were little more than mythology or folklore, to use two words she frequently used.' Her exchanges with FitzGerald were followed by what one of those present euphemistically described as 'a good dinner', meaning the food was accompanied by a surfeit of alcohol. According to Donlon: 'The next morning began for most of us rather badly, because we had undoubtedly over-indulged. The hospitality had been very generous and there were some sore heads around the place – I believe not confined to the Irish delegation.'

Up at dawn, Thatcher testily told her officials that Fitz-Gerald was still pushing unacceptable proposals for joint authority. One of those officials was Goodall. According to his own account of the meeting:

She really exploded and went on about the Irish and I sat back and thought that I didn't really like this. I withdrew my attention and I obviously withdrew my eyes. Her eyes suddenly swivelled round on me and she said, 'Mr Goodall!' So I sat up pretty sharply. She said, 'Wouldn't you like to go and be an ambassador somewhere else a long way away?' So I said, coming back to earth, 'Where would you suggest, prime minister?' And she said: 'Indonesia, perhaps?' I said to

Robert Armstrong afterwards, 'Why did she suggest Indonesia?' He said, 'Oh, it was the greenest place she could think of.'

Armstrong was to add that Thatcher had a double reservation about Goodall, both because of his family and because of his home department: 'She was suspicious of David, because she knew that he had Irish origins – and of course he came from the Foreign Office and that was always fatal. But in fact she had a very high regard for him, and when he finally left the Cabinet Office she very much missed him.'

She instructed her officials to rebuff FitzGerald, Goodall recounting: 'We were then told to prepare a very stiff note. We emphasised in the note that we were still serious about the business of trying to reach an agreed outcome, but that the whole question of shared decision-making was simply not on.'

Powell described this as 'a sort of missile aimed at the very heart of the Irish negotiating system', Donlon concurring that it 'certainly sent some shivers down our spines.' The note stated sternly:

The position of the British side throughout the talks has been and remains that joint authority, or arrangements tantamount to or apparently suggestive of joint authority, are unacceptable to the British government. At no time has the British side accepted the contention that it was essential that the Irish nationalist role be that of an equal participant in decision-making, either at the ministerial commission level, or at the level of devolved government. Nor has it ever entertained the suggestion that the Irish government might be a participant in decision-making as part of an interim executive chaired by the Secretary of State for Northern Ireland.

When the two sides met that morning, Douglas Hurd laid out the British suggestion: a security commission for Northern Ireland, where, in his words, Dublin ministers 'would be able to raise all their concerns about all kinds of matters to do with order in the province.' FitzGerald was not receptive to the idea. He recalled: 'Margaret Thatcher said then that the role of the security commission would, of course, be purely advisory. I said that wouldn't do, we'd need to have a clear role on appointments and complaints. And she said, "That's not on, that's not on, that's joint authority, you can't have that."'

Just as the word alienation had earlier caused problems, the apparently innocuous word 'involving' now led to difficulties. When FitzGerald said to Thatcher that she seemed to be envisaging arrangements involving the Irish, 'she jumped at me and said, "involving, I never used that word."' As Donlon remembered the exchange: 'She hit the roof. She immediately turned to Robert Armstrong and said: "Robert, have you been using that word? Does that appear in any document? If that appeared in a document I am in trouble in the House of Commons."'

At this point, FitzGerald made what he thought was a major concession. He offered to amend Articles 2 and 3 of the Irish constitution, which Unionists had long attacked as an offensive claim to jurisdiction over Northern Ireland. The articles could only be changed by a referendum, but FitzGerald indicated that, in exchange for significant movement on the British side, he was prepared to consider this. The idea stirred little enthusiasm on the British side, however, with Hurd thinking that 'the price would turn out to be too high.' Powell voiced a different reason: 'We frankly doubted whether Garret FitzGerald's government could get it through the Irish Parliament. We thought it would probably lead to the collapse of his government.'

Thus the whole thing, in Nally's words, 'just fell to pieces.' As the Chequers meeting broke up, FitzGerald remembers Thatcher approached him: 'She said I looked depressed, and I said I was depressed, yes, because things had gone backwards and we weren't getting very far. That obviously worried her, for as we left she tried to cheer me up.' What happened in the next few hours did nothing to cheer the dejected Taoiseach: in fact, it sparked a real crisis in Anglo–Irish relations. Some of the options which FitzGerald had put to Thatcher had come from a nationalist forum which had met in Dublin over a period of many months. The New Ireland Forum had taken submissions from many shades of opinion, acting in effect as a think-tank for nationalist Ireland, in which senior figures from all the major constitutional parties debated the way ahead.

When Thatcher was asked about what had emerged from her meeting she was brusque and undiplomatic in the extreme. She replied briskly: 'I have made it quite clear that a unified Ireland, that is out. A confederation of two states, that is out. Joint authority, that is out.' Never noted for her extreme sensitivity to opinion in other countries, the tone of Thatcher's comments was nothing out of the ordinary for her. To Irish nationalist ears, however, this rebuff, delivered as it was with a forthrightness which bordered on vehemence, came across as both injury and insult.

The trouble for FitzGerald was that he walked into his own press conference without hearing any of this, for interference had prevented him picking up her comments on his car radio. He recalled: 'I went in to my press conference totally unaware of what had happened, but the journalists had all come from her press conference. They knew, and I was tackled at once on what she'd said. As I didn't know what she'd said, I was in an impossible situation. I looked pretty weak at that stage.' Donlon, watching from the back of the room, winced as he saw FitzGerald's predicament: 'I saw his face drop – it was as if somebody had hit him a blow in the solar plexus.'

Thatcher's words, which became known as 'Out, out, out,' were taken as an affront by all sections of opinion in the Republic. Powell was to say of it: 'This must have been a pretty rude shock to the Irish, it can't have been easy for Dr FitzGerald to swallow what was said. It was all part of her approach – she believed you had to lay down your bottom line loud and clear. One of the great advantages of Mrs Thatcher is that she was frankly unembarrassable. She said what she thought, she said what she meant, and she was proud of not being diplomatic.'

Most Irish nationalists, however, felt that she had gone beyond the bounds of diplomatic decency. A wave of anti-British anger swept across the south, so intense that many, including Armstrong, feared the idea of any kind of Anglo–Irish deal had been swept away: 'There was a period of some weeks in which I wasn't at all sure that it would be possible to go on with the negotiations,' he said.

But things steadied, and Armstrong and others persuaded Thatcher that they should try to retrieve something from the diplomatic wreckage. Over lengthy dinners and discussions, the British and Irish cabinet secretaries and other officials sketched out compromises and inched towards agreement throughout 1985. The British prime minister made an effort to mend her fences with FitzGerald when they met again in December, as Powell was to recall: 'Of course Mrs Thatcher was quite capable of playing nice cop as well as nasty cop, and I think she felt she was probably almost too hard on Garret FitzGerald. When they attended a European summit in Dublin, I remember her saying to him, "Garret, I've been doing my best – I've been smiling all day for you."'

They made progress, though in the light of the earlier disputes over words such as alienation and involving – and above all, 'Out, out, out' – they came to pay the most particular attention to vocabulary. When the idea took shape of a new institution to give the Irish input into British policy, 24 different words were considered for its title. The two sides worked through suggestions such as committee, commission and even, briefly, conclave before settling on their final choice. Nally remembered being in full flight when Armstrong interrupted him and said, 'Conference – conference is the word. Anglo–Irish intergovernmental conference.'

It was also agreed that Dublin should have a physical presence in the north. Although in the end government offices were pressed into service, it was a closely guarded secret that the Irish had acquired a house near Belfast. Donlon said:

We went so far as to buy quite a substantial house, but the British side were very negative. They said, 'No, no, you can't do that, that is just too obvious, it is like an embassy, it is almost like a colonial governor's residence – you can't have it.' We had now bought it – to be fair, without consultation in detail with the British side – and naturally enough when they said they couldn't secure it we were left with no alternative but to agree. We held on to the grand property for about two years and eventually sold it, I am happy to say to the Irish taxpayer, at a profit.

Meanwhile, Unionists grew increasingly anxious about all the negotiation which was going on behind closed doors, with occasional leaks, sometimes accurate and sometimes not, provoking Protestant alarm. A sense of calm was, however, imparted by James Molyneaux, then leader of the main Protestant political grouping, the Ulster Unionist party. He believed assurances given to him by senior Conservatives that nothing untoward was in the air.

Ulster Unionist MP Ken Maginnis recalled: 'Some of us used to go to Jim Molyneaux to raise all these rumours with him, and we'd find Jim totally unperturbed. He'd talked to some of the people who were close to Mrs Thatcher, and we were constantly being reassured that all these rumours were without foundation. Even on the day before the Anglo–Irish Agreement was finally decided, it was the same story.' But eventually even the taciturn and unworried Molyneaux became concerned, and went to see Thatcher. He recalled: 'What she said was, "But you see, Jim, this is not joint authority, I assure you it's not joint authority." And I said, "No, but it will lead to joint authority – there are going to be enough loose ends there for them to catch on to, so don't let us fool ourselves."'

When the terms of what became known as the Anglo–Irish Agreement were published in November 1985, virtually every Unionist felt Thatcher had betrayed their cause: some even burnt her in effigy. The document was a political and security hybrid. Thatcher was most interested in its security implications, in particular the idea that it would open a new era of north-south security cooperation; FitzGerald and Dublin placed much emphasis on its political provisions.

Hillsborough was a venue chosen with meticulous attention to detail, because of the significance and sensitivity of the event. It was chosen at the last minute from a shortlist of three, the others being Dromoland Castle in County Clare and the Royal Hospital at Kilmainham in Dublin. One of the attractions of Kilmainham was a large picture of King William III, the great Protestant and Orange hero, portrayed with his wife Mary. Dromoland Castle was the most luxurious venue, Dermot Nally recalling: 'I think Dromoland had ordered something like 60 or 80 lobsters for the post-signing dinner – I am not sure what happened to the lobsters afterwards.' The lobsters were, in fact, a subterfuge designed to mislead, amounting in fact to a particularly expensive red herring.

In the end, the two governments settled on Hillsborough. Thatcher herself added the final touches to the setting, scrutinising an enormous watercolour painting and asking what it depicted: Robert Armstrong was able to tell her it showed the playing fields of Eton. Goodall remembered: 'The prime minister examined the ornaments behind and looked at the pictures to make sure they didn't send some wrong message. Then she started to rearrange the furniture. She said, "I think we want this table moved," so she and Garret got hold of a table between them. We all stood around and Peter Barry, the Irish foreign minister, said to me: "You have to be a prime minister to move furniture around here."'

Next, the two prime ministers sat down. Finding themselves with some time to spare, Thatcher, perhaps wishing to avoid another 'Out, out, out' debacle, suggested a mock question session. Armstrong recalled:

She suddenly had this bright idea, that in order to rehearse themselves Dermot Nally should put questions to her and I should put questions to Garret – the more awkward the questions the better. It was a bizarre scene – here we were firing questions at the other one's prime minister. It was a measure, I think, of her respect for him and his for her, and their joint respect for the two of us, that this could be done. There was a real sense of friendship about it.

Goodall recalled it as 'a pretty weird experience, really. I'd never been to Hillsborough and I found this very elegant eighteenth-century mansion with high wrought-iron railings, in front of which was gathered an enormous crowd of vociferous activists led by Ian Paisley himself. His voice, I must say, carried practically to Belfast, and they were shaking the railings and roaring disapproval. We could hear this background noise even during lunch.'

The document signed that day was, by any standards, a historic one, giving the Republic a significant role in the running of Northern Ireland. The Agreement opened with a statement by the two governments that any change in Northern Ireland's status could only come about with the consent of a majority of its people. It added that if, in future, a majority clearly wished to have a united Ireland, that decision would be respected and put into effect. The idea that Unionists would regard this as a historic advance would, however, prove to be a forlorn hope.

The Agreement then unveiled intricately crafted new structures, at the heart of which was an inter-governmental conference – Armstrong's word had been accepted – which would be jointly chaired by the Northern Ireland Secretary and the Dublin Minister for Foreign Affairs. This was to be serviced by a small secretariat of British and Irish civil servants based at Maryfield, a closely guarded office building on the outskirts of East Belfast. At the inter-governmental conference, the Irish government could put forward views and proposals on almost any subject: the Republic was given no executive power, but the Agreement committed the two governments to making 'determined efforts' to resolve their differences within the conference.

Almost everyone was surprised that Thatcher was prepared to sign such a document. She had the reputation of being one of the few British politicians to retain any personal commitment to the Union between Britain and Ireland, and, as the European Community had ample cause to know, she was famously jealous and protective of British sovereignty. That sovereignty was technically untouched by the Anglo–Irish Agreement, yet its nationalist tone was obvious to everyone.

Thatcher had not got her joint security zone; FitzGerald had not got his joint authority. It was a compromise package, but it was inspired by a vision: a new era of Anglo–Irish cooperation, in both security and political terms. Every concept, every paragraph, every sentence and almost every word in the tightly written Agreement had been endlessly parsed and negotiated over by ministers and civil servants.

Thatcher assumed Unionists would welcome the fact that she had stitched into an international agreement the consent principle – the concept that Irish unity could only come about with the consent of a majority in Northern Ireland. She explained on television: 'The whole purpose is to get more stable government in Northern Ireland, with a fair deal for each and every citizen, and to reassure the Unionists that their future is all right because the border is accepted, that it could only be changed by a vote of the majority.'

But far from being reassured, the whole of Unionism was outraged. Their reaction was best expressed by Unionist MP, the late Harold McCusker, who conveyed to the Commons the deep hurt he felt had been inflicted on him:

I stood outside Hillsborough, not waving a Union flag – I doubt whether I will ever wave one again – not singing hymns, saying prayers or protesting, but like a dog, and asked the government to put in my hand the document that sold my birthright. I felt desolate, because as I stood in the cold outside Hillsborough Castle everything that I held dear turned to ashes in my mouth. I never believed that the Agreement would deliver me, in the context that it has, into the hands of those who for 15 years have murdered personal friends, political associates and hundreds of my constituents. It would have been better if my children had never looked at the Union flag or thought that they were British or put their trust in the House of Commons, than spending the rest of their lives knowing that they are now some sort of semi-British citizen.

His distress and anger was practically universal among Unionists, who believed the document – 'the Diktat', as Unionist newspapers called it – weakened Northern Ireland's place within the Union. Their opposition was so deep, in fact, that it lasted for years. Protests took many forms, ranging from political boycotts to mass rallies and demonstrations. The sense of crisis led to closer contact between Unionist political parties and loyalist paramilitary groups, two elements which had often been critical of each other. Publicly, the politicians and the illegal groups stayed strictly apart; privately, however, they were in close touch. Confirmation of this came from David Ervine, a loyalist who would later himself enter the political arena. Then a representative of the paramilitary Ulster Volunteer Force (UVF), he remembered meetings involving senior Unionist political figures and illegal groupings such as his own.

There was much militant rhetoric. Paisley declared: 'All I can say, if the British government are determined to reject the ballot box, then they are making the choice of anarchy, not us. And we said that to Mrs Thatcher – two buttons, Madam, you can press either one: democracy or anarchy. This is not the time for words, it is the time for action. Where do the terrorists return to for sanctuary? To the Irish Republic. And yet, Mrs Thatcher tells us that that Republic must have some say in our province. We say Never, never, never.'

Some working-class loyalists defined action as violence. Protestant paramilitary groups such as the UVF and Ulster Defence Association (UDA) had claimed hundreds of lives during the 1970s, but their killing rate dropped in the 1980s, dwindling to an average of around a dozen a year. The Anglo–Irish accord brought new recruits and a revived militancy, however, as tensions and fears rose in the Protestant backstreets.

Johnny Adair, a Protestant from the tough Shankill Road area of Belfast, one of the heartlands of loyalist militancy, was among the impressionable young men. In later years he would rise to the top of the UDA's assassination squads. He remembered: 'It was a time when people like myself thought, this is it, we're going to be sold down the river – very shortly here it's going to be a united Ireland. That's why so many of us responded and came on to the streets.'

While Thatcher saw herself as a Unionist, her relations with Unionists were clearly problematical. Looking back, Powell said: 'There was nothing in the Anglo–Irish

Agreement that should have given the Unionists a moment's loss of sleep, but I'm afraid it didn't work out like that. She would frequently say that surely her commitment to the Union was sufficient guarantee to the Unionists that she would never give away anything that would jeopardise their interests. This was a constant refrain for her, and she was bitterly disappointed when the Unionists, by their reaction to the Anglo–Irish Agreement, did not take it at face value.'

Faced with an eruption of Unionist and Protestant outrage, everyone seemed to have forgotten that the purpose of the Anglo–Irish Agreement had been to stop Sinn Fein and the IRA. Intended, among other things, to tackle the issue of nationalist alienation, it had produced Protestant alienation on an almost unprecedented scale.

For Unionists, it gave rise to profound political trauma. They saw it as striking at their own sense of Britishness, and saw it too as Britain entering a compact with their ancient opponents. They regarded it as a deal done in an underhand way, with the prime minister taking far-reaching steps without consulting Unionist leaders. Thatcher herself tended to regard the accord as a security initiative, rather than a historic new beginning. Foreign Secretary Sir Geoffrey Howe later reflected: 'It took a gigantic struggle by many far-sighted people to persuade her; but although her head was persuaded, her heart was not.'

Unionists saw the Agreement as a victory for constitutional nationalism, and constitutional nationalism agreed with them. It represented, in fact, an unprecedented new partnership between London and Dublin. In the years which followed, that partnership had tense moments during many political and security crises, but though battered it was not broken. From then on, the Northern Ireland problem was essentially viewed from an Anglo–Irish perspective.

4
Death and dialogue

The Agreement was to have profound effects on the politics and psychology of Northern Ireland, and indeed on Anglo–Irish relations, but for some time its deeper significance was masked by the cries of loyalist angst and the din of war. The next few years were to produce much drama, and much violence.

Republicans debated the exact significance of the Agreement, but at the same time the IRA's sinews of war were being strengthened to a fearsome extent. Eluding the surveillance of the British and Irish security agencies, the IRA smuggled in large stocks of weaponry from Libya, whose leader, Colonel Gaddafi, was both sympathetic to their cause and hopeful of causing trouble for the British government.

Gaddafi had provided guns and money to the IRA in the early 1970s, but his interest appeared to have cooled until 1984, when his relations with Britain sharply deteriorated. As a result he renewed the relationship, giving the IRA large stocks of modern military hardware. Four separate shipments of arms made their way from Libya to Ireland in the mid-1980s, bringing the IRA around 1,000 rifles as well as formidable weapons such as Semtex plastic explosive, heavy machine guns firing armour-piercing rounds which could cut through even protected police vehicles, Sam-7 missiles and anti-aircraft guns capable of downing helicopters and planes, and even flame-throwers.

The new weapons meant the IRA was able to step up its violence, not just in Northern Ireland but also in England and Europe. The Libyan armament was brought into play only gradually, but as it came into greater use the IRA killing rate rose from 37 in 1986 to 58 in 1987 and 66 the following year.

The IRA aim was to reverse the pattern of security force casualties. Over the years patterns had changed, so that most security force fatalities came from the police force, the Royal Ulster Constabulary, and the Ulster Defence Regiment (UDR), both of which were locally recruited. The casualty rate for regular British troops had gone down. In the years 1985 to 1987, for example, nine regular soldiers were killed compared to 71 police and UDR members. The republicans coldly set out to kill more British troops, calculating that this was the way to increase the impact of their violence on British political and public opinion.

The IRA thus stepped up violence in England, attempting to move from the previous pattern, which was generally one of hit and run, and instead establish an ongoing presence in Britain, with IRA members and supporters waging a sustained and, in effect, continuous offensive. They attacked a wide range of targets, including military personnel, who tended to be more relaxed in Britain than in Northern Ireland. This approach was further extended to mainland Europe, where British troops came under attack in Germany and neighbouring countries. In Northern Ireland, the IRA staged a series of what they termed 'spectaculars' in which prominent people or large numbers of security force personnel were killed. These included the 1985 incident in which nine RUC officers were killed by a mortar bomb at Newry police station in County Down, and the 1987 assassination of a senior judge and his wife in a border landmine attack.

Yet the escalation of IRA violence could also produce results which were major setbacks for the republican cause. The most striking of these was the Enniskillen bombing, which took place on the morning of Remembrance Day in November 1987, as large numbers of Protestants gathered in the Fermanagh town in readiness for the annual parade and service. A large IRA device hidden in a community hall just behind them exploded without warning, demolishing a wall and bringing down tons of masonry.

The final death toll was eleven, but more than 60 other people, aged from two to 75, were injured. Five of the dead were women. The IRA had desecrated an occasion set aside for the remembrance of the dead, and the world condemned them for it. Two themes flashed round the world in the wake of the bombing: one was that the IRA had killed 11 Protestant civilians as they gathered on Remembrance Day; the second was the almost super-human display of Christian charity and forgiveness shown by a local man, Gordon Wilson. He gave an account of how he lay trapped in the debris holding his daughter's hand, in a radio interview which is remembered as one of the most poignant and affecting moments of the troubles. They talked for a while, but then Marie said, 'Daddy, I love you very much', and fell silent. Wilson survived the ordeal, but his daughter did not. After her death, he summoned the strength of character to say, 'She was a great wee lassie. She was a pet, and she's dead. But I bear no ill will, I bear no grudge.'

A few days after the bombing, a senior IRA source

acknowledged the damage it had inflicted on his movement, saying: 'Politically and internationally it is a major setback. Our central base can take a hell of a lot of jolting and crises with limited demoralisation, but the outer reaches are just totally devastated. It allows the Brits to slot us into the category of terrorists, and that's bad. People in the IRA just feel sick.' Martin McGuinness concurred: 'It was a total and absolute disaster. I felt absolutely gutted by it. My initial reaction was, these people have lost their lives, innocent people in the town of Enniskillen, so my thoughts were obviously for them and for their families. As time moved by and the funerals took place, people sat back and reflected on what had happened and the enormity of all of that. Obviously, it was going to deal a damaging blow to Irish republicanism.'

Thatcher visited Enniskillen shortly afterwards, Powell commenting: 'She resolved that the whole ceremony should be restaged and she would be there. That was quite a brave thing to do, after all, given the personal risk she was at, given the personal risk to many others. At that moment the iron really entered her soul: she thought that the time and political capital that she had invested in the Anglo–Irish negotiations was negated by the continuance of terrorism.'

Battle was joined in earnest with the republicans, the loyalists and the security forces all stepping up their efforts. This led to an extraordinary sequence of events in one month, March 1988. It began in Gibraltar, when three IRA members, one of them a woman, were shot dead by the SAS in disputed circumstances, in what came to be regarded as one of the most controversial incidents of the troubles. Although the IRA unit was intent on staging a bomb attack against British soldiers, the fact that they were unarmed when killed led to widespread criticism of the authorities.

The bodies of the three dead republicans were flown to Dublin and then driven to Belfast, thousands lining the route taken by the coffins. Many thousands more attended the funerals in West Belfast, but in Milltown cemetery mayhem broke out when, to general amazement, a lone loyalist gunman, Michael Stone, a stockily built man with long hair and a moustache, launched a one-man attack on mourners. In other attacks, Stone had helped create a new pattern in which the targeting of randomly chosen Catholics was expanded to include prominent republican figures.

He had earlier targeted Martin McGuinness. Now prepared to speak frankly about his activities, he recounted:

After the Enniskillen bombing, which was an outrage, which was sacrilege, it was put to me, and I willingly took to the task of getting myself down to Londonderry, the Brandywell, i.e., Mr McGuinness's home, to have a look at him for assassination. He was targeted because he was the then head of Northern Command of the IRA. That was in the files I read, so the buck stopped with Mr McGuinness, so he himself had to be sanctioned, i.e., assassinated.

I took particular interest in McGuinness's house, as I intended shooting him through the bathroom window. I decided not to shoot him at the school because of the children. It was decided to give him a 'head shot' at a newsagent's shop in Bishop Street, as this was the most convenient place to do it as he went to the newsagent every morning. I arrived at the scene at about 8.35 a.m. and parked about 20 feet from the shop. I had a .38 revolver in my pocket and an Armalite rifle across the back seat covered by a blanket. I sat there until 9.15 a.m. McGuinness failed to turn up. I went back to Belfast.

The funerals of the three IRA members killed at Gibraltar gave the would-be assassin a second chance. Stone explained: 'I knew there'd be funerals; I knew it would now be Milltown cemetery. I'd been in there over the years. All the loyalist volunteers had been in over there – it was part of the basic training. I said, "It's only two people we're after here, that's McGuinness and Adams, so we'll go for a close quarters." So it was more or less left down to me.'

Stone arrived in the cemetery, which was crowded with mourners, loaded down with grenades and handguns. Republican funerals were often accompanied by a heavy security presence, but on that day, apparently entirely coincidentally, the RUC and army had pulled back a considerable distance. Stone, surrounded by thousands of republicans, was on a near-suicide mission. He continued: 'As the cortège came in, and the mourners came in, I'd actually positioned myself on a path, on the left of the roll of honour, and I planned to shoot McGuinness and Adams, two head shots, as they passed the roll of honour. That was their Cenotaph, and that's where they were going to die.'

But at the critical moment, Stone's view was obstructed by some of the thousands of mourners. McGuinness, Adams and other senior figures then gathered around the republican plot which contains the bodies of many IRA members, most of them killed in the troubles. Stone went on: 'Once the oration began, I pulled out two grenades, lobbed them over actually the head of the mourners.' The result was chaos and confusion, thousands scattering to take cover in the wake of the completely unexpected and unprecedented attack.

After throwing grenades and firing shots, Stone then jogged between the headstones towards a motorway several hundred yards away, pursued by hundreds of men and youths. On the way he periodically stopped, firing shots and throwing grenades to hold his pursuers at bay. Describing the scene, McGuinness said: 'I saw him taking off down the graveyard, then I took off after him, but I was a long way behind, younger people . . . had charged after him and as they ran after him he was firing shots at them and he was throwing hand grenades.'

Stone recalled: 'They were throwing bricks and I was throwing grenades and I sort of had the upper hand. And when they were exchanging insults, I actually called Gerry, I says, "Gerry, come on!" One guy got pretty close, he seemed to know what he was doing, he was ducking in and out behind the headstones. And for a second, he produced a target, and I shot him once and he died.'

He eventually reached the motorway, but by that stage had apparently exhausted his supply of grenades and ammunition. An incensed crowd overpowered him and beat him unconscious before police arrived and saved his life. Most of this extraordinary scene was televised.

Stone had killed three men and injured many more people. He recalled: 'My head swole up and I could barely see out of one eye and I went, "Yeah, fucking brilliant!", because I'm lying there thinking, yeah, brilliant. Because militarily it was unsuccessful. I didn't achieve the objective, I'd actually failed in my mission.' His actions were nonetheless enough to place him in the pantheon of loyalist paramilitary heroes: his name and likeness would, in the years that followed, be painted on backstreet Belfast gable walls.

More was to follow. One of those killed by Stone was a member of the IRA, and as his subsequent funeral made its way to Milltown a car carrying two British army corporals unaccountably drove into the cortège. Mourners besieged the car, assuming that its occupants were loyalists intent on a repeat attack. Dozens of them rushed forward, kicking the car and attempting to open its doors. The corporals were eventually pulled from the car and punched and kicked to the ground. They were then dragged into a nearby sports ground, where they were again beaten and partially stripped. Finally, they were driven to a patch of waste ground and shot dead. The sequence of events is still remembered as an almost unreal period of instability and polarisation.

Yet, even as the horrific violence raged, behind the scenes there was debate and introspection, particularly within republicanism. The Libyan connection had left the IRA better armed than ever before. Violence was certainly causing great disruption, but Enniskillen had demonstrated that terrorism had its political limitations, and could easily be counter-productive. Sinn Fein had established a foothold in the political system, but in a series of elections it had reached a plateau of around eleven per cent of the vote: enough to cause some disruption but not enough to paralyse or overthrow the status quo. On a much more profound level the Anglo–Irish Agreement presented a formidable challenge to the republican movement, since it seemed to undermine many of the assumptions which had kept the IRA campaign alive for so long.

It certainly contained a counter-insurgency function, promising, as it did, closer security cooperation between

London and Dublin, but it had much deeper implications. Sinn Fein had always characterised the Unionist tradition as a British creation, saying that London relied on the Protestant population to help administer Northern Ireland as a British colony. The republican charge was that Unionists had developed a veto on British policy, and that London would not dare challenge Protestant strength. But this old pattern was now shattered. Britain was clearly intent on forging a new deal with constitutional nationalism, and in doing so was prepared to stand up to fierce Unionist opposition. The daily expressed anger of Protestants at the Agreement was an unmistakable sign that Britain was prepared to press ahead, even in the teeth of Unionist anger.

Sinn Fein's Danny Morrison summarised the republican attitude: 'We wanted British withdrawal – that's what we were fighting and dying and going to jail for. But we also saw that the Agreement was a concession, although we were not going to trumpet that. It was a concession because it was a move slightly away from Unionists towards nationalists. We were prepared to pocket any benefits that came from it, but continue to push and demand for more.'

Furthermore, the Agreement demonstrated that the republican view of the south was ludicrously out of date. Since its inception, republican purists had refused to acknowledge the legitimacy of the southern state. The signing of the Anglo–Irish Agreement was a body blow to this view, since the accord was very obviously a deal struck between two sovereign states on equal terms. Britain's formal acceptance of the legitimacy of Irish nationalism gave Sinn Fein much food for thought.

The Agreement was clearly posing the most fundamental of questions to all concerned: on one reading, it had redefined the whole Irish question. Hume emphasised the theme that British interests had changed:

I put out a statement immediately, saying the most important part of the Agreement was that the British government had now declared neutrality on the future of Ireland. Because I knew from my experience, both as a politician and as an historian, that the traditional IRA attitude and their reasons for violence was that the British were in Ireland defending their own interests by force. While that may have been true historically, centuries ago, it was no longer true in today's world.

The IRA had traditionally claimed it was engaged in an anti-colonial, anti-imperialist freedom struggle: suddenly, the supposed imperialist power had made an important move which suggested it did not expect to stay in Ireland for ever. This raised the question, in thoughtful republican minds, of whether a continuation of violent action represented the most effective way ahead.

Republican leaders acknowledge that this was a seminal period for them, and one which would, in time, lead on to the peace process. The flavour of the debate is recalled by some of the leading figures. Pat Doherty, a senior republican who was national organiser of Sinn Fein said: 'We had a meeting of the organisers with Gerry and we were talking about political development and the obstacles, and of course there was a fairly intense debate.' Doherty wondered: 'How are we ever to prove that politics could work, unless there was a plan and a coherent strategy?' Morrison contributed: 'What the republican movement wanted to be associated with was a desire for peace, even though it was fighting an armed struggle against the British presence here. They certainly wanted to emphasise the fact, because now, you see, the movement was highly armed.'

Adams made a key point: 'I made it clear that there was no military solution – there had to be a political solution as this was not a military problem, it was a political problem. We needed to challenge our political opponents, we needed to challenge and try and work out alliances with them and try and isolate areas where we didn't agree, but work out cooperation in areas where we did agree.'

The problem was that IRA violence had made Sinn Fein political pariahs, even to fellow Irish nationalists: there was no formal public contact between them and the Irish government, or the SDLP or the Catholic Church. What contact there was tended to be fleeting and furtive.

One of those attempting to build bridges between the republicans and the rest of nationalism was Father Alex Reid, a Redemptorist priest based at Clonard Monastery in the Falls Road district of Belfast. One of the key figures in the peace process, he shunned publicity for many years before agreeing to describe his role to Brook Lapping. He remembered: 'The SDLP and the Dublin government wouldn't talk to Sinn Fein unless the IRA stopped, so you were in a Catch-22 situation. And the Sinn Fein people could do nothing about creating or developing an alternative unless they could talk to the Irish government and the SDLP.' So it was that in late 1985 he wrote letters to Hume, recalling: 'The essence of the proposal was that the nationalist parties would agree through dialogue among themselves, which is where we were stuck. These letters were actually designed to try and persuade others to talk to Sinn Fein.'

Hume recalled receiving the letter: 'I got a message from

a priest who told me that what I was saying was very interesting to Sinn Fein and that they would like to talk to me about it, and would I talk to them.' Father Reid was pleased with Hume's response: 'He was the leader of the biggest nationalist party and he could have written a polite reply or sent some local person to see us. I will always be very grateful to Mr Hume because he didn't know me, but he actually phoned the day he received the letter and said he would come down the next day. He spoke to us as if he had known us all our lives. Basically he came in and said yes, he would cooperate.'

Hume reasoned: 'One of the things about the republicans who used violence was that, while we disagreed with them fundamentally, they actually believed in what they were doing. Therefore, if you've got the fact that the reasons for violence no longer existed, you had a real chance of getting the violence stopped.' The result was a series of meetings, heavily criticised from many points of the political spectrum, between teams from the SDLP and Sinn Fein in Belfast monasteries. Hume was forced to defend himself: 'I'm a politician, politics is the alternative to war, politics is about dialogue, I'm about dialogue. I'll talk to anyone about it, that doesn't mean I approve of what they stand for.'

The debate went right to the heart of the difference between Sinn Fein and their constitutional rivals, the SDLP. Mitchel McLaughlin of Sinn Fein declared:

Can you argue that constitutional and peaceful means have succeeded, when the evidence was to the contrary? I mean, I was there on October 5th 1968 when the first civil rights march in Derry was attacked by the RUC. I was there at the battle of the Bogside, when the British Army came on the streets. I was there on Bloody Sunday, when the British Army shot up a civil rights march and murdered 14 people. So those are the arguments that we gave to the SDLP.

Seamus Mallon replied for the SDLP: 'I remember saying, where are you getting? Are you winning this war? Have you any hope of winning this war? You certainly can continue it, but are you going to win? Or are you going to get to a stage where you're never going to be defeated? Is that your victory? Because, if that is your victory, then it's not in the name or in the wishes of the Irish people.'

Sinn Fein contended that Britain was a colonial power occupying and exploiting Northern Ireland for its own benefit. At the monastery, Hume argued that this was no longer true: 'I said very clearly to Sinn Fein and to Gerry Adams and company that the British had declared their neutrality on the future of Ireland in the Anglo–Irish Agreement.' Morrison replied, 'Oh, how can you say that? The British are not neutral.' McLaughlin concurred: 'How would you define British neutrality in Ireland when their army was on the street, when you had emergency legislation, when you had people being killed on a weekly basis – was that neutrality?'

Mallon came back: 'I remember saying what Britain has been seeking for some considerable time was a way with honour of getting out of here, and shaking the dust of what they would regard as this terrible place off their feet.' Morrison conceded, 'There was some merit to some of the things they were saying, although this business of the British being neutral was a nonsense.'

The talks tailed off after eight months, most observers regarding them as a fruitless exercise which had run its course and failed. Yet, in the years that followed, contact was maintained between Hume and Adams, regularly and discreetly. It was a dialogue which was to prove to be one of the most important wellsprings of the peace process. Adams was to say that the most important outcome of the talks was 'that John Hume and I kept talking. We kept talking before and we kept talking afterwards. We developed enough trust in each other, and in each other's personalities, to continue that dialogue through some awful incidents.' Over the next few years the fighting would continue, but so too would the talking.

Hume set out to strengthen his hand with Adams. He approached Peter Brooke, the thoughtful new Northern Ireland Secretary, asking him to say something to help prove to Sinn Fein that the British government was indeed neutral. Brooke was already interested in Sinn Fein's thought processes, making a point of assiduously reading its newspaper, *Republican News*.

Hume said: 'The British government no longer had any economic or strategic interest in being in Ireland, and therefore I said to Peter Brooke, the British government should say that.' Brooke confirmed: 'We did discuss whether the way in which Sinn Fein were representing the British position as being a colonial one could in fact be contradicted. We were seeking to convey that this was just fundamentally false.' He agreed that the time was right for a new clarification, and went on to produce in a speech a short but hugely significant statement: 'The British government has no selfish strategic or economic interest in Northern Ireland.' It was brief, it was concise, yet it would turn out to be a milestone in the slowly developing peace process.

5
The message

The IRA was planning another attempt on the life of Margaret Thatcher in November 1990, the same month that Brooke made his speech, when she departed from Number 10 and thus left the Anglo–Irish scene. Her resignation meant the attack would be directed against her successor, John Major.

First, however, Major received a less violent communication from the republicans. He recalled: 'I'd been prime minister for two days, I think, when a letter arrived from Gerry Adams of Sinn Fein. It was the Sinn Fein case in straightforward terms – that he believes that the British should leave Ireland and there should be a united Ireland. But there just seemed a flavour about the letter: it might be possible that Sinn Fein were looking for a way out of the last 20 years, that they were looking for a way to end the violence.'

As Adams remembers it: 'It was a Dear John. It struck me, something I just read somewhere, that Ho Chi Minh or someone like that had, through all the decades for the liberation of Vietnam, continuously written to the colonial power. It just struck me that here we were, and we'd never made any attempt to proactively engage the British prime minister.'

Adams was also to reveal that a first copy of his letter to Major was, ludicrously, addressed to the wrong Downing Street, a small street in the heart of the fiercely loyalist

Shankill Road district. Adams shook his head as he remembered: 'I wrote a letter and gave it to one of the highly trained staff that we have around this place, and it was dispatched to John Major, Number 10 Downing Street, Belfast. I got a very nice reply from the person at Number 10 Downing Street, Belfast.'

Just ten weeks later, the IRA sent a very different sort of message, in the form of a republican attack which struck at the very heart of government. Major recalled: 'We had a cabinet meeting on the Gulf War, and the War Cabinet, the most senior and most involved members of the cabinet, were there with senior civil servants, Robin Butler and many others.' Butler, who had been in the same room as Thatcher when the Brighton bomb went off, now found himself in the same room as Major in another serious incident. He remembered: 'We were discussing, as it happens, at that moment, the risk of Iraqi terrorist action in London, and whether there was any possibility that they would launch terrorist attacks. And I remember very vividly that the last word John Major used, before the explosion, was the word "bomb."' Major's memory is: 'There was a moment in which everyone seemed to freeze and then someone shouted, "That's a mortar!"'

From a specially prepared transit van abandoned at a carefully chosen point in Whitehall, just 200 yards away from the War Cabinet meeting, the IRA had launched an attack which only narrowly missed its target. Charles Powell recalled: 'I was sitting right next to John Major at the cabinet table. I put my hand on his head quite instinctively and pushed him down under the table. Indeed, I was going down pretty fast myself, and various other members of the War Cabinet were adopting not altogether heroic poses, hardly surprising.

'Thank goodness we had replaced the cabinet room windows only very recently with non-shatter glass, otherwise I think you would have had several dead people in the cabinet room. There was a lot of noise, smoke, then the most frightening feature of all – the cabinet room door burst open and a number of middle-aged and rather overweight Metropolitan policemen emerged, waving elderly revolvers which none of them had ever fired in anger. It seemed to me that this was getting really dangerous. The press was told that the War Cabinet had continued almost without a break – well, that was one way of putting it.'

Major remembers: 'We stayed crouched under the table for a short while, and then we left and went to different parts of the building. I went down to a secure room. But it was very close. Another ten or twelve feet nearer and it would actually have come through the cabinet window, and half the cabinet, I think, would have perhaps not survived it.' Northern Ireland Secretary, Sir Patrick Mayhew, made an ex-soldier's comment: 'A very near miss had been secured by the IRA. A little bit of correction for line would probably have killed a large part of the cabinet, if not the whole lot.'

The double message from the republicans was that, while they were interested in talks, they were also intent on prosecuting their campaign. The Armalite and ballot-box strategy had, it seemed, been refined to one of operating with a talks invitation in one hand and a mortar bomb in the other.

Back in Belfast, loyalist groups were maintaining their own campaign of violence. Johnny Adair, who had recalled hearing incendiary rhetoric from loyalist politicians at the time of the Anglo–Irish Agreement in 1985, had by then risen close to the top of the UDA, also known as the Ulster Freedom Fighters. Adair, who acquired the nickname of Mad Dog, said in an interview of one attack which killed five Catholic men: 'That was just a message to tell the republicans, that do this to us and we'll do this to youse – that's an eye for an eye and a tooth for a tooth. I led from the front, I was not an armchair general. The Ulster Freedom Fighters trained their recruits and armed them heavily, and took the war, for once, to the IRA and Sinn Fein.'

Another senior loyalist said: 'We certainly felt we were winning the war. When we saw the tricolour over coffins, the beret and gloves on top of that, we felt encouraged that these people are not unbeatable, that they bleed the same as we bleed, and they will die the same as we die.'

David Ervine maintained republicans were becoming so worried about their casualty rate that they offered a deal: 'We won't kill you if you don't kill us.' The loyalist response was stark: 'We were getting to the bastards, and the answer to the Provos at that time was fuck off, no way,' he said.

But despite all the shootings in Belfast and the mortar attack on Downing Street, republicans remained interested in a dialogue with the British government. Adams recalled that 'a practice developed almost of semaphore.' Both the government and the republicans got into the habit of sending each other their speeches, drawing attention to their most important points. Republican attention was drawn, for example, to a speech by Mayhew in which he referred to welcome signs that some in Sinn Fein were voicing their wish for a peaceful solution and a desire to follow a constitutional path. Both sides then came to believe that some better form of dialogue was desirable, using a long-established but only infrequently used channel known as 'the link'.

This had been reactivated by Peter Brooke, who recalled: 'I used to have these regular weekly briefings with John Deverell, who was the head of the intelligence service in the province.' An MI5 veteran who had risen to senior rank, Deverell had for more than a decade been concerned with monitoring and combating the IRA in Northern Ireland, Britain and on the Continent. As head of intelligence in Northern Ireland, he oversaw and coordinated the activities of the RUC's Special Branch, military intelligence and MI5 itself. This meant he was at the centre of an extensive web of clandestine activity. Hundreds of Special Branch officers and hundreds of army intelligence operatives were targeted on the IRA, trying to find out all they could about the republican movement. His job was to put all the pieces together.

Brooke continued:

We met alone in order to discuss issues like telephone warrants, but they were good occasions, because it provided an opportunity for an exchange. On one occasion he did catch me by surprise by telling me about the link which existed in the Londonderry area. That was totally news to me, but it was brought to me because we had to decide whether to reactivate it, as the British individual within that link was going to be retiring from the service. We would need to introduce somebody else in, and that was something for which they required a deliberate ministerial decision on my part. I was the one who was going to be in the firing line if news broke that it existed. We did have a proper debate about it, because it was a real decision, a Rubicon that I personally was having to cross, but I was satisfied that it was a proper thing for me to do.

The next move involved Deverell and John Chilcot, who, as permanent secretary at the Northern Ireland Office, was the most senior civil servant in Belfast. Chilcot recalled with a smile: 'I remember John Deverell arriving at a particularly useful time – I think the sun had just gone over the yardarm. And he did have this message through the link which contained the potentially quite dramatic phrase, as it were authorised by Martin McGuinness: "The conflict is over, but we need your advice on how to bring it to a close."'

Chilcot's immediate reaction – 'apart from pouring John a decent-sized Bushmills whiskey and also one for myself' – was to inform Mayhew and Major. Mayhew gave an initial judgement: 'At face value it looked as though we really were, as John Chilcot suggested, nearer to an end to violence than we had been for the last twenty years.' Major's reaction was: 'It was a message I was delighted to receive, but it immediately raised questions – was it authentic?'

Chilcot gave his judgement: 'The prime minister asked us quite explicitly, was this message authentic? Did it come from McGuinness, was McGuinness speaking for the IRA leadership? What we told him, having worked it through and done some digging, was that yes, it was authentic, it was from McGuinness and it was spoken with authority.'

The research carried out for the Brook Lapping programmes has, however, established definitively that this was quite wrong. McGuinness was speaking the truth when he declared: 'I sent no such message, and sent no message which in any way indicated that that was the mood of republicans at that time.'

The message, as we shall see, was the work of a number

of hands, none of which belonged to McGuinness. It was first drafted by 'the link' – three Catholics in the city of Londonderry, who for many years played an extraordinary clandestine role. One was close to the IRA, another was particularly trusted by the intelligence agency, MI5, and the third, Denis Bradley, was a former priest who knew McGuinness well. The three had in the past acted as go-betweens, a conduit between the highest levels of the IRA and the British authorities, especially in the mid-1970s. The link's route to the British government had previously been through a British intelligence officer, Michael Oatley. The new man was an MI5 agent they all knew as Fred, or Robert.

Having received what they thought was authentication of the message, Major called together a few trusted advisers to work out its exact significance and how to react. Major recalled that they sought to put themselves into the minds of Adams and McGuinness. Looking back, Mayhew set out the dilemma:

The question was whether these people were generals in an opposing force in military terms, or whether they had truly recognised that a military approach was not going to get them what they wanted, and they were now going to try to lead their followers down a political road. We had to move back from the previous position of successive governments, which had been, 'Well, we will give you five years and we will see how you behave over the next five years and then perhaps we will talk.'

Mayhew further believed that the government would be playing for the highest of stakes, even mentioning the possibility of civil war:

My advice was that we should take this further but with due caution, [as] potentially damaging and very weakening, handle with care but with hope. There were very proper concerns – what would be the effect if this got out and nothing came of it? What would be the effect amongst our supporters in the House of Commons? What would be the effect, more importantly, amongst the majority of people living in Northern Ireland, who were always afraid that the Westminster government would get sick of the whole business and try to railroad them into the Republic against their will, and if that suspicion and fear was fed, well, then one could visualise even civil war.

Chilcot advised a pragmatic approach: 'If you set a long time condition, a period of rehabilitation in which no violence took place, it would not happen. It wasn't realisable, it wasn't deliverable for the republican leadership, and wasn't realisable for us.'

Other ministers who viewed the whole thing more as a danger than an opportunity included the Home Secretary, Kenneth Clarke, a senior minister who had not been closely involved in Northern Ireland. He said: 'I took the very cautious view. I was deeply suspicious, having had no direct dealings with McGuinness or the IRA in the past, and I found myself spelling out what seemed to me the obvious very, very, high risk in this and that it wasn't something that John should embark upon.' Major, however, decided the message should be explored and investigated rather than rebuffed, saying: 'We decided to send a pretty substantive and pretty encouraging reply. We didn't brush their letter aside, and I think the tone of the reply, as much as the substance of the reply, encouraged the possibility that we might move further.'

The prime minister's reply was sent off on a Friday evening; some involved had thought of waiting till Monday, but officials were anxious to get it off their plate. On the Saturday, after it had been despatched, came the Warrington bomb. Two IRA bombs placed in litter bins in the Lancashire town killed two children: three-year-old Jonathan Ball and Timothy Parry, aged twelve. The killings led to a particularly strong wave of revulsion throughout Britain and especially in the Republic, where tens of thousands of people attended a peace rally.

In the wake of the deaths of the children, the government reconsidered. Mayhew spelt out his attitude: 'We were in the presence of a hard cop, soft cop, kind of approach. I knew well enough, of course, that there was a school of thought in republican circles that said the only way to get the Brits to move is to kick 'em. Was this the Brits being kicked? Nothing could have been less propitious at that moment.'

Major disclosed: 'I very seriously considered pulling the plug on the whole enterprise and just dropping it. I was very close to it indeed, when I saw the real horror of what had happened at Warrington.' Chilcot described Major's state of mind: 'You're asking, in John Major's case, a British prime minister and an Englishman, to try to reach a judgement about the potential direction of development of republican politicians, query former terrorists. That's a big gap to judge across, and so you need some bits of evidence to help you to cross it.'

Major's reply to the republicans, consisting of nine carefully constructed paragraphs, had meanwhile been passed by Fred through the link to McGuinness. He was noncommittal: 'I went along and met with the contact, and the nine-paragraph statement was handed to me. And I

said, "Yeah, this is very interesting, grand," still very sceptical about where it was all leading.'

Chilcot set out to gather evidence of the IRA's intentions. He said he instructed Fred to go back and ask the
link for proof of IRA good faith, in the form of a short
ceasefire. He believed that if there was an agreement that
events on the ground would be favourable – a euphemism
for an absence of violence – for a period of weeks, then
direct dialogue might be possible. He summed up: 'It was,
if you like, a test of the republican leadership's capability
to control their own movement, and a wish to do that,
but also an indication of where they were heading.'

There is dispute over whether what Fred did next was
authorised by ministers, but there is no doubt that a direct
encounter then took place. McGuinness and Gerry Kelly,
a senior republican who had once been convicted of bombing the Old Bailey in London, met Fred in a house in
Derry. McGuinness remembered what Fred said:

Fred was very keen to persuade us that the British government
were serious about engaging in real and meaningful negotiations with us. The British government's attitude about Ireland was that Ireland should be as one – and those were his
exact words. I was quite convinced from my contacts with
this person that he was a bona fide representative of the
British government, and that this was a person who could
have a message on the desk of the British prime minister
within seconds.

Kelly maintains that Fred said: 'Everyone knows we agreed
that there is going to be Irish unity, it is an inevitability.
What we want is to make that process easier, we want to
convince the IRA that armed struggle is not necessary.'
Fred then broached the subject of a ceasefire, though he did

not use that word, McGuinness reporting: 'He indicated to us that they wished events on the ground to quieten for a period of several weeks, I think two weeks was mentioned specifically. The word ceasefire in fact wasn't even mentioned, cessation wasn't mentioned.'

Fred had avoided the word ceasefire not through nervousness, but tact, since all of those around the table knew that a mid-1970s IRA ceasefire had convulsed the republican movement. This feeling was so strong that republican Young Turks later ousted the former leadership of Ruáiri Ó Brádaigh and Dáithí Ó Conaill and seized control of the movement. Those Young Turks were headed by Adams and McGuinness, who claimed that, during the first ceasefire, the British 'probably came as near at that time to defeating the republican struggle than at any other time.'

Instead of ceasefires, they had, in fact, helped to construct the theory of the long war, accepting that the IRA campaign would be long and difficult. Fred was keen to explore the possibility of ending violence, but he was also keenly aware that the Martin McGuinness who sat poker-faced across the Derry table that night had spent almost two decades refusing to contemplate another ceasefire.

Gerry Kelly remembered: 'You know it is okay this guy saying it in a private room, so we did ask questions about, well, who else knows about this, was he really speaking for the British government? He was very adamant about that. Are you speaking for the British prime minister? Very adamant about that.'

This time it was McGuinness's turn to take a message back to his colleagues. Adams was pragmatic: 'We can't rule it out, and we could also see merit in the IRA taking the moral high ground. Part of what we were eventually arguing was that there were times when there aren't any IRA operations for a month or for longer periods. So if this happens sometimes in the ebb and flow of armed struggle, why not do it in a deliberate way?'

But while the republicans mulled this over, their bombers were highly active. A large bomb placed at Bishopsgate, in the heart of London's financial district, in April 1993, caused huge damage, estimated at well over £300 million. Yet still the British offer lay on the table. Little happened for some weeks and then, out of the blue, Bradley was summoned to a meeting, where McGuinness gave him a message with an offer of a two-week ceasefire to allow talks. McGuinness explained: 'The contact, like ourselves, understood the hugely important significance of this. This was mould-shattering. The IRA were prepared to take this absolutely massive step for them and bring about a period of quiet – in effect, accede to a request from a British government. That was absolutely huge, immense, massive within the process.'

Fred passed McGuinness's message, with its offer of a two-week ceasefire, to London, where Major called together a few key colleagues for a late-night meeting at his room in the Commons. Once again Kenneth Clarke was highly dubious: 'I always took the view,' he remembered, 'that I'll believe this when I see it – if this can be turned into a serious peace process with these people on terms which are remotely satisfactory to Irish policy as a whole.'

Major was to say it was helpful to have 'that sceptical voice' present. Chilcot remembers that the prime minister would have preferred to have more to go on from the republicans: 'I think John Major felt that he was entitled to something more than a mere two-week ceasefire. The wording perhaps didn't take the republican leadership, if they were ever put the question by their own supporters, any further than that. But I think all the contextual surround would be that this ceasefire, if it prospered in terms of getting into dialogue, would then be extended indefinitely, and would be as it were the end to violence.'

Mayhew, too, wanted to take the exercise forward, but Clarke argued that two weeks was simply not enough. Major weighed the arguments: the republicans had offered a ceasefire, but they had also killed two children in Warrington and set off a bomb at Bishopsgate. He certainly had a sense that a great opportunity was to hand, but at the same time the IRA had made it clear that though they favoured talks they were in the meantime intent on maintaining their violence, both in Britain and Northern Ireland. Major concluded that two weeks would not do, with Chilcot saying of the continuing violence: 'That in a sense raises the price for a British government to enter into dialogue – and part of the payment of the price is in time.'

So it was that Major concluded a longer ceasefire was necessary. 'We fixed upon the period of three months,' he said. 'That, we thought, was a sufficient firebreak, but it was not too long to be a deterrent. Not too long to look like a government ploy, but a sufficient period to show their good faith.'

Just then, however, the IRA set off a large bomb at the Opera House, Belfast, causing much damage to the downtown area. In British eyes, it was simply one bomb too many, Mayhew exclaiming: 'Well, I mean one after another, after another. A time comes, and it came after the Opera House one, when I'm afraid everybody said, "Well that's it – at least for the time being, that's it." And there's no means, at this point in time, of saying when it can be revived, because who can argue now against those who believed all along that this was hard cop, soft cop stuff.' And so the British reply specifying a three-month ceasefire was put in the file, and never sent.

In Derry, McGuinness waited for a response that never came. The ceasefire offer had been truly ground-breaking in IRA terms, and the republicans found the silence that followed it puzzling. To their mind, attacks such as the bomb at the Opera House represented simply business as usual: in their mentality, the logic of the fact that a cease-fire might be in the offing was that violence would continue until the moment it was actually agreed.

McGuinness recalled: 'I sat back, the days passed, I made contact with the contact. I said, you know, "What's going on here, what's happening? Why has there been no response? What's wrong, is there a problem?" There was nothing, and then eventually it became clear to me that it wasn't going to happen – that the British government had moved along this route, that the IRA had called their bluff, and the British government backed down.' The two sides had seemed to be moving towards each other, but in the event, real dialogue did not take place. In retrospect it can be argued, however, that their dealings through the link were a vital preliminary to the eventual engagement which was to come.

6
'The link'

The story of 'the link' is one of the most extraordinary to come out of the troubles. The IRA and the British authorities were for decades locked in mortal combat: the republicans killed hundreds of members of the security forces, while London retaliated by killing scores of IRA members and imprisoning many hundreds more. Yet, right through the ferocity of the conflict, a direct channel of contact remained open from the British cabinet to the leaders of the republican movement.

It all came to light with an exclusive story in the *Observer* newspaper in November 1993. Exactly what passed between the government and the republicans continues to be in contention, for after the existence of the link was eventually revealed, the two sides issued differing versions of their communications. Each published detailed accounts, each accusing the other side of deceit and forgery. The government claimed the 'conflict is over' message had been sent by Martin McGuinness: he maintained it had not. Mayhew said that 'what has been said to the IRA in private is exclusively what has been said in public. They have been told in private that we have meant what we've said in public.' The government claimed that any meetings with the republicans had been unauthorised: 'It was a spook freelancing,' Mayhew's press officer told journalists.

The government's case was weakened when it was

forced to concede that documents it had published were incorrect. Responding to queries about the discrepancies, Mayhew announced that a number of 'errors' had come to light. A more direct piece of evidence about the accuracy of the government's public position came during a conversation between one of the authors, Eamonn Mallie, and a former government minister. Pressed on the accuracy of what had been set out by the government the minister said: 'Of course we fucking lied. What could we do?'

What follows are the words of Denis Bradley, a remarkable man who, with others, played a remarkable role in working to bring the troubles to an end. Bradley, the one-time priest, tells the story of what happened, giving a unique insight into a subterranean structure which, unknown to the wider world, had existed for decades.

McGuinness's mother and Bradley's parents came from the same area near Buncrana in County Donegal, and as a priest Bradley had officiated at the wedding of McGuinness and his wife, Bernie Canning, in Buncrana. McGuinness and his family attended Long Tower Church, where Bradley was a curate for years. According to Bradley, a senior Catholic RUC officer in Londonderry, Frank Lagan, suggested in 1972 that there should be a line of communication between republicans and the government. Bradley and two others become involved at that stage, working first with senior civil servant Frank Steele. His understudy was Michael Oatley, an MI6 officer who took part in talks with the IRA in 1974. Bradley remained in the chain up until 1978, when it became dormant, but became reinvolved at the time of the 1981 hunger strike.

In 1990 McGuinness approached Bradley and expressed concern about one of the men involved in the link, a local man who dealt directly with the British. Bradley agreed to become reinvolved, to assure McGuinness that any business would be transacted properly.

Norma Percy and her colleagues interviewed Bradley for many hours, the transcripts of their conversations amounting to some 25,000 words. They also interviewed, on an off-the-record basis, his two colleagues in the link. What follows is an account which, of necessity, has been heavily edited, but which retains Bradley's original words.

The republican movement is a strange beast. It can be a very vicious beast, as we've all known, watching 30 years of war. It is a strange beast in that it trusts no one outside of itself – even me, though I was very close to some of the people over the years because, historically, that's the position I was put in; I was a Catholic priest. You particularly trusted somebody like me who was on the ground, and you trusted me more over the years as you saw where I was coming from, because you knew you could interpret who I was and where I was coming from, and what I was looking for was peace and the end to war.

It's important to understand that myself and Martin McGuinness have had a long and complex relationship, which I suppose had at the centre of it a lot of trust and a lot of understanding, but also one which had a lot of arguments involved in it.

I had longed for, maybe even prayed for, Martin McGuinness to begin to think politically, but his reaction always was, politics is game-playing. I think there was within that psyche an understanding of politics as a dirty game. Then he came to me one day and talked politics and talked about having political ambitions, though he wouldn't have used the words political ambitions. I said to him, 'Are you now interested in politics?' and he said, 'I've always been interested in politics,' and I nearly fell off the chair. I thought, we have had a road to Damascus conversion somewhere here. The conversion from politics being game-playing to actually having an interest in politics is a major, major shift.

This is the beginning of something that can be built upon, this is entering into a new reality. Knowing him as well as I knew him for all those years, and having argued with him for all of those years and having had major rows at times, I thought once that change begins to take place in him it will take place in other people – but perhaps it has already taken place in other people, and he is reflecting what is happening and it can be built upon.

I was told that Fred had arrived in Northern Ireland, that the link or the back-channel had been very quiet, cold for quite some time. I hadn't been personally involved, and I was told that Fred had arrived and that Fred was talking very positively about a new change within the British mentality. He wasn't saying that it had all changed, he wasn't saying that anything was going to be easy. But what he was describing was a total change: that enough people within the various hierarchies of British politics and British intelligence were now beginning to look at the possibility of re-engaging with republicans.

I also felt that the British would use and abuse whenever it suited them, so I was extremely sceptical. But if there was a reciprocal change on the British side, then it couldn't be ignored. My weakness, and the weakness of the back-channel, was that we wanted peace. That's always a weakness, because you cannot walk away from a possible opportunity. Even if you sometimes know that the opportunity is not going to go the full way, you have to grab it because your bottom line is that you want peace and therefore that leaves you exposed. So our weakness always was that people could use us and abuse us, because they would have thought that we would always be there. There had been often arguments amongst the three of us in the link that we were too soft, that we were too available. When the republicans wanted to say they didn't like us or didn't really trust us, they could do that, and they could also tell us nothing. The British could do the exact same things, and we had no access to the actual centres of power.

So we had to build up antennae which were way and beyond normal antennae, we had to suss things out from the subtleties of a word, from the subtleties of how a word was spoken or how a sentence was put forward. We became quite good at that, but we still were very weak. Therefore, when Fred came talking with his new box of Smarties, my reaction was that I'd seen these Smarties before and I remained to be convinced that it would go through to that degree.

Fred came with a speech which Peter Brooke was about to deliver, and said this was an indicator of goodwill, of their willingness to re-engage and to begin the process of building up some semblance – small as it may be – of trust between republicanism and the British government. He said this speech was going to be delivered in a couple of days' time. Would we please get it to the republican movement, so that they can have it to know that it's happening, because we believe that the content is extremely important.

I read the content, and there was a statement within it that the British had no selfish or strategic position within Northern Ireland, that they wanted to be reasonably neutral and that they wanted to try to work out a solution. Now that's only a sentence, but within this type of reality that type of sentence has major implications. Because if you analyse that historically, it is the first time ever that the British government said, 'We have no selfish and strategic position vis-à-vis Northern

Ireland, we are people who want peace, we want to work out a solution within Northern Ireland.'

And I thought there was a basis for a solution, it was there within that document. Peter Brooke was not alone giving this document, but he was actually beginning to use what I would call tonality – the way he said things was very different from what was being said in the late 1980s.

Republicans took it, and I remember talking to McGuinness afterwards, who read the sentence and interpreted the sentence extremely well. He said, 'Yes, if that is true that is a major, major shift.' Now he didn't trust it, had major reservations about it, it's only words on paper, what does it mean? But you could see that things were changing, and that things could begin to happen. So Fred was now an interesting player within this process.

One of our people was a major player with the British – we always sent him into the field to play with the British, and if he didn't convert you with passion, he converted you with boredom. He would have talked to you like many's a politician till you had nothing left to say. He wore you down, he was extremely good at doing it, the type of thing that I wasn't particularly good at. He would have bombarded them with material, he would have talked to them about the politics, about the history of Ireland, about the history of British–Irish relationships and so forth.

I had had a situation before when I was told: 'Denis, when you see us – meaning MI6 – re-engage in this situation seriously you will know that the British are beginning the process of re-engagement again. Anything else that happens between now and then is only play-acting.' That had left a deep psychological impression upon me, because I had come to the conclusion that the intelligence people move within the British establishment before the politicians move. The politicians will not make their movement without having their intelligence people out on the ground doing their pre-negotiations before the politicians will move. That is part of how the system worked.

There was always a fear in this type of world that people had been 'turned'. We thought we were capable of turning MI6 agents, turning them in the sense not of making them into spies in that old John Le Carré-type war, but turning them into philosophical, theological converts who believed there needed to be engagement.

I think that there was a suspicion that one of our people had been turned, so when Fred appeared, Martin McGuinness was very reluctant to engage in the process. I had to use the relationship that I had with him to actually persuade him to re-engage, to keep it going, not to break it off, that things were beginning to change; and that while I hadn't been a member of the trio for about six years that I personally would re-engage to reassure him that things would be okay.

One day Martin McGuinness arrived into my office with one of the other members of the link, and they talked about republicans possibly re-engaging in the link. He described to me again his old suspicions of the 1970s and his difficulty with one of our members, and [said that] he personally wasn't comfortable with him. He was suspicious of all of these situations because he had to be – it would be naive not to be suspicious of them.

I remember pleading with him for quite some time that this was bigger than this personality clash; that 1974 was understandable, but you couldn't live off the fears of 1974 for ever, that there had to be a re-engagement at some stage, and that now was as good a time as any. The signals were beginning to come out from all sides that engagement would be possible. I remember saying to him, 'Look, Martin, I've been out of this for six years, but I personally will go back in. You know me well enough, I won't tell you lies. While you and I may shout and argue with each other, we trust each other enough to know that nothing untoward will happen and I'll protect your back as well as I can.' He said he would think about it. You had to know McGuinness well enough to know that 'I'll think about it" meant yes. So we were back on board.

We were dealing with two groups of people who were very suspicious of each other and who were looking for the downside of everything before they would look for the upside of anything. It was quite clear for a number of months that the British government, through Fred, through Peter Brooke's interventions, that things were changing, that they wanted to engage. We were being assured by Fred on a daily basis that this was a reality.

On the other hand, the tonality, the type of speeches, the type of responses that were coming from republicanism were now a million light years from where they had been a year beforehand. They were talking about Europe, they were talking about the island of Ireland growing together economically, they were talking about contextualising the conflict.

We were aware, through Fred and other sources, that in fact republicanism was engaged in a dialogue with the Irish government. We were also aware that the SDLP were now engaged, specifically through John Hume, in a dialogue with republicans, and that all of that reality was now in situ. The one danger was that it could die off through the actual first steps being taken, and that it was hard to know how that first step was going to be taken. When you spoke to any of them individually they said, 'It's too dangerous for me to turn round, I have too much of a history here, I could get stuck in the back or stuck in the front if I turn round, if I engage.' So it's as if they were all in the one room but they weren't facing each other. Our job as mediators, if we were any good, was to get them to turn around and face each other.

The 'conflict is over' message

We were frustrated: they had been in that room for quite some considerable time now, and weren't even acknowledging that there were other people in the room. So, out of all of that, we said we needed to do something and we said right, let's write something. We didn't often write: it's very dangerous to write in this type of situation, because you can be accused of leading policy and creating policy rather than either interpreting it or sending it on to the next person.

So we said, let's write something and we wrote something. I was sitting at the desk, I was the one with the pencil. I claimed to be the writer among the three anyway, because if the others had written it I would have said the grammar's not good enough. So we all spoke about it, talked about it, threw out sentences and so forth. My memory of it is that it was a vague, vague statement describing the fact that they were all in the room together, that things were ready to move and that really the conflict, or the war, was over.

We didn't use those words – the war is over – but I put them in a vague, vague way that this conflict was now coming to an end, that people were anxious for this engagement to take place, engagement being political talks.

I have a memory of that day, I have a memory of the mood amongst the three of us, I have a memory of the depression. I have a memory of the need to move out of that frustration. It was an interpretation of what was happening among all of the parties. It would have used words like, the conflict was drawing to a close, and it is clear that there needs to be a new political engagement – words of that style.

We sent it. We gave it to Fred, and I will swear to the day I die that Fred added the words, 'we need help to get out of this conflict'. I think Fred knew that with those words he could turn the rest of the people in the room round to engage with each other. Fred was doing what we were doing, and adding on to it to make sure that it happened. I have no evidence of that, Fred never told me that, but he would need great persuasion to persuade me that he didn't do it.

It became quite clear quite quickly that the British were prepared to engage, and so it was a matter of saying that meetings will have to take place. It meant that for the first time since 1974 the British representatives would have to meet the republican representatives. Therefore, a date and time was set up eventually: Fred had to go back, make sure, come back to us, say if this happened who would meet, who would not meet, the republicans had to be told that a meeting was possible, now would they be prepared to have the meeting.

It wasn't too difficult by this stage to get the republicans to agree to meet, because they were now of the mentality that that type of meeting would have to begin and that they were going to suss out the ground. They weren't gonna trust us to say that the British had changed, and they weren't going to trust Peter Brooke saying that things were going to change. They were actually now demanding a face-to-face situation before any of these realities could be taken on board.

So Fred took a couple of weeks to set up the meeting, and it was to take place on a particular evening at, I think, six o'clock. My greatest memory of that is arriving in the house in which the meeting was supposed to take place and receiving a fax to say that the meeting was called off. Now, at this stage we knew that two representatives from republicanism were actually in situ, ready to be picked up.

21 March 1993: the meeting with Fred

There were to be two people coming to that meeting from the British side. One of them was obviously Fred, and the other was to be, as we understood it, John Deverell. John Deverell was the immediate superior to Fred, who was head of intelligence in the north of Ireland, therefore if we were having him at the meeting we were actually getting in to the heart of British intelligence. To this day I am not too sure why John Deverell didn't come, but at four o'clock a fax arrived saying, meeting off, internal difficulties. And then on the phone it was explained to us by Fred that John Deverell was not coming.

We always handled our own security situation. When a meeting was taking place with the republicans, or with the British, we handled the security situation. We decided where they would meet, how they would meet, who would pick them up and so forth, because you were always in danger of either being interrupted by the media or by security people.

We arrived at the house early that afternoon to brief ourselves as to how we were going to control this, how it was going to be talked over, what was going to happen. One of the questions, for example, was whether we were going to sit in, whether anyone was going to object to this. We had come to the conclusion that we would sit in, that it was important that we be present.

I remember being very excited and slightly afraid, afraid it would go wrong, afraid that people wouldn't engage in the way that I had hoped that they would engage. It was nerve-tingling, but it didn't last too long because a fax came in saying the meeting wasn't going to happen, that the British side weren't coming. I remember that feeling, the disappointment, the frustration, the anger of it not happening. I remember somebody shouting, 'Get on the phone.' Within the next hour there were about six phone calls. We were shouting and roaring, saying, 'This must not happen, this is disastrous, if this meeting doesn't take place we have to break this off for ever.' We could not allow ourselves once again to be put in the situation of bringing these two electric wires so close together, and suddenly when we're about to connect them somebody says, 'Oh, I'm pulling this one away.'

Then, about six o'clock, Fred said, 'I'm coming, the meeting will take place.' Fred did come, but he was on his own. There wasn't too much time to discuss why he was on his own, but he did say something about internal difficulties. Whether John Deverell had actually personally pulled out or whether he had been told to pull out was not clear to me.

Fred was sitting there while one of my other colleagues was sent, as was our wont, to pick up the two people who were to come. I knew McGuinness would be at the meeting but I didn't know who else would be: republicans didn't tell you things like that. So he was sent off, and he came back about 15 minutes later to say they weren't coming to the meeting. Now this was becoming an extremely frustrating day: first we had the British not coming to the meeting, then we had one of the British coming, and now we had the republicans not coming.

One of my colleagues conveyed to me that, Bradley, you have to get into your car and go and persuade these guys to come to this meeting. What I don't remember is how Fred ended up with me in my car. There was too much passion, too much frustration around to remember details like that, and it was all happening too fast anyway. I do remember driving through Derry to the house where I knew Martin McGuinness was, and thinking, 'Oh, here goes again.' It's not very good on the nerves, that type of situation. Fred came with me and I don't remember all that much about our conversation in the car. I do remember thinking, 'You're a brave man. If I was in your position, would I do this?'

Anyway, we arrived, by this stage it was kind of duskish, the lights were on in the city, I remember driving into a small street, parking the car and getting out and knocking and Martin opened the door. And before he knew what was happening I had Fred in the sitting room with myself. I do remember walking into the room and seeing Gerry Kelly sitting there watching television. Before anybody knew it we had Kelly, McGuinness, Fred and myself and I think one of my other colleagues in. I said, 'Look, there's been all kinds of mix-ups, you know, this meeting was supposed to take place. There are not two British representatives, but this is Fred, he's arrived and this is too important, I don't think we can just let this go like this.'

By this stage I was meeting two very hostile faces. I do remember that Martin's face was getting a bit angry and that Gerry Kelly's face was reasonably hostile. I remember saying, 'Look, I think you two need to talk.' There was a small kitchen off the living room and I said, 'Look, I think we should go out here and talk for a few minutes.' I don't think there was a word spoken between Fred and Martin and Gerry at this stage. I think I blustered – keep this going, keep it talking, and I took the centre of concentration away so that nobody could say anything too fast.

I remember getting upset in the kitchen. It was a very narrow kitchen, and I remember Fred sat down and I stood. I said to Martin and Gerry: 'Look, the three of us in the link have been working with this man for quite some time, and here he is. All right, there were supposed to be two, I acknowledge that, I accept all of that, but look, we're at a delicate stage, this is too important to be blown out of the water because one other person hasn't arrived.

'This man has come, you know him in the sense that you know what he's been working at for the last couple of years. What I want you to do is to listen to him for a while. I'm gonna leave the room now, I'm gonna go out into the living room and I want you to talk to each other, ask whatever questions you have to ask and make up your own mind. But I am telling you, I'm pleading with you, that this meeting should take place, you just can't let this go.'

Within about ten minutes the door opened, Martin come out and looked at me rather staringly and said, 'Okay, we're gonna meet.' I don't think I hugged him, but I came close to hugging him. I think I might have put my two arms on his two arms and said, thank God, or thanks, or something of that nature.

I do remember driving back to the house where the meeting was to take place. I was slightly more relaxed now, and I said to Fred, 'You're a brave man.' He had gone where no other man that I'd ever met from MI6 or MI5 or any of the British agencies have ever gone, in that he was prepared to get into a car with me and go right into the heart of the Bogside.

At the meeting I said a few words at the very start and handed it over to Fred very, very fast – like getting rid of a burning coal. I don't know how long Fred talked, but it was as good a performance as I think I have ever experienced in my life. He was superb. He talked about the history, he talked about 1974, he talked about the underlying hostilities that existed not just from obviously the military position, but from the political situation, saying that the republicans were obviously going to be very hostile, were not going to believe everything that was said.

He was coherent, but it wasn't over-smooth. He was extremely good at taking the sore points and talking about the sore points – 1974, the fact that John Deverell was supposed to be at the meeting but didn't come. He said he appreciated that it wasn't easy on the republican side, that neither was it easy on the British side, that there were all kinds of different interpretations of what should happen. But he wanted to assure people that there was a different climate, that people were now open within his organisation, within the British political body, for a re-engagement with the republican movement. He did all the things in an introductory fashion that were necessary to defuse the hostilities and to make people listen.

I do remember him talking very well about 1974, that he would have to accept that the British had not played that completely straight and that he could appreciate himself the type of hurt that that would have resulted in. He said that if this republican leadership were lost to the political process that irreparable damage would be done, and it would be very difficult to gather it up again.

He talked about the difficulties that British governments had, that it was important they understood that what appeared to be the case wasn't always the case. That it was a very large, complicated organisation and that sometimes you would hear somebody say something from the British government, and somebody say what appeared to be contradictory.

And that you had to appreciate that these things took time, and that there was a methodology and that sometimes he was as frustrated by that as they were. That he was only one part of that and that sometimes it took time to get all of the body politic engaged.

But he very quickly went on to say, and I remember this specifically, that the British government was now of the mind that this engagement had to take place with republicans. That it had to take place with integrity, that it wasn't going to be without its difficulties, that it wouldn't roll the whole situation over overnight, but that this was not going to stop this time. He was very good on that. He said, 'I'm not telling you, wouldn't be honest for me to tell you, that if we engage and if we can work out something that it's all going to be okay. There will be many difficulties, difficulties we can't even perceive at this stage, but I am assuring you that the body politic believes now that this engagement is going to happen. If it can be successfully undertaken it will have an inevitable output.'

I think the first question to him then was, 'What do you mean by that?' And he said that some of these people liked the whole European dimension, that within the new changing Europe, within the different relationships between the British and Irish islands at the moment, there's an inevitability that's taking place. That there's an inevitable change, and that inevitable change is going to result in some form of unity. And I remember thinking, hmmm, interesting.

He spent about 40 minutes or so going through all of this stuff, taking on the sore points. He dealt with them in a fairly general way, not tying anything down. He was great, he was absolutely wonderful, because had he said, 'Look, excuse me, we're about to enter negotiations with you and you're gonna have to be a united Ireland in six years' time or ten years' time,' they would have walked out of that room not believing a word. They would have said, 'We're being conned here again.'

They then began to ask questions like, who was this coming from, and he said it was coming from the highest office – I don't think he said the highest office within the land, but something akin to that, that this was coming from the very top. He was asked: 'Has this been cleared right up to the top?' He said, 'Yes, this is cleared right up to the top.' Again he kept it in fairly vague terms, he wouldn't have said, for example, that John Major had cleared it.

Now there was a break in the conversation and I and one of my other colleagues grabbed him in a room and we said, 'Are you sure this is cleared by Major?' And he said, 'This is cleared right up to John Major.' Back in the room, he was asked what this would mean in practical terms, would this be a set of meetings, and he said yes. Who would be at those meetings? His initial thing was that it would probably be someone at the level of Quentin Thomas initially, and himself or whoever, John Deverell, but within a few days John Chilcot would join the meeting.

But, and this was I suppose the core of his task on that night, he said: 'None of this can happen in an atmosphere and in a reality of violence. No British government will ever meet you while there's bombs going off in the street. Just can't happen, we couldn't survive it, and morally they wouldn't see it as correct. Now, if there was to be a ceasefire, then that changes the whole atmosphere; these talks cannot take place unless they are within the atmosphere and in the context of a ceasefire. Now we realise that you have difficulties with that, so what we are proposing – and it was a very definite proposal – is that the minute we are told that that ceasefire was about to happen, discussions could begin happening one minute afterwards. In other words if the ceasefire was called at nine o'clock on a Monday morning we could engage in discussion one minute after nine o'clock.'

Now he also said very clearly that it was their analysis, it was their opinion, that negotiations could not be kept from the press for longer than one week, and therefore they would have to be prepared for it coming out after a week. The second thing that he was asked, and which he was very specific about, was that the initial contact would not be with John Chilcot, but that Chilcot would join the talks two to three days in. It was up to the republicans to appoint their own delegation; the British would not have any input into that. They would not demand or refuse anyone to be there.

The other thing that was asked was where it should take place. He said they hadn't decided upon that, but what had been mentioned was Norway or Sweden, or possibly Scotland. The south of Ireland would give them major difficulty, [as] that would be a territory where they would not be comfortable having those meetings. So the reality would probably be either one of the Scandinavian countries, or Scotland. It wasn't dwelt upon too long, but what was made very clear over and over again was that two weeks was demanded and needed for those meetings to take place. They would start not at the end of the two-week ceasefire, but one minute after the ceasefire was officially engaged in.

My memory of the end of the meeting was being first of all absolutely exhausted. It had been a long day, there had been many emotions, and yet I had a realisation that something very important had happened. I knew that McGuinness and Gerry Kelly were very impressed by Fred – you just tell, you can tell those things. I knew that something very important had been put into this equation; I knew that the ball was now very strongly within the republican court. My own assessment was that they wouldn't turn it down, they would run with it, and that Fred had done one hell of a job. In fact he'd done two jobs that night for which he deserved immense credit. One was that he had gone with me in a car and gone into a place where few other people would have gone.

Secondly, his performance in persuading these people that things were about to change, that there was a way through these difficulties, and that a way out of the war into some kind of peace was actually on the table.

I'm always aware of Unionist sensitivities, and I remember thinking if a Unionist was sitting in this room, how he would feel – would he or she feel utterly betrayed? I had two thoughts. I thought Yes, they would, but on the other hand, there's nothing been said in this room tonight which is actually not politically real, in the sense that the general thrust of what has been talked about is where things are inevitably going and there is no rowing back from this. So Fred actually had not sold anyone out, other than to the political momentum that is happening in the world, and particularly in Europe, at this time. And his performance was good, not just at the level of how to engage the two people, but it was good in the broader political context in which we're now living. There was one important moment in the meeting when he had this break for people to go to the toilet and so forth, and somebody asked Fred how he was feeling. I do remember him saying, 'I didn't know Gerry Kelly was going be at the meeting, but I'm glad he's here. I think we have enough strength within republicanism if we go with this that they'll buy it.'

I also remember, at the very end of the meeting, going up to McGuinness and saying, 'Look, Martin, thanks.' McGuinness and I had many a battle, but he always knew where I was coming from and I think he trusted that that night. I think I'll be eternally grateful for that.

Later Gerry Kelly said to me, 'You know, you were way out of line tonight bringing him down into that house. It doesn't matter what the outcome is, you were way out of line.' I said, 'Sure, it's my job to be way out of line. I would be useless to people like you unless I go over the top.' He was in some ways confirming for me what the role of mediators is – you can't go out of line too often, but every so often, at the appropriate moment, you have to go over the top. Otherwise you're useless.

My two colleagues went to London and had a meeting with Fred and John Deverell, and came back quite convinced that things were okay, that they were going ahead. From my perspective, what was interesting obviously was there was always this suspicion in the back of your head – was Fred flying solo on this? We were now into the situation of where it was going to take place, we were now being told that mileage measurements were being taken from pick-up points to Ballykelly not far from Derry, that logistics were being examined about what kind of van it would be, how many seats should be on it, all of that.

April 1993: the ceasefire offer

I remember making provision for babysitters for my own children, in the sense that if I was going to be away for a week or fortnight or whatever, it was going to have implications at a family level. I remember lying at nights beginning to think how the process would work. How much would they allow us to be involved? We structured meetings in the sense of saying that we would have to have a room to ourselves in which we could actually meet among ourselves, all of those type of mediation preparations would have taken place. But we were still waiting on the response from the republican movement.

Word came to me that a meeting with McGuinness was on. I was quite nervous and tense and expectant all at the same time. It was my judgement that the response would be a positive response, but there was always the fear that it would be conditional and that there would be something else written into it, that it would be half-hearted, that it would be surrounded by the type of demands that weren't capable of being met.

McGuinness came in and he said, 'Somebody needs to write this down,' so I was given the task of being the scribbler to write it down. And he started to read out a statement. Now, it wasn't a matter of taking out a statement and reading it, he had little bits of notes from different places, and I was amazed at the logistics of it. But he read it and it took some time to actually read it, wasn't that long a statement but it took some time to do it, and I remember the excitement mounting in me as he dictated it and as I wrote it.

The statement was to be given to the British with a very strong warning that not one single word of this was to be changed. I think that warning was repeated on three or four separate occasions, Martin looking at me specifically. And I do remember very strongly the feeling inside my guts when the word came that they would give us two weeks' ceasefire. I thought, this is the beginning of the end. No matter what happens now, no matter what difficulties there are, there is going to be a major, major shift in this whole thing. I remember thinking, it's over. I remember the elation of that moment, I remember the change inside my stomach, the sensation of knowing that this is the beginning of the end, that things will never ever be the same again, because now two massive changes have taken place. First of all the British have engaged, and secondly, republicans have now offered the ceasefire to begin the process of engagement, and that changes all things for all time.

After that we went into what appeared to be a retrograde situation for quite some time. First of all, the British began to pull back on the situation. We now began to get rather negative overtones about internal difficulties within the British system, elections coming up, maybe this should be slower, maybe we're going too fast – words that were actually not particularly helpful. My memory tells me that they had actually tied it down to a specific house in Limavady (near Londonderry), where the meetings were going to take place. But they didn't actually take place, and the British began to roll back the situation. Fred began to get very, very annoyed. I think that he began to feel he had been betrayed, that for internal difficulties and for internal reasons that Major was being got at. That he had put himself out on a limb with full blessing, and now he was being made to look the person who was dishonest, disloyal, untruthful.

September 1993: telling John Hume

We were now reaching a situation which was utterly impossible to live with. My greatest memory of it is sitting in that same room where that first meeting took place and saying, 'We have to blow this out of the water, we have to get this out into the public. All of these people are now in this room, all of these people are now looking at each other, all of these people are now ready to engage, and for internal political reasons within the British system at the moment we are actually not going to get this engagement.' Our weakness, which was our strength, was the fact that we were secret. The fact that no one knew of our existence, the fact that we were undercover in that sense for all those years, had now to be blown apart.

The British had asked for something, had received it and now weren't running with it for their own reasons which were not all that clear to us. You were actually beginning to sense an uneasiness within either the British cabinet, or within the higher echelons of the British civil service who would have been involved in this. They were saying roll back, take it easier, it's not politically expedient at this moment of time; it may be better in two to three months' time. Knowing republicanism, that was a no-no. We could not bring [it] to this emotional intensity, bring it to this level of engagement and then say, well, excuse us, gentlemen, it really doesn't suit the other side at this moment of time. That was not liveable for us, and I don't think it was sustainable for the leadership of republicanism at that time.

Fred was particularly annoyed, and felt betrayed. He had been away on a holiday and he came back and he reported back to us. But he was now on the side of dialogue, he was on the side of getting this thing moving. Fred reported to us that there had been a very serious meeting in Downing Street with, I think it was Hurd and Major, the secretary to the cabinet and perhaps a few others.

He told us that Kenneth Clarke had been pulled in because he was considered to be an important element. The reportage was that he was advising caution on the part of the prime minister. You now had a situation where Fred looked to be the person who actually had brought us to this point but was reneging, or wasn't actually bringing the full weight of the cabinet with him, and had gone ahead of the cabinet or the prime minister.

So Fred did something which I think was honourable and right for him at that time. He wrote a personal note to Martin McGuinness explaining his own position, and we gave that to Martin McGuinness saying that everything that he had said was, in fact, the truth.

We three in the link discussed it for days. We needed to find a methodology of getting this out into the public arena, and the decision was finally made that the person that we should divulge it to was John Hume. We knew that intense negotiations had been going on between John Hume and Gerry Adams. We knew of the dialogue that was taking place between Belfast and Dublin. We knew all of that and Fred knew of it. Fred knew every meeting that took place, he knew most of the details of what happened at those meetings. He was enormously well-informed.

So we called John Hume, asked him to come, and we sat down and we talked for about two to three hours and told him the whole story. We told him more than the whole story. We in fact showed him the Hume–Adams document which the British had given to us, which, in the public arena at that time, didn't exist. We were informing him that, unbeknownst to him, there were other talks taking place, that the British were engaging with the republicans. We told him the whole thing – that the engagement had taken place, what the British had asked for, and that the republicans had responded positively. And this was news to him.

First of all, he was amazed at the level and the detail of contact. I know he was amazed by the fact of what the British had asked for, and what they had received. He was amazed at the fact that we showed him the Hume–Adams document. I think that he was confused and slightly relieved.

It was quite obvious what we were doing was handing this very hot coal into John Hume's hands. We were saying, 'Look, we have brought this ball, we have brought it in our way and you have a lot of hot coals in your hands at the moment. Here's another.' We all could foresee John Hume walking into the White House and saying to Clinton: 'Excuse me, do you realise that the British asked for two weeks' ceasefire and got it? And they haven't acted upon it, having asked for it – and what are you going to do about it?'

Nobody was saying Fred had done wrong. Nobody had sacked Fred, nobody had pulled Fred out of this equation, saying he was solo flying. Fred was still at the heart of this, and being informed of the top-level meetings between John Major and so forth. We were now facing timing issues about whether it should take place in October. My two colleagues went to London and had a meeting with Fred. The upshot of it was that the British said that they were prepared to release to the republican movement the detailed outline of their strategy and their policy.

We went to another meeting, met John Deverell and Fred. We checked the whole process again, that the British were serious, not just serious, but that all of the things that had been said at the meeting with Fred were in fact British policy. That, despite whatever difficulties they had, we were still on line for this, and this releasing of this document to the republican movement was a step further down the line to negotiations, face-to-face negotiations. We took the document and we came back to Derry and asked for a meeting with Martin McGuinness. Martin was not pleased with receiving the document – in fact, he was very angry with receiving the document.

Within a week we were asked to a meeting with Martin and Gerry Adams and, I think, Gerry Kelly. There was a long discussion about this in which we were told that it was probably better at this stage that we disappeared. That it would probably be better if that source of engagement disappeared and they entered into their own direct dialogue. And would we give them the numbers and the fax number and the telephone number and so forth for Fred. And at that stage I said to Gerry Adams, 'I don't mind us going, but your timing is atrocious.' He said: 'You might be right, but that's the way these things happen.'

Fred is a Scot who would be about 62 now. I think he fell in love with Ireland. I tracked all these people down the years, Steele, Oatley and Fred; they were all seduced by Ireland, its people and its history. Fred pulled the whole thing together. He did so at some risk and cost to himself within his own organisation and within the establishment. I think a statue should be built to him in Ireland.

7
Hume–Adams

While one channel of communication had closed down, other avenues of contact were still open. The outside world did not know it, but in 1988 the then Taóiseach, Charles Haughey, had opened secret talks with Adams and others in Sinn Fein, via his aide Martin Mansergh and a senior Fianna Fáil politician, Dermot Ahern. Mansergh was to recall of Sinn Fein:

The point was made that northern nationalists were alienated from Dublin. They claimed that if British troops were stationed in Dundalk, the popular reaction would be the same as in the north. They needed an alternative political strategy, if violence were to stop. The view was expressed that the Anglo–Irish Agreement was not worth the candle, as the cost of the provocation of Unionists was not commensurate with any substantial gain. We naturally stressed the total unacceptability of violence to the people of the south, and pointed out that it was the single most potent divisive factor weakening Irish nationalism, with northern nationalists, nationalists north and south, and the Irish-American community all divided on the question of the legitimacy of violence, thus preventing a political combination for electoral or other purposes.

Dermot Ahern was left with an abiding memory of the talks:

All during the discussions, it was quite obvious to me that Adams and the others were people who were on a hook and wanted to get off the hook, while at the same time not giving on the core principles they felt very strongly about. One of the things that I think convinced us was something which came out very strongly from Gerry Adams himself: that he was going into his 40s, that he'd seen nothing but violence from his early life. He was endeavouring to ensure that his children and his children's children didn't go through that in the years ahead. I got the impression that he and the others could see that the violent campaign was not progressing the cause of Irish republicanism or nationalism.

But I was never convinced, and we were never convinced, that he and the others had the wherewithal to stop the atrocities. We felt that while their intentions were good in that regard, they just were not able to convince the people who were pulling the triggers or planting the bombs to stop.

While the republican contacts with Dublin produced few tangible results, another channel was to prove to be of huge significance. It was a process which, though at first strictly secret, would later become known to the world as Hume–Adams. Although the SDLP–Sinn Fein talks of 1988 had not reached agreement, party leaders John Hume and Gerry Adams had ever since remained in contact. The two had certainly not found common ground on the question of violence, or indeed on the question of whether the British were neutral or not, but they had come to know each other's minds. Hume had, moreover, asked Peter Brooke to make his statement that Britain had no selfish strategic or economic interest.

On one level these were only words, but on another they had established the beginnings of a new template.

Hume now conceived an ambitious extension of this idea, thinking of the possibility of a single declaration that all sides might accept, which might encapsulate the essence of the positions of all sides. His ultimate hope was that, by providing a new focal point on which agreement might be built, the end result could be a ceasefire. Adams put the concept of the people of Ireland's right to national self-determination at the centre of his position: this was generally seen as code for a united Ireland, with little or nothing in the way of recognition of the rights of Unionists and Protestants. Hume gave a subtle new twist to this, arguing that self-determination could only be achieved through agreement. He recalled his argument: 'The British government were not preventing Irish unity. The situation was now that Irish unity was a matter for those Irish people who wanted Irish unity persuading those who didn't.' Adams was to concede of Hume: 'Where he's very good is the reality that there is a large number of people here in this part of the island who are pro-Union, and you just can't ignore that.'

The republicans argued that Unionist consent for a new Ireland was desirable, but insisted that Unionists could not have a veto on the future. In seeking to ensure they would not have a veto, they advanced the idea that the British government should take on the role of persuaders, attempting to convince Unionists that their future lay in a united Ireland. They also, in line with tradition, wanted the British to withdraw, having first set out a time frame for their withdrawal. The difficulty was how to square this with the position, as laid out in the Anglo–Irish Agreement, that any change in Northern Ireland's status could only come about with the consent of the majority.

After many rounds of talks, Hume had a fair idea of

what might be feasible. On 6 October 1991, he picked up a pen and a piece of lined white paper and did something which was to prove a vital step in the peace process. He wrote out a draft declaration to be made jointly by the British and Irish governments. It was to prove the first in a long line of such drafts, which would, in December 1993, culminate in the Downing Street Declaration. Few realised at the time of this declaration's appearance that it represented the final draft in a process which had secretly been under way for years. The intention was to find common ground in everyone's ideological positions, and to reconcile what had always appeared irreconcilable. Under the heading, 'A strategy for peace and justice in Ireland', Hume wrote as follows:

Aim: A joint declaration by both British and Irish Prime Ministers

1. Leaving the past aside and regretting the pain and suffering caused by past failures to settle the relationships of the people of both islands satisfactorily.

2. Recognising that the implementation of the Single Market and the coming into being of European Union with the effective removal of all borders fundamentally changes the nature of British/Irish relationships. Further recognising that future developments which leave both parts of Ireland as the only part of the new Europe with no land links with the other regions, will intensify the common ground between both parts of Ireland and intensify the need for maximum cooperation to achieve maximum benefit from European Union.

3. Regret, however, that there remains a serious legacy of past relationships – a deeply divided people on the island of Ireland. This is a major concern of both governments and

both deeply regret that these are the last remaining such divisions in the new European order.

4. Both governments recognise that these divisions can only end with the agreement of the people North and South in Ireland.

5. Both governments therefore commit themselves to using the maximum resources to create the atmosphere in which such agreement is made easier. Both governments find it unacceptable that these are the last remaining divisions in a Europe that has already ended many more deep and bitter quarrels. They will, therefore, promote intensive cooperation at all levels in order to strengthen the process of agreement.

6. The British Government reiterate yet again that they no longer have any selfish political or strategic interest in remaining in Ireland. Their sole interest is to see peace and agreement among the people who inhabit the island and they will devote all their available resources to that end.

7. For its part the Irish Government recognises that the traditional objective of Irish nationalism – the exercise of self-determination by the people of Ireland as a whole – cannot be achieved without the agreement of the people of Northern Ireland. It would, therefore, commit itself to working for institutions of government North and South which would respect the diversity of the people of Ireland but allow them to work their substantial common ground together in order to build the necessary trust for an agreed future.

In order to pursue that strategy, the Irish Government would set up a permanent Irish Convention to plan and implement the steps and policies required to break down the barriers which divide the people of Ireland and which prevent the exercise of agreed self-determination. If the British Government refuse the joint declaration, the Irish Government would proceed to set up the Convention with the

additional objective of planning and implementing the policies required to persuade the British Government to adopt
our strategy and objectives. Membership of the Convention
would consist of elected representatives of all parties in Ireland who share the objective of a united self-determined
Ireland.

This draft contained many of the key features of what
would, after many changes, become the Downing Street
Declaration, including self-determination, an assurance
from Britain that it had no selfish interest in remaining in
Ireland, and a heavy emphasis on the need for agreement.
In setting out these points Hume was building on a number
of elements, one of which was material from his 1988
debates with Sinn Fein. The document set the Northern
Ireland problem firmly in an Anglo–Irish context, drawing
on the Anglo–Irish Agreement and envisaging the two
governments working ever more closely together. It also
stressed the European dimension. Peter Brooke had set
out, in his speech of November 1990, that Britain had no
selfish strategic or economic interest: Hume augmented
this by saying it had no political interest either.

The offer of a Convention to be set up by the Irish
government was another element which could be traced
back to the 1988 SDLP–Sinn Fein talks. In those discussions, Hume suggested that an IRA ceasefire would be
followed by a conference, convened by the Irish government. The document did not explicitly demand an IRA
ceasefire, but it was obvious that it was intended to produce
one. It was also implicit that Sinn Fein would be admitted
to mainstream Irish political life, for the proposed offer by
the Irish government to set up an Irish Convention was an
open invitation to give up violence and enter constitutional

politics. Hume's pro-Europeanism, meanwhile, was reflected in the heavy emphasis on the European dimension.

None of this amounted, in terms, to fulfilment of the traditional republican demand for a British declaration of intent to withdraw from Ireland. But it cast Britain in a very different light from the colonialist and imperialist power of Sinn Fein's standard analysis. On the contrary, it made clear that Britain was anxious above all to secure agreement; that it viewed the problem in an Anglo–Irish context; that it intended to manage the problem jointly with Dublin. It also, arguably, amounted to a strong signal that Britain did not expect to be in Ireland for ever and a day.

The crucial part of Hume's draft lay in its seventh point, in which he sought to address the republican demand for Irish self-determination. This could not be achieved, he wrote, without the agreement of the people of Northern Ireland. This was a very subtle concept, for in effect it entwined the principles of self-determination and consent. It thus combined, at least in theory, that which republicans sought with the Unionist demand that the majority opinion should prevail within Northern Ireland.

The importance of this was that it offered the republicans something which they had never had before: a chance to fit the northern Protestants into their theoretical scheme of things. Although, as we shall see, republican thinking was evolving quite fast, it still lacked any way of rationalising the very obvious divisions between Unionist and nationalist. Sinn Fein had strayed so far away from the original eighteenth-century republican vision of uniting Protestants and Catholics that it had actually suggested giving resettlement grants to those who did not want to live in a united Ireland.

Hume was offering a way of making the reality of the division more digestible in terms of nationalist doctrine. The principle of self-determination would be recognised and acknowledged, but nationalists would be conceding that Unionists had rights. Partition would still be in place, for the moment at least, but it would continue not because Britain insisted on it, but because Irish nationalists were, in the exercise of self-determination, granting Unionists the right to choose it. The border would therefore exist by nationalist choice, rather than British imposition. It was not an easy concept, but it was obviously a serious attempt to address republican concerns.

A few days later Hume took the piece of paper with him to Dublin and showed it, still in longhand, to Haughey, explaining his thinking behind each point. The Taoiseach listened attentively: he was fully aware of Hume's continuing contacts with Adams, and realised that the document had been put together in the hope of meeting republican concerns. After a while Haughey pressed a buzzer and the two men were joined by his adviser, Martin Mansergh, who took the document and embellished it with diplomatic language.

Shortly afterwards, two more key figures were drawn into the process. One was Dermot Nally, and the other senior diplomat Seán Ó hUiginn, known to possess one of Ireland's most formidable minds. This Dublin team set to work on Hume's draft. First, Mansergh produced an alternative document, then Hume and the Dublin team amalgamated them into one. This document retained the structure of Hume's and dealt with the same subjects in the same order, but was slightly longer and contained more verbal flourishes.

This first document was to be sweated, argued and

fought over in many different versions as the months went by. The republicans insisted on inserting into it a time frame for British withdrawal, in line with their traditional position. It then went to Albert Reynolds, who had taken over as Irish Taoiseach and who instantly saw merit in the Hume–Adams process, but believed it needed more work. His verdict: 'When I studied the document, I felt it was too green. The IRA always held their traditional view – Brits out, give us the date. So that runs contrary to the whole principle of consent on which any new project would have to be based. That was the foundation stone of any new project. How can you say on the one hand – Brits out, give us the date – and at the same time accept the principle of consent?'

His cerebral adviser, Martin Mansergh, concurred on the consent point: 'I don't know that this seemed at all obvious to the republican movement, but it certainly was absolutely obvious to us.' After more drafting and redrafting, Sinn Fein called a halt, insisting that it had gone as far as it could. The draft they ended on was unacceptable to Reynolds, which meant it stood a vanishingly small chance of being acceptable to John Major. Yet Reynolds clung tenaciously to the idea that the declaration process could bring real progress and decided, in his parlance, to give it a go. He said of what the IRA described as their bottom line: 'I got this draft, this is it, they wanted it presented to John Major. I told them again that I didn't see it making any progress, but, if they insisted, and to show my good faith, I was prepared to take the draft to John Major.'

Reynolds and Major knew each other from European finance meetings and got on particularly well. 'I liked Albert a lot,' Major would recall. Reynolds hoped to build on this relationship, as his press officer Seán Duignan would remember: 'He always had this feeling about John Major that if he could get his undivided attention, if he could get him away from his advisers, he could convince him. This was a feeling that Albert Reynolds constantly repeated to me: "If I can get him away from these people I can convince him, I can bring him along."'

Reynolds certainly had a highly individualistic prime ministerial style and approach: he was a hands-on Taoiseach, much given to sorting things out on a one-to-one basis. Bertie Ahern, his eventual successor as leader of Fianna Fáil, gave a flavour of the unique Reynolds approach:

Albert doesn't follow notes in the formal way of accounting to the Cabinet. Albert would say, 'Well I've been in touch with that fellow, I've been in touch with him and I'll ring him' – that's his style, he'd do it himself. Albert would come in with the sheet [agenda] and the civil servants, but then he would never look at the sheet. He'd be saying, 'Well I'll be on to your man, I'll have those two down to the office; those two fellows met me and I met them in a room, and I had to get rid of my car and my bodyguards, then I had to get my daughter to give me a lift down and the security guys were going the other way.' He'd say these kind of things, it was very horrific, but that's the way Albert went on.

At first, Reynolds proposed taking the extraordinary step of flying to London, or having Major fly to Dublin, so he could hand over the document in person, in an effort to emphasise the importance he placed on it. Major recalled with a laugh: 'I didn't think that was a very good idea. Heaven alone knows what would have been thought. It would never stay secret, and of course it would immediately arouse all sorts of suspicions – conspiracy theories, never far away from the Irish question, would absolutely abound. All hell would break loose. So I said, "Come off it, Albert, we can't do that."'

Instead, Major had Butler fly to Ireland. Butler, survivor of both the Brighton bomb and the Downing Street mortar attack, flew into Baldonnell military airport near Dublin while Reynolds drove to meet him. They met in a spartan office, Reynolds recalling, 'We had two mugs. He was coffee, I was tea.' Butler studied the document, then asked: 'What makes you think this is going to work?' He saw at once that there were points which would be very difficult for the British government to accept.

Reynolds remembers: 'He asked me if I genuinely believed that I'd get a response from the IRA because they were very, very sceptical about anything that was produced would draw the type of response that we would all be hoping for. That was a full cessation of violence – a ceasefire, not just for a week or a month, but for ever and a day.' Butler remembers: 'And then he said, "The Army Council have seen this and this would be a basis for peace." And with that I took the document back.'

Major's reaction was immediate: 'I had a look at it and it was just awful,' he was to recall. 'It was completely unacceptable. It had everything in it that we couldn't possibly accept – we couldn't be persuaders for Irish unity, we needed changes to Articles 2 and 3 of the Irish constitution, we weren't at all keen on pan-Irish authority over things that were legitimately the responsibility of the United Kingdom.'

But Reynolds, the irrepressible salesman, was not prepared to give up on the project, and at his next scheduled summit with Major, in 10 Downing Street, he made his pitch in person. 'I gave it my best shot. I said I would and I did,' he recollected. 'I said, what was the price of peace – was it not worth everybody going the extra mile, taking the extra risk?' Butler recalls what Reynolds argued: 'Don't let the British government have any illusion that the IRA have been defeated. They haven't been defeated and they won't be defeated. Unless we can get a peace by a process of this sort, we won't get peace at all.'

Major had a liking for Reynolds, describing him as 'dear old wheeler-dealer Albert', but his insuperable problem with the document was that it contained a time frame for British withdrawal from Northern Ireland. Over a Downing Street supper he stressed this point to Reynolds:

I said to Albert, 'This isn't going to work. You simply can't do that. The principle of consent in Northern Ireland is absolutely fundamental to any agreement we can have. And there's no possibility of me now, or at any stage in the future, or any British government I can think of, actually agreeing to a time frame to remove ourselves from what we consider part of the United Kingdom.'

That wasn't on, and I had to say to Albert it wasn't on. I remember saying to Albert, pointing to the document and saying, 'Well, where are the constitutional guarantees we were promised?' And Albert picked up the document and looked at it, and he said, 'Well they're in there, they're a bit oblique but they're in there.'

Reynolds recalls the exchange: 'I said, "Look, principle of consent is there, it's enshrined in the Anglo–Irish Agreement, it's there in the document, it's there a number of times in the document in various ways. You might prefer to have it up in lights, but it's just not possible to do that."'

Mayhew, who was present, clearly remembers the occasion: 'The Irish view was, it's there, it's implicit, but don't go and sort of spell it all out or you'll frighten the horses. John Major held out, absolutely firmly: "No good." Never got hot under the collar or anything like that – it was a very friendly meeting – but "make no mistake, Albert, no good as you're trying to run it at the moment."' Major recalls Mayhew adding: 'Well, the reference to a united Ireland isn't oblique, that's quite explicit. We've got to take great care of our audience.'

As Reynolds had predicted, the wording of that particular Hume–Adams draft had been turned down. But Hume's ground-breaking idea of a joint declaration by the two governments, which would help induce the IRA to call a ceasefire, won through. The two governments began to rewrite it, in secret. Hume waited all summer to hear what had happened to his brainchild; but no one told him what was going on.

In September 1993 Hume planned a trip to America. But just as he was about to leave, he received startling new information. Denis Bradley of the link told him that other talks were going on without his knowledge, which came as a surprise to Hume. The three members of the link had decided to tell Hume, because they feared the IRA's offer of a ceasefire was being ignored by the British and would be withdrawn. They hoped Hume could bring American pressure to bear on the British.

Hume did not publicise the ceasefire offer, but he did go public about some of his own activities, issuing a joint press release with Adams just before he left for the USA. This said they had given the Irish government their draft peace proposal. Adams explained their motive: 'We frankly didn't know what was happening. The only way to unlock the deadlock, the log-jam, the minimalist pace, was to say publicly that the governments had not responded to us.'

The Hume–Adams announcement caused a firestorm of publicity. The public and the media knew next to nothing about all the subterranean contacts going on behind the scenes. Public, political and media interest reached an intense pitch, the topic dominating news bulletins in Britain and Ireland, with many politicians and newspapers criticising the idea of Hume's working with Adams. The public was essentially in complete ignorance of what Father Reid had been up to, of Denis Bradley and the back-channel between the British and the IRA, and of the succession of draft declarations. Bringing even a part of all this into the public domain appalled Dublin, where one source said there was 'a sense of absolute fury.'

A similar mood prevailed in London, Major recalling: 'Almost anything that came out of a dialogue between John Hume and Gerry Adams, then had the support of the government in Dublin, was almost bound to be complete anathema to the Unionists.' This was highly relevant to Major for two reasons. First, he did not want to stir Protestant anger and create security problems. Second, he was acutely aware that, with a wafer-thin majority in the Commons, the survival of his government could depend on the support of the bloc of Unionist MPs, headed by James Molyneaux.

Major and Molyneaux were both frank and revealing about the one-to-one negotiation they held in advance of a vital European vote, in which Major could not count on the support of some of his particularly anti-European MPs. Recalling the circumstances in which he invited Molyneaux to Number 10, Major said: 'We were just coming up to an absolutely crucial vote in the Maastricht debate. It was a vote so crucial that if we had been defeated upon it I would have resigned, and it was a couple of hours before I was going into the Chamber to speak. I was finishing the notes for my speech and the projections from the government whips at that time were that we were likely to lose.'

Major was justifiably nervous, since Molyneaux and his party would instinctively have strongly disapproved of many of the things the government was involved in, especially its secret contacts with republicans. But he had to explore every avenue which might keep his government alive.

Molyneaux remembers arriving at Number 10 following Major's invitation: 'I went over without delay. The prime minister was at the cabinet table, where he usually did work, with papers in front of him, obviously drafting the speech he was going to make – the most important speech of his career perhaps – within about an hour.' Major recollects: 'And we sat there in silence for a moment and I was clearly waiting to see what the Ulster Unionists were going to do in this crucial debate that afternoon. And Jim said, "I might be able to offer you nine." And I said, "Nine abstentions?" which is what I thought he would probably be able to offer.'

Molyneaux remembered the occasion with a grin: 'And I said, "No, if we're lucky, it might be nine for." So then he did this sort of mock counting sort of thing – it was this kind of a joke we had between us about lack of formal education. "But that would be eighteen," he said. So I said, "Yeah, yeah, so it would be right enough."'

Then, after a pause, Molyneaux said, according to Major: 'But we mustn't do a sordid deal.' Molyneaux remembers Major being surprised by this tack. Major recalled: 'And I said, "Of course not, but I'm gonna be asked why you have suddenly delivered these crucial votes in this crucial debate." He remembers Molyneaux giving a wry smile and looking around the room. 'What about telling them the truth then?' said Molyneaux. 'Which is?' asked Major. 'Nothing was asked for, nothing was given,' the Unionist leader responded. The prime minister, who must have privately been hugging himself with delight at the realisation that his government was about to survive, and without having to resort to some grubby deal, said: 'Great.'

When Molyneaux delivered the votes as promised, few believed he had not made such a deal. Seamus Mallon of the SDLP rose indignantly in the Commons to declare: 'History will show that, down through the years, sordid deals have cost the lives of countless people in the north of Ireland. Does not the prime minister have a duty today, now, to tell this house what deal he did with the nine Ulster Unionists?' Recalling that moment, Molyneaux would laugh out loud as he recalled Major's response: 'John just got up and with a broad grin said: "Well, let me clear up the matter for the honourable gentleman so he's in no doubt. Nothing was asked for, nothing was offered and nothing was given." ' From his Commons seat Molyneaux nodded in confirmation: he had indeed made no deal with the prime minister, but by saving the government he had earned huge personal and political credit with him.

Three months later, he had occasion to draw on that credit when the prime minister invited him back to Number 10 to test his reaction to the fact that the British and Irish governments had been negotiating a joint declaration. The last time London and Dublin had signed up for a joint deal, Unionist and loyalist anger had spilled on to the streets. So how, Major wondered, as he and Butler waited for Molyneaux, would the Ulster Unionist leader react to another Anglo–Irish initiative?

Molyneaux remembers the encounter: 'The prime minister was alone, apart from the Cabinet Secretary. They both looked a little uneasy.' Butler concurs: 'We were apprehensive. We showed him the document that we'd been working on, which Albert Reynolds had first given us and which we amended, to see what his reaction was.' According to Molyneaux's recollection, he first asked about the origin of the paper: 'And Robin Butler looked as if he was going to say something, when the prime minister said, "No, I'll handle this. It has come to me from someone who has a fair bit of authority on the other side of the fence."'

Major recalls Molyneaux's verdict: 'It's a very green document. It's a very republican document. There's a lot of Hume-speak in here.' Major got the message very clearly: Molyneaux did not regard this as a basis for doing business. Hardly coincidentally, Major put the document to one side. But as the London–Dublin politicking continued in Belfast, events on the streets were to grab the headlines.

8

Downing Street Declaration

———

While London and Dublin searched for agreement, savage violence erupted to make October 1993 one of the most awful, yet most crucial, months in the troubles. It began in confusion mixed with hope, then plunged into violence and near despair, almost as dark as any period of the troubles. The death toll was the highest of any month since 1976.

An IRA bomb went off on the Shankill Road around lunchtime on a Saturday, at a time when the road was thronged with hundreds of shoppers. It was aimed at Johnny Adair and other leaders of the paramilitary Ulster Defence Association, whom the IRA thought were meeting in offices above a fish shop. IRA members attempted to place the bomb in the shop, in a very risky operation which carried a high chance of causing civilian casualties.

In the event, the bombing did not go as planned, for as IRA member Thomas Begley was putting the device in place it detonated prematurely, killing him and nine Protestants. Four women and two children were among the dead, but no UDA members were killed because the upstairs office was empty at the time. The explosion demolished the old building. In the aftermath local men, police, firemen and ambulancemen tore at the rubble in a search for survivors, but the elderly building had collapsed like a house of cards. A young police officer who arrived quickly at the scene said later:

I was one of the first in. I remember an old man being recovered. His head was the first thing to appear from the rubble, and that was quite a frightening experience. I knew he was still alive because his eyes were blinking. An ambulanceman put an oxygen mask over his mouth but by the time he left the rubble he had died. After he was moved, we continued to remove rubble from where we were standing, but unknown to anybody we were standing on other bodies. As the rubble was being removed – and it will stay with me until I die – I saw a young girl's foot. I knew it was a young girl's foot because her shoe size was about three or four. It poked through the rubble, and I wanted to stop digging then, because I knew I was going to see quite a horrendous sight; and in fact I did.

A paramedic recounted: 'The scene was horrific. There was one lady lying in the road with head injuries and half her arm was blown off. She later died. But the worst part for me was when we unearthed the body of a young girl. I will never forget seeing that face staring up out of the rubble.'

The bombing was one of a series of IRA attempts to assassinate leading loyalists such as Adair. Loyalist killings were running at a particularly high level, and had developed a new feature. In addition to the standard pattern of loyalist attacks on random Catholic targets, loyalists had begun to target members of Sinn Fein, together with members of their families and friends. In the five years leading up to the Shankill bombing, 18 people with Sinn Fein connections were killed by Protestant extremists.

At this point, Northern Ireland descended into something close to sheer dread, as loyalist gunmen went on the rampage, killing six people in a series of shootings. The

UDA then attempted to match the Shankill death toll with a Saturday night attack on a bar in the quiet, mainly Catholic, village of Greysteel near Londonderry, a week after the Shankill bombing.

Eye-witnesses to the attack have spoken before now, but what follows is an edited account of a Brook Lapping interview, conducted by David Alter, not with a survivor but with one of the gunmen. He had been a member of the UDA for less than a year when he was told to make himself ready for the Greysteel attack. Here, in his own chilling words, is his story:

Around 1990, 1991, I just sort of decided that maybe it was time I did something or tried to do something. I started selling magazines to raise money for prisoners, but I knew in my own heart that I wanted to go further. But I didn't want to rush things, so I went and started off selling magazines, and as time went on it just progressed. I actually ended up waiting for over a year before I was accepted into the ranks of the UFF [Ulster Freedom Fighters]. That was at the start of 1993.

I was asked was I sure, had I thought about it and I said I had. I then had explained to me the different things that I would be asked to do, that I would be asked to kill people. I could be asked to maybe plant explosives, stuff like that there. He asked me was I sure, could I deal with that – having killed somebody? He said to me that do you know that you could end up in jail for a long time, or worse you could be dead, end up dead? And I said yes, that I'd accepted that. That this was just part of the risks.

When I joined, myself and another person had to go somewhere and meet these people. And I was just told then and there, you're now a member of the Ulster Freedom Fighters. There was no swearing-in ceremony or anything secretive about it, it was oh, you're in, and that was it. When I heard about the Shankill bombing on the news, I think it was just shock, really. After the initial shock had died down, there was just anger and rage that this has been carried out. I think it was just purely sectarian. I mean, the IRA have this great thing that they're not sectarian. But I believe they're just as sectarian as they claim the loyalists are. And I just, at that time I just wanted to get revenge.

On the Wednesday after the bombing, the commander had come up and said that there was going to be something, something was going to happen. There was going to be an operation and we're asked would we carry it out, which we readily agreed. We were then taken to another location, where we were briefed on what weapons we would be using and how to use them. At a later date, we were then informed what the target was to be.

The target wasn't going to be a member of the IRA or Sinn Fein. This was going to be, you know, an eye for an eye, a tooth for a tooth. I knew then that it was going to be directed at ordinary people, what could be deemed as ordinary people, the nationalist community. The statement from the UFF leadership had said that the nationalist electorate were going to pay a heavy price for the Shankill bombing.

We were told then to go to a certain location. We stayed the night there, and early on the day of the shooting we were picked up. We were more or less split in twos. That was for security, so that if there was an informer within the ranks, that person would not have the opportunity to contact the RUC or other security services. Then we were told what the target was to be. The commanding officer said that it was to be the Rising Sun. The operation just was to go in and spray the bar with gunfire, and that was to kill as many people as possible.

We carried out a recce. We stopped off at the bar itself. Myself and another person went into the bar to check it out, to see the layout. We actually went into the lounge bit first and we realised we were in the wrong place, and came out and entered the front bar. We ordered some food, and then just generally looked around, see where was the best place to go in. After we got our food we just came out, and we decided to go into the lounge that night, because the layout of the bar made it too risky for us to go in there. So we went back to the safe house and we just sat and waited. We left, I think it was around about nine o'clock – we were actually a bit late, so we were. We had to travel to where the boiler suits and weapons were.

When we got to the bar I think more or less my mind was blank. Things seemed surreal as if we was in a dream kind of thing. Maybe that sounds funny, but it's the best way I could describe it – just nervous, butterflies. When we reached the bar, myself and the other gunman got out of the car and went in. I remember one of the customers saying something, and then shooting and firing my gun once. It jammed and I couldn't clear it, and then everything was quiet, things seemed to be going in slow motion. I can't remember hearing gunfire, although I knew there was gunfire happening. It seemed to be ages, take for ages, in fact it was just a matter of seconds, minutes.

My memory then is coming out of the bar and getting into a car and driving off. I can remember bits in the bar, just looking around me and people lying on the ground, that is really it. As we were driving away I felt dejected and kind of down, because I felt that I hadn't done what I was supposed to do because my gun had jammed. I have heard people before talking about gunmen driving away from shootings shouting and cheering, but I didn't feel elated or anything like that. All I can remember is just saying, oh my gun jammed, my gun jammed.

I mean, at the end of the day I don't think it is right, you know. I mean it's a war but I don't think that people should revel in the fact that they are killing somebody. It is a job and it has to be done. I did feel that the retaliation had been achieved at the end of the day. I would rather that it was an IRA man or a Sinn Fein member that we killed, but I mean, they have always claimed to be protectors of the nationalist community and that bomb was planted in the name of the nationalist community. It was seven killed, I mean, there was two Protestants killed in that bar and we regret that. But I mean there was a war going on.

The driver of the get-away car, interviewed for the first time, was to say there were mixed emotions in the car as the UFF men made their escape. There was no gloating, he said; it was just a matter of getting home: 'We passed three police cars on the way back, which was a nerve-wracking occasion. I do actually remember looking down to the main road and just seeing a sea of blue lights flashing with their sirens, the emergency vehicles, and thinking to myself, what have I done.'

What he and the others had done was to take lives which ranged from a teenage girl to an 81-year-old pensioner, one of the oldest victims of the troubles. Although one gunman's weapon had jammed, the other fired 44 shots, killing eight people and injuring 19 more, splashing the floor and walls with blood.

The Shankill bomb, the Greysteel attack and other incidents left 23 people dead in the space of a week, plunging Northern Ireland back to the worst days of the troubles. The 23 funerals produced moments of great poignancy and high political drama. A moving example of this at the human rather than political level came at one of the Greysteel funerals, when Hume broke down in tears after being approached by the daughter of a victim. He recalled: 'A young girl who was from one of the families that had lost a loved one came up to me and said to me, "Mr Hume, we prayed for you last night in our house, and we prayed that you would be successful in the work that you're doing, so that what happened to us will not happen to anybody else."'

Another funeral, that of the IRA man killed by his own bomb in the Shankill fish shop, generated intense controversy. A wave of condemnation was directed at Adams for helping to carry the coffin of the dead bomber. Adams was to explain: 'I just knew that I had to go to the funeral, it wasn't an issue, and I knew when I went to the funeral what was I to say – that I wouldn't carry the guy's coffin? That would be a huge insult to his family. You have to remember that he had parents and family as well.'

Although many at first assumed the peace process was over, it turned out that the killings had the opposite effect. When the first waves of shock and anger died down, there was renewed determination in many quarters to keep the process going. Major was to suggest that the violence actually gave fresh impetus to a process which was about to expire: 'The process was on a knife-edge. I think it would have broken down had not the Shankill and Greysteel tragedies intervened.'

When Reynolds and Major met a few days later at a Brussels summit, the Taoiseach was desperate to keep the joint declaration idea alive. But first the two prime ministers spoke their minds to each other about Adams and his role at the Begley funeral. Reynolds was to recall Major saying: 'What's this about? How do you expect me to continue with any process when I take up the papers this morning and in every paper on the front page is Gerry Adams carrying a coffin?'

Reynolds said he responded: 'John, look, what you have to understand is this – if this man didn't carry that coffin, he couldn't deliver that movement. He's no good to you or me if he didn't carry that coffin.' Major was to comment: 'I understood that, but it didn't mitigate the feelings that people had. And that bomb destroyed any vestige of a possibility that the Unionist community would accept anything that had a Hume–Adams label on it. I said to him in terms, "Albert, this has got to be the two governments, we can't be seen to be dancing to the strings of any third party."' Reynolds, anxious above all to keep the declaration process in play, agreed to go along with this: 'I was quite prepared to say clearly and unequivocally, Hume–Adams document – no. It is not on the table, it's gone. I was doing that to make sure that the document that the two governments had exchanged was still on the table.' The two prime ministers issued a statement that, despite John Hume's 'courageous and imaginative efforts', they would not adopt or endorse the Hume–Adams proposal.

At this stage Irish nationalist opinion took a decisive hand, reacting angrily to the impression that Major had, in effect, closed down the idea of Hume–Adams. The pressure on Reynolds and his ministers was tremendous: in effect, the Irish government was forcefully instructed to stick with the Hume–Adams talks process. The overwhelming feeling was that there was promise in the initiative which should not be thrown away. Reynolds's office was deluged with an unprecedented flood of angry letters and phone calls, accusing him of betraying Hume and throwing away the chance of peace.

The message was driven home at the Fianna Fáil annual conference, held in Dublin in November. Mentions of Hume's name drew thunderous applause, while ministers and TDs (Member of the Dáil) were buttonholed by delegates and told they should be supporting the SDLP leader. The *Irish Times* reported:

Among much of the Fianna Fáil rank and file, John Hume obviously still has the stature of a demi-god. The SDLP leader could hardly have expected even his own party to give him the kind of accolades he was accorded this weekend on the floor of the ard-fheis. A motion calling for government support for the SDLP leader unleashed a wave of pro-Hume emotion that washed over the delegates and led to passionate declarations of belief in the Hume–Adams initiative.

One delegate said it was nothing short of a disgrace that the government showed no respect for the Hume–Adams proposals. How, he asked, could they be so cool about something that involved a possible end to violence? The mere mention of John Hume's name brought a round of applause. While there was no orchestrated challenge to Mr Reynolds's leadership, waves of dissent were washing about because of a perceived failure to champion the cause of sundered brethren in the north. There were loud voices warning against letting John Hume be hung out to dry.

The irony, of course, was that Reynolds was already working to keep the peace process alive, though after the Brussels meeting he was pretending not to. The sheer force of public opinion, however, left him with little choice: from that point on he not only had to pursue the initiative, but to be seen to do so. Reynolds's aide, Seán Duignan, recalled what the Taoiseach was saying privately at the time: 'Reynolds afterwards claimed to me that it was for the optics, and that John Major privately accepted that they were declaring Hume–Adams dead in order to keep it alive. There was a problem with getting John Hume, in particular, off the pitch. He is so revered not just in nationalist circles in the north, but in the south, that Albert Reynolds very quickly realised that this was simply not on. Being a good politician, Albert Reynolds took that message very quickly.'

Mitchel McLaughlin of Sinn Fein observed:

Albert Reynolds had come to the conclusion that John Major wasn't going to sign up for it, and came back to announce that. They had indicated that to us – we knew what he was about to say to his party conference. But the popular reaction to every reference to Hume–Adams reversed Albert Reynolds on it and convinced him that he should have one more try. At an instinctive level, nationalist Ireland knew that this was the correct way to go. Albert Reynolds picked up that message, and then ran with it very very forcefully – to his enormous credit he went back into battle again and he has to be given credit for changing John Major's mind.

Hume, however, was incensed at the apparent shelving of his initiative, angrily challenging Major across the floor of the Commons: 'The prime minister describes me in that statement as courageous and imaginative. Why has he rejected my proposals before he has talked to me about them?' Major replied coolly: 'I reached the conclusion, as we set out in the statement over the weekend, that it was not the right way to proceed.' Hume's deputy, Seamus Mallon, was to say: 'It was a very lonely moment for John Hume and myself sitting on those benches, because the two prime ministers had actually, if I can use a political term, shafted him.'

Not long afterwards, Hume indulged in an unusually close form of political contact: 'I met John Major in the bar in the House of Commons a few days later. And I walked up to him and caught him by the coat and said, "If you accept that document and make that joint declaration there would be peace within a week, yes. Gladstone failed, Lloyd George failed and Churchill failed. If you succeed you will go down in history as the prime minister who brought peace to Ireland. Take the leap."'

Major remembers the incident clearly: 'He took me by the lapels very emotionally, seeking a peace in Northern Ireland, for it passionately mattered to him, and said – you can achieve it.' Major now moved, though not as Hume had urged. He finally replied to the IRA's offer of a ceasefire, but said two weeks was too short, and instead offered talks following a three-month ceasefire. He emphasised his approach in a high-profile speech at the Lord Mayor's banquet in London's Guildhall, often an occasion for major policy pronouncements. He declared: 'If the IRA end violence for good, then, after a suitable interval to ensure the seriousness of their intent, Sinn Fein can enter the political arena as a democratic party and join the dialogue on the way ahead.'

Major also attempted to seize the initiative on a second front. Only days before he was due to meet Reynolds, he despatched Robin Butler to Dublin, with a bombshell in the shape of a radically restructured version of the joint declaration. It shifted the emphasis to the calming of Protestant fears and toned down the green rhetoric. It was to be an unhappy meeting, as both Reynolds and Butler would testify. Reynolds remembered: 'Robin Butler came to see me on a Friday night, late on a Friday night. He asked me to stay in the office and I did. And he produced this new document.'

Butler recalled: 'I could tell from his body language when he got it that this wasn't going to go down very well, and he opened it and he glanced through it and he pretty well exploded immediately. I got a bigger roasting from him than I ever had in any meeting with a member of another government, and I'm quite sure Albert Reynolds knew exactly what he was doing when he was giving me that roasting.' Reynolds confirms:

I lost my temper with him, I got very angry and I said, look, I never, ever will join you in that strategy. And I am not, under any set of circumstances, going to start with a new document here and now. Eventually I got it out of Robin Butler that they wanted a total reversal of strategy. They wanted me to join with them in taking on the IRA. And how they were going to tackle them, that they were never going to do this and all of that. But I just could not believe my ears. I just couldn't believe it, I said, 'I'm not taking that and I'm not buying it. If that's the idea that you have, forget it.'

Butler, bracing himself, then informed Reynolds of another piece of delicate news. The Cabinet Secretary had to tell the Taoiseach that the *Observer* newspaper would be running a scoop that Sunday, revealing the story of Major's dealings with the IRA through the Derry link. The already roasted Butler recalled: 'I then had to break to him this story about our approach from the IRA and our contacts with them, and the reason why we'd had to keep those a secret.'

Reynolds again expressed anger and incredulity: 'And here they were, for a number of years, talking behind the scenes. Me never told – the Irish government never told – and here we are in confidential discussions.' Duignan, looking back, remembered: 'I was struck by the extraordinary resentment between the two sides at this time and the distrust that evidently welled up: the British insisting that they were talking about one draft, and the Irish saying "No, no, no, we are talking about something that we compiled and that you agreed we would talk about." There was Irish distrust of perfidious Albion. At one moment I remember Dermot Nally saying, "They think they are talking to the King of Lesotho."'

Another senior government aide, Fergus Finlay, also had a vivid memory of Nally's reaction: 'Dermot Nally is one of the most mild-mannered of men, but on this occasion he was raging, absolutely furious – volcanic – in a way that I had never seen him. It all reminded me of a remark that Garret FitzGerald once made about the difference between Irish and British negotiating styles. The Irish, he said, always asked for far more than they hope to get, and the British always promised far more than they expect to deliver. I just saw it as a try-on.'

Mansergh would say of the secret British contact with republicans:

It was clearly a matter of deep embarrassment to them. The embarrassment was that they had told us nothing about it. I was told afterwards by a senior British official that the reason for the contacts was that the British government wanted to check out for themselves what John Hume was saying to them. John Hume is the type of person who likes to take a fairly optimistic assessment, and I think each government wanted their own direct contact with Sinn Fein so that they could form their own independent judgement.

Eventually tempers cooled and a scheduled Anglo–Irish summit took place in Dublin. As it opened, both governments concluded that a joint declaration was the only way forward. To make it work, the Irish needed enough to mollify Sinn Fein, while the British needed enough on the consent principle to satisfy Unionists. It started badly. Reynolds was furious to find Major still pursuing the new British draft, while Major blamed Reynolds for a stream of what he regarded as unhelpful leaks to the Irish media.

Irish government aide Fergus Finlay recalled: 'We lined up on either side of a long dining-room table in Dublin Castle. Almost immediately, Albert Reynolds accused John Major of bad faith. No documents had been tabled at that stage, the documents were only in the background.' Albert Reynolds said: 'I'm not gonna discuss it; I'm not gonna discuss the latest draft that we got from you because it represents bad faith on your part. Either that's off the table or we're just out of here, we'll end the summit now.'

The two then met in private session, while outside, officials and other ministers waited anxiously. One of Reynolds's ministers, Mrs Maire Geoghegan-Quinn, said: 'At one stage we thought that was it – they're going to go home, they're just not prepared to allow Reynolds to do what he wants to do. Reynolds always believed that Major always wanted to do it, that he wanted to do the big thing, the big deal, that he wanted to be the prime minister that cracked this finally, but that he was not being let do it.'

Behind closed doors, Reynolds led the charge with some distinctly undiplomatic language: 'Look, John, this is bad faith in any sense of the word. I can't buy it, I won't buy it. We'll have no summit and we'll leave it at that if that has to be it. I'll be gone out of here. Am I being fooled all the time? Am I being fooled by my friend John Major all the time? I mean is this, was this an act that we were going through over previous months? What does he take me for – a stupid effing so-and-so? That's the way it was, high-tempered stuff.' Major counter-attacked Reynolds over the press leaks:

He sat there looking at me in a bit of a sulk over the problems we had had. I had a big pile of newspapers under my arm which I slammed down on the table. I said, 'Well, where do you think this came from, Albert? You know the difficulty this caused with the Unionists – whereabouts did that come from, it couldn't have come from London, must have come from Dublin. When this sort of nonsense breaks all over the press, how can I stop the Unionists believing that we are reaching all sorts of deals that they would never find acceptable? If this goes on we just won't reach a deal.'

The venting of all this spleen helped clear the air to some extent, and the two prime ministers emerged ready to do business. When Fergus Finlay asked Reynolds how it had gone, the Taoiseach replied: 'Well, he chewed the bollocks off me, but I took a few lumps out of him.'

The meeting continued, but all was not plain sailing. Finlay recalled: 'At some point John Major was holding a pencil in his hand, and the pencil snapped between his fingers. Everyone could see that he was biting his tongue to control some kind of outburst. And he in turn pretty well said that Albert Reynolds had no right to prevent them tabling ideas if they thought that the ideas were important. To which Albert replied that, as far as he was concerned, it was too late in the day for that: "You're just making a fool out of me. If you carry on like this, this dialogue will go on for ever and get nowhere."'

Major remembers the pencil incident:

There were moments of great frustration. No Anglo–Irish negotiation is ever short, it's never explicit. An Irish official reintroduced a point that had been cleared off the table, or I thought we'd cleared off the table, an hour or two ago. I was pretty frustrated and I clenched my fist and banged the table – pencil broke in my hand and scurried right across the table. I think everybody thought it was a piece of ill-temper. It wasn't, it was sheer frustration.

It may have been a good thing – it may have ruined the pencil but I think it concentrated minds. The flavour of the meeting was that that sort of thing happened, on both sides, on a number of occasions but everybody knew what was at stake and everybody stuck at it.

Finlay, speaking of the British draft, recalled: 'We all sat down round the table and began discussing the Irish draft, as if nothing had ever happened, and the matter was never referred to again.' The change in the British line led to some confusion among the media and those who were briefing them. Duignan recalled:

It was bizarre because the Downing Street press secretary, Gus O'Donnell and I were briefing in the one room, within feet of one another, and we repeatedly contradicted one another. The journalists were going back and forth saying, 'Do you realise you are contradicting each other?' I was briefing that the Irish position document was the one that was being discussed within a few feet of us in the chamber. Gus was saying exactly the opposite, it was another document. At some stage it seems that the British conceded. The first I knew of that was when Gus calmly changed tune and simply said, 'Yeah, the Irish document is now the document that is on the table.' It was very strange.

Butler summed up the extraordinary meeting:

At the beginning of the summit, I think both sides were not only aggrieved with each other, but were very doubtful whether we could carry any initiative forward. By the end of the summit, we genuinely had got to the position where both sides thought that there was something worth negotiating about. The move that we'd made was to return to the Irish draft. The movement that they'd made was to show that they were prepared to take our concerns about it seriously, and to negotiate further on important points. That was not the end of the tunnel, but it was light at the end of the tunnel, and I think that both sides were genuinely relieved by that. There was a feeling of bonhomie that came from the release of what had previously been tension over a situation which was very uncomfortable.

Foreign Secretary Douglas Hurd said: 'I wrote in my diary that night that Albert Reynolds was testy, determined and twinkling – twinkling. I had the sense that he was enjoying himself and I rather warmed to that. I also had the sense that he wanted an agreement; I warmed to that too.'

Not all points were cleared up, the two prime ministers instructing their officials to find ways round the remaining difficulties. The officials did as they were told, but every word was fought over: even punctuation was subjected to debate. One issue arose over the British statement, first made by Brooke three years earlier, that they had 'no selfish strategic or economic interest in Northern Ireland.'

Finlay explained: 'We thought that that phrase would be immeasurably strengthened by the inclusion of a comma between the word "selfish" and "strategic". And we tried very hard to get that comma in. It would have strengthened things. There were people even then in the republican movement saying to us, "They mightn't have any selfish strategic interest, but do they have an unselfish strategic interest in Northern Ireland?"' Butler recalled with a smile: 'We felt that, since it was our statement, we ought to be able to put it the way we wanted to, and in the end the Irish government accepted that.'

By this stage, the scope of the joint declaration was being extended. The original idea was to produce a text that would wean the republicans away from violence, and this remained its primary purpose; but the concept arose that it should be addressed to Unionists and loyalists as well. The Protestant community was notoriously insecure and fearful of political innovation, and people in both London and Dublin worried that a document addressed exclusively to republicans would spark off a wave of anxiety. Increases in loyalist anxiety often led to a rise in loyalist violence, which all sides were anxious to avoid.

There were, in addition, interesting stirrings within the loyalist paramilitary underworld which some were hopeful of encouraging. The UDA was becoming, if anything, even more militant, with control of the organisation moving to a group of Young Turks who had a real appetite for killing. Within the UVF, by contrast, some more thoughtful figures were emerging, with many ex-prisoners questioning the value of violence and expressing interest in exploring a political path. (The drop in UVF violence led UDA men to describe the UVF contemptuously as 'the peace people'.)

Dublin had long maintained a discreet network of private contacts with Protestant and Unionist figures, including politicians, clergy and others, and two of these now came to the fore. One was Dr Robin Eames, who as Archbishop of Armagh was head of the Church of Ireland; the other was the Reverend Roy Magee, a Presbyterian minister based in East Belfast. Dr Eames, who had a reputation as a political prelate familiar with behind-the-scenes activity, had access to John Major. He was also known to be in close touch with many other sections of opinion, including important figures in the Ulster Unionist party. The party would not officially talk to Reynolds, but Dublin attempted to use Dr Eames as a line of contact to senior Unionists, and the churchman became a regular visitor to the Taoiseach's office.

Reynolds related: 'He was a good balancing voice. It was obvious that he had a very clear view as to where he wanted to see his people going. I clearly recognised that he would have close contact with the leadership of the Unionist party as well, and would be in a position to give me a very strong input as to what their fears were and how those fears could be accommodated. I showed him drafts of the declaration.'

Reynolds also sought and received input from Roy Magee, in whose East Belfast parish both the UDA and UVF had many members. He knew some of the most important paramilitary figures. In the early 1970s, he had himself been involved in Unionist politics as a member of Ulster Vanguard, a hard-line loyalist grouping. He therefore had a track record of commitment to Unionism, though in his work in the 1990s all recognised his aim was ending violence. He was in touch with the CLMC – the Combined Loyalist Military Command – an umbrella organisation which represented the three major Protestant paramilitary groups, the UDA, UVF and the smaller Red Hand Commandos.

One evening in late 1993, Mansergh, watching television, saw Magee talking about the loyalist paramilitants, and recommended to Reynolds that contact should be made with him. Reynolds, aware of Magee's contacts with the paramilitants, established a personal relationship with him, thus setting up yet another line of secret contact, this time between the Irish government and the extreme loyalists. Reynolds recalled:

Roy Magee used to come and see me in my own office. The two of us talked at length from time to time, with nobody present, no record kept, so there was a matter of trust between the two of us to build up a good relationship and to make others feel that their voices were being listened to in Dublin as well. Maybe every couple of weeks there would be telephone communication between my office and Roy Magee.

I became absolutely convinced that I could accept the messages coming from the loyalists, just the same as I would accept them coming from the other side. I was telling Roy Magee that my view was, and my good feeling was telling me, that there was a distinct possibility of getting the IRA to call a ceasefire. I wanted to take the other side on board as well and see could we move them towards a ceasefire as well.

Although loyalist violence was running at a high level, Magee assured Reynolds that opinion was changing and developing within the loyalist underworld. Reynolds believed that at least some of the loyalists wanted to move into politics. Magee felt his dealings with Reynolds were valuable, but later revealed there had been one almost comic misunderstanding between them. He brought to Dublin a text from the loyalists which contained six points, including the right of free political thought, the right to pursue constitutional change by peaceful means and the right to equal opportunity. Reynolds, eager to show himself willing, said he agreed with all the points and would include them in the declaration. The misunderstanding arose because Reynolds assumed the points were what loyalists wished to be reassured about. In fact, however, they were points which the loyalists were prepared to offer to Catholics and nationalists.

Magee explained: 'I presented six points. He assumed that what he was being told was what loyalists wanted written into a Bill of Rights. What they were saying was, "Here is what we would want to see written into a Bill of Rights to make sure nationalists would be comfortable." They were in fact conceding them, which is different.' The misunderstanding about these points went right through the system in Dublin. They went forward for inclusion in the text of the declaration and were eventually incorporated in what was to become the Downing Street Declaration, where they are still to be seen, a lasting reminder of how misapprehensions can occur in the most carefully constructed chain of communication.

Chilcot was to sum up the position which had been reached by late 1993:

The prospect of re-engineering all-party talks, excluding the non-constitutional parties, Sinn Fein and the loyalist parties, by then was a dead duck. Things had gone too far forward, really, too much progress had been made. The only game in town was to get the real result, which was peace, however imperfect and perhaps not permanent, but nonetheless to get it and with that some kind of political settlement. Anything less wasn't really worth going for, and I don't think anybody was seriously thinking of going for it.

As the joint declaration was reaching its final form, John Major arranged a late-night rendezvous with James

Molyneaux. At an earlier encounter, when Major and Butler had shown Molyneaux an early draft of the document, the Ulster Unionist leader had quietly but firmly signalled his disapproval. Major had then shelved the drafting process, but had later returned to it. The Unionist leader's response would be vital, since open opposition from him would make the document more controversial and actually reduce its chances of success.

Major recalls Molyneaux's reaction: 'He was pretty apprehensive at first, as he began to read through the document. In particular, he would have liked us to have taken out "no selfish or strategic interest."' Molyneaux remembers: 'The prime minister said: "But you know why it's got to be there." And I said, "Yes, I know why it's there. Britain has no selfish interest in remaining in Northern Ireland, we're not a colonial power any longer."' Major recalled fondly: 'And he looked at me in a typical Jim way and said, "I won't expostulate about this, but I'm not gonna go out and advocate it." And that really was as much as we could have hoped.' The encounter was a vital one, in that it helped clear the way for the joint declaration to be finalised.

The text which was finally agreed between the two governments was a masterpiece of diplomatic ambiguity. It reconciled the irreconcilable in one serpentine paragraph, which laid out: 'It is for the people of the island of Ireland alone, by agreement between the two parts respectively, to exercise their right of self-determination on the basis of consent, freely and concurrently given, North and South, to bring about a united Ireland, if that is their wish.'

For republicans, it said they could 'bring about a united Ireland.' But for Unionists, only 'on the basis of consent.'

For republicans, it said, 'the people of Ireland alone' must decide; but for Unionists, 'North and South' must agree. Neither side would be wildly enthusiastic about the formulation, but perhaps both might be able to live with it.

Ten days before Christmas 1993, Reynolds flew to London for the signing ceremony. Only six months earlier, at Baldonnell military airport, the joint declaration had been no more than a glint in the Taoiseach's eye. By now, it had become the basis for a momentous new Anglo–Irish understanding, a milestone in troubles history. The two governments then proceeded to the final technicalities. Finlay recalled:

The agreed draft was brought to Albert Reynolds very late that night. He decided he was happy with it, but asked us to check one more time that this was the agreed draft. My recollection is that the very, very last draft was faxed back to London and came back immediately, unamended and unchanged and then we were all happy. We flew over to London the following day. We landed in Heathrow Airport, were brought in by motorcycle police outriders, all the way into London. Somewhere on the outskirts of the city one of them hit a traffic island and I gather he ended up in hospital. But we lost him – we just whizzed by, I'm afraid, watched him lying in the road and went on, on our peace-making mission.

Ministers and officials sipped champagne in Downing Street. Butler would recall going up to Reynolds and making a remark with real feeling. Reynolds, too, remembered the moment: 'Robin Butler came in when everybody was having their glass of champagne and everything, and said to me: "I never thought I'd see the day. We've come a long way from Baldonnell, because I didn't give you a hope in hell of ever making it through."'

Duignan felt Major was somewhat tense and nervous, and that the occasion had no atmosphere of celebration. He later recalled: 'I remarked to Martin Mansergh that the occasion had all the strained bonhomie of a shotgun wedding reception, but Mansergh said it was just their natural British reserve.' Duignan spotted one particularly reserved figure in the gathering – Mayhew, who held continuing doubts about the whole declaration process. Duignan wrote: 'Sir Patrick made no attempt to conceal his lack of enthusiasm. He remained separate from the milling politicians and officials, gloomily staring out windows for much of the time.' Mayhew responded: 'I was entirely content with the text of the Agreement. I may have been just a touch anxious about the elation of certain Irish officials and perhaps I was slightly worried as to what that might portend.'

Mansergh gave this judgement on what became known as the Downing Street Declaration: 'Together with the Anglo–Irish Agreement, it was the catalyst for peace. It did mean that nine months down the line republicans had to make up their mind whether they were going to fish or cut bait. So it was one of the highlights of the peace process.'

The Declaration was intended to usher in an era of peace and goodwill in Northern Ireland. The question was whether it offered enough to secure the first vital step, an IRA ceasefire. For the IRA and Sinn Fein it was a moment of truth, representing as it did the considered view of the British and Irish governments, hammered out over so many months. The fact that London and Dublin could agree on something so substantial, within weeks of the deaths and despair of the Shankill and Greysteel attacks, was in itself an achievement for politics and negotiation, and a reaffirmation of the strength of the Anglo–Irish relationship. The Declaration was widely welcomed in Britain, the Republic and internationally; the Unionist community, after a period of uncertainty, decided not to take great exception to it.

For the Protestant community at large, the fact that IRA violence continued and even at times increased did nothing to ease community relations, and meant most Protestants and Unionists did not believe the IRA was heading for a cessation. A general Protestant consensus emerged, however, that the Declaration was not a particularly dangerous document.

The spotlight was therefore on the republicans. The two governments had declared, formally and publicly, that Sinn Fein could enter the political processes if the IRA gave up violence. But the Downing Street Declaration was not at all what the republicans had aimed at and hoped for when that process began. Much of the document was concerned with reassuring Unionist opinion, and in its formulation on consent Reynolds had gone further than any previous Taoiseach in enshrining the right of a northern majority to say no to Irish unity. There was no trace of any British intention to withdraw; on the contrary, Dublin had joined in setting out a formal guarantee that unity could only come about by consent. The republicans, in their first draft, had wanted Britain to make a unilateral move committing itself to Irish unity and British withdrawal within an agreed period. That document suggested that the consent of Unionists was to be sought for such an arrangement, but did not make this a prerequisite. Here consent had been elevated to a point of the highest principle.

Major added to the Declaration a series of comments designed to reassure Unionist opinion, telling the Commons:

What is not in the Declaration is any suggestion that the British government should join the ranks of the persuaders of the value or legitimacy of a united Ireland; that is not there. Nor is there any suggestion that the future status of Northern Ireland should be decided by a single act of self-determination by the people of Ireland as a whole; that is not there either. Nor is there any timetable for constitutional change, or any arrangements for joint authority over Northern Ireland. In sum, the Declaration provides that it is and must be for the people of Northern Ireland to determine their own future.

Although the Declaration excluded the elements listed by Major, many in the republican camp were taken by surprise that he had participated in any such exercise, for they had thought it unlikely that Reynolds could talk Major into making any announcement which so publicly and directly addressed republican concerns such as self-determination. A month earlier, a senior republican had said privately: 'Major just hasn't the balls for it, hasn't the bottle for it. He's the wrong man in place at the wrong time.'

But Major had cooperated in producing the Declaration, and furthermore had addressed republican theory in a serious and substantive way, and one which had the approval and support of constitutional nationalism both north and south. He acknowledged Irish self-determination, subject only to the operation of consent, and formally declared that Britain had no selfish strategic or economic interest in Northern Ireland. Many republicans had assumed that

Major's desire not to offend the Ulster Unionist party, with its nine Commons votes, would prevent him from going so far.

The Downing Street Declaration in itself was clearly incompatible with traditional republican theory, yet Sinn Fein reacted not by rejecting it but by calling for clarification. The party announced it was setting up a peace commission to organise a process of consultations with as wide a range of opinion and individuals as possible, before giving its definitive response. Pat Doherty of Sinn Fein recalled:

I was actually in Belfast on the morning of the announcement of the Downing Street Declaration. There was a whole crowd of us in a small room, and there was a sort of a silence and an anger. One of our members, who we regard as mild-mannered, was outraged, absolutely outraged, but the rest of us were saying, 'Well, you know, that's realpolitik.' We knew it was going to be difficult – it was very difficult to find a sense of our core values in the Declaration. What we had to do was bridge the gap from where that document was at, to where it should be at, that was our task. I suppose in a sense that summed up what we were saying to our base – that we were now dealing with the real world.

There was concern about the prisoners, there was concern about what this emerging political consensus meant for the IRA. Where was the struggle going? Were we sure, did we trust – you'd often hear this word – did we trust the Irish government, did we trust the SDLP? And you'd have to explain that it's not a question of trust, it's a question of dealing with them, dealing with the fact that they were a reality. But we were confident and strong enough that we had an analysis that was deep enough.

In all of the debates we've had, in all of the meetings we've had with our base, I would leave the meeting with two almost contradictory feelings. One was an unbelievable belief in the leadership that was sometimes quite frightening, that they had a real trust and belief in the leaders. And the other one was a real fear of the process that we were in – that there may be a mistake made and we may end up being outmanoeuvred by bigger and more powerful forces. I suppose there's a contradiction in that, but there's a reality in that as well.

Martin Mansergh was to comment: 'In a sense Sinn Fein leaders were riding two horses at the same time in trying to reassure the wider leadership that this was still consistent with core demands. But they probably realised that, in practice, it was heading in the direction of a negotiated political settlement that would, certainly for the time being, fall considerably short of Irish unity.'

The Declaration had placed those republicans who wished to fight on indefinitely in a difficult position for the document had, in itself, increased the odds against a military victory for the IRA. The two governments had jointly laid out a position of self-determination coupled with consent, and even the most militant had to recognise how slim were the chances of changing that through violence. The two governments were generally judged to have made genuine efforts to tackle the issues which mattered most to the republicans. A decision to fight on as before would clearly produce a wave of anger in nationalist Ireland, which would blame the IRA, and no one else, for continuing the conflict. A senior Dublin source said of the Declaration:

It gave the Provos an involvement, an entry to the political process. It gave them the possibility of saying, 'We can influence events, we can become involved in discussion.' Its major achievement was that it did that without, at the same time, alienating the Unionists to a point where they would resort to open violence – in other words, there was a balance in it. We did allow it to be diluted: the serious dilution as far as the Provos were concerned was the absence of the time frame and on the British acting as persuaders. But those points were simply non-negotiable for the British.

Dublin continued to maintain discreet contacts with Sinn Fein, who had deputed McGuinness to keep in touch with the Irish Department of Foreign Affairs. McGuinness remembered:

On one occasion I was going into their building at Stephen's Green in Dublin, and there was one of these Dublin tourist buses outside, an open-top bus, full of Japanese and Americans and Germans, with a guy who was giving them a tour of Dublin. I was attempting to get into the building without being seen and suddenly I hear, through the loudspeaker on the bus, the man saying, 'And the chief negotiator for Sinn Fein, Martin McGuinness, is now entering the Department of Foreign Affairs.' This was all over Stephen's Green – I couldn't believe it.

London, however, maintained its distance. On a pre-Christmas visit to Belfast, Major brusquely brushed aside the republican request for clarification, declaring: 'There is a gauntlet down on the table. It is marked peace. It is there for Sinn Fein to pick it up. The onus is on them. There is no need for fresh negotiation. There is no need for any indecisiveness. There is no further clarification needed; we are not being drawn into negotiations. I am not playing that game.' While this was effective as a television soundbite, it led to a stalemate which lasted for months.

9
The American connection
_____

While there was little movement on one front there was furious activity on others. Politically, there was a huge development when President Bill Clinton involved the US administration in Northern Ireland matters in a way which delighted Irish nationalists. But while the Dublin government was greatly pleased, the British government was absolutely appalled.

The Clinton era of close involvement in the peace process began at a time when London sought to pile maximum pressure on republicans for a positive response to the Downing Street Declaration. But Dublin and Hume took a different view. They specifically supported the idea of having the US allow Adams, who had been banned from America for many years, into the country. It would, they thought, provide a practical and striking demonstration to republicans that diplomacy and politics could deliver more than violence.

The issue had first appeared on the Clinton radar screen back in April 1992, when, during the presidential election campaign, he had been invited to the New York Sheraton Hotel for an Irish-American forum. Clinton, then Governor of Arkansas, was to face a highly sceptical audience. The night left a vivid impression on Clinton, who would recall: 'I was exhausted. It was late at night and it was almost like I was being put through an oral exam for a Ph.D. in Irish politics.' Among the gathering was politician

Peter King, who, unusually for a US Republican Congressman, was an outspoken critic of British policy in Northern Ireland and a supporter of Sinn Fein. He recalled the standard response of senior US politicians to the Irish question: 'I wasn't expecting much, because I had never heard a national politician in America say anything but the most banal or non-controversial things about Ireland. It was either, I wore a green tie on St Patrick's Day, or my cousin came from Killarney.'

Some of Clinton's audience supported the IRA, or its political wing Sinn Fein, and were there pressing for the interests of Irish republicans. One of the most pointed questions of the evening came from Martin Galvin of Noraid, which represented Sinn Fein in the US. He asked Clinton: 'If you were elected President, would you direct the State Department to allow a visa to Gerry Adams?' This was a delicate question, in that the US authorities had for years refused to give Adams permission to enter the USA. As Peter King remarked of the occasion: 'So you have Martin Galvin, who was in a way the voice of the republicans in the United States, and you have the guy running for President of the United States, talking about Gerry Adams, who in British eyes was this arch-terrorist.'

Although, as he admitted, Clinton was not well-versed in Irish affairs, his instincts were more radical than those of any previous American politician running for President. Clinton would say of that meeting: 'There were lots of questions and they weren't exactly hostile, but they were highly aggressive. I came to see it wasn't so much directed aggression against me, it was just this accumulated frustration these people had. They thought no politician in either party would ever do anything but show up at the St Patrick's Day lunch.

'So here Galvin bores in on the ultimate question, the visa question, and I had the feeling that we ought to try to do something.' His response at the time was: 'I want to give you a precise answer to the question. I would support a visa for Gerry Adams. I think it would be totally harmless to our national security interests, and it might be enlightening to the political debate in this country.' Looking back, Clinton would muse: 'I'm not sure at the time I understood all the ramifications of what I had said.'

The question of allowing Adams and other republicans to enter the US would later become a key issue in the peace process. No one realised it at the time, but it was to lead on to Clinton, during both of his terms of office, taking a greater interest in Northern Ireland than any other US President. At the time of the Galvin question, however, it made Clinton's aides highly nervous. One of these was Tony Lake, who as National Security Adviser would later find himself immersed in matters Irish. He said of the Clinton answer: 'He committed himself to supporting a visa for Gerry Adams, actually without the advice of his foreign policy team. It came as something of a surprise to us. All of us, in early 1993, recommended against giving Adams such a visa because IRA terrorism was continuing.'

By early 1994, Major had no reason to believe that Clinton would change US policy. Once in office, Clinton had shifted position, twice refusing Adams a visa, so that what he said at the Sheraton Hotel meeting looked like just another politician's empty campaign promise. Major certainly thought so, later saying of Adams: 'We had signed the joint Declaration but he hadn't supported it, he was equivocating on it and demanding clarifications but he expressly hadn't supported it, he hadn't renounced violence. It never occurred to me that he would get a visa – I saw no conceivable reason why he should.'

But Major had reckoned without the power and persuasiveness of a new breed of Irish-Americans. Tens of millions of people in the US describe themselves as Irish-American; few of these had any detailed interest in the Northern Ireland problem, but many held to their ingrained image of Britain as a colonial power of occupation, exploiting Ireland. To the traditional guilt of the emigrant was added the image of their ancestors having to leave the old country because the British callously allowed the famine to kill millions of native Irish. With the British historically cast as the villains of the piece, many Irish-Americans simplistically assumed when the troubles began that the IRA were in the classic mould of anti-colonial freedom fighters intent on driving out an army of occupation.

In the early 1970s this translated into large donations of dollars sent openly to the republicans, as well as a surreptitious flow of arms shipments. In the late 1970s Dublin and Hume had made a severe dent in all this by recruiting powerful Irish-Americans, such as Senator Edward Kennedy and the late Tip O'Neill, then Speaker of the House of Representatives, to oppose support for violent republicanism. In doing so, the Irish nationalists also astutely harnessed Irish-American political influence in the cause of constitutional nationalism. This new alignment had been shaken, but not destroyed, by the surge of anti-British feeling and support for republicanism generated by the 1981 hunger strike.

By the early 1990s a new phenomenon was emerging: corporate Irish-America. People of Irish descent had risen to some of the most powerful boardrooms of America, where they commanded large amounts of investment money and, very often, sizeable personal fortunes. Many wanted to do something for the land of their ancestors; most of all they wanted, if they could, to help rescue it from the long cycle of violence. One such figure, who possessed both business acumen and political antennae, was Niall O'Dowd, who had emigrated to the US in the 1970s and had become a successful publisher. A close associate of O'Dowd's was Bruce Morrison, a former Congressman who led a successful campaign to have the number of visas for Irish emigrants increased, and who was friendly with Clinton. O'Dowd said: 'I had information from my own contacts that were here, that Sinn Fein were interested in a new departure in America, in opening up the possibility of an American intervention in Northern Ireland.' He flew to Dublin to discuss with a republican contact the idea of bringing an influential Irish-American group to meet Sinn Fein:

I'd never met him and I set up a meeting with him in a hotel in Dublin. Because I'd never met him the basic thing was that he would have a pint of Guinness, and I would recognise him. We sat down and we talked and – he's a man of few words, and I did all the talking. I basically put to him the idea that we would create a new opening in America. I said to him that everyone in Northern Ireland was frozen in place and an American dimension would create a whole new dynamic within the peace process.

I said to him, 'Look, here's my plan. You guys call an unannounced ceasefire, for the period of which our delegation will be in Ireland. We will bring that message. We will inform the White House in advance of that ceasefire, as an example of your good faith.' He took it very seriously and said he would come back to me, and that he would give it very serious thought, and would talk to his colleagues about it. I got the feeling that I was pushing an open door in some ways, that they had thought through at great length what the situation was, and how they might extricate themselves from what was increasingly becoming a war that nobody could win.

This was reported back to the White House by what O'Dowd referred to as a cut-out. He was in touch with Edward Kennedy's Foreign Policy Adviser, Trina Vargo, who in turn briefed Nancy Soderberg of Clinton's National Security Agency. O'Dowd explained: 'The purpose was to give the White House deniability. Trina then agreed to go to the White House because they wanted deniability – they didn't want to be associated in any way with a group of amateur diplomats who were going over to Ireland. It was a strange world – you're groping around in the semi-darkness a lot of the time. You know the White House is out there, you know the IRA's out there, and you're trying to make shapes out of shadows really.'

The unannounced IRA ceasefire duly took place, lasting for ten days and taking the security authorities completely by surprise. Martin McGuinness recalled: 'The Irish-Americans clearly indicated before they came that it would be most helpful if a period of quiet could be arranged to facilitate their visit, and we went off to see what we could do in relation to all of that.'

In September 1993 the Irish-Americans arrived, knowing that high on Sinn Fein's agenda was a visa for Adams, who, with McGuinness, met them at Sinn Fein's West Belfast headquarters. Niall O'Dowd related the Sinn Fein pitch at the meeting, describing what McGuinness said:

'He said to us that he had been stopped on his way to the meeting, that he had been harassed, and that he wanted to make it clear that we were in a war zone. The helicopters were overhead, 30,000 British troops were on the streets, and that things were very tough in his community.'

The visiting delegation made their own points, Bruce Morrison recalling: 'The one message I wanted to convey was that the label "terrorist" was drowning out their entire message. That was my experience as a member of Congress, and so somehow that had to change, and in my view the way that changed was what the IRA had just done, for our visit, which was stop.'

Sinn Fein's leaders indicated that the IRA would stop their war only if they believed they could get more from Britain through politics, saying that they needed the US administration's backing to strengthen their hand. Adams remembers arguing: 'We had shared objectives. We were people looking to develop the international dimension, particularly in the USA, and they were people from that constituency looking to make a contribution.' McGuinness adds: 'We talked about visas for Gerry Adams and for leading Sinn Fein representatives. We talked about opening our own office in Washington, and we talked about how we could make all of that happen.' O'Dowd liked what he was hearing, but was optimistic: 'I said I thought we could deliver the White House. I wasn't quite sure in what guise, but I said I was confident that we could deliver the White House, for the first time in the history of the Irish conflict.'

But the White House was not yet ready to welcome Adams, partly because of the strong feelings of Senator Edward Kennedy, who had great influence on America's attitude towards Ireland. He recalls: 'I was against the visa. I'd been strongly opposed to the IRA and violence, and had maintained that position in the United States Senate.' But things were changing. Clinton had chosen St Patrick's Day, 17 March, to announce the appointment of a new ambassador to Dublin, Senator Kennedy's sister, Jean Kennedy Smith. She was open to the arguments of Albert Reynolds, who now threw his weight as Taoiseach behind the idea of allowing Adams into the States. He explained: 'I was going to give it all I had to try to get it. He was banned out of New York, but if we could get him in and be seen to win the diplomatic argument on the world stage, supported by Washington, it would be a big step forward.'

When Kennedy visited Dublin in December 1993, to spend New Year's Eve with his sister, he paid a courtesy call to the Taoiseach. Jean Kennedy Smith remembers:

It was more of a social conversation really, but at the very end I asked the Taoiseach to tell Ted what he thought about a visa for Gerry Adams. And he said, 'I think you should go for it because I think he wants peace.' The argument from the Taoiseach was very persuasive, in that he felt that the big thing that Gerry Adams wanted to avoid was a split within the republican movement. He knew that at this time he did not have the power to dictate to the IRA that they were going to go on the path of peace.

Reynolds remembers: 'He was surprised to hear about me changing government policy to go and support a visa for Gerry Adams, because he had been implacably opposed to it.' According to Kennedy: 'I remember asking him whether he was absolutely personally convinced, to a moral certainty, that Gerry Adams was against violence and for moving the political process forward, and he spent

a good deal of time telling me how he came to this conclusion.' Kennedy found this persuasive, but before
making up his mind checked with Hume, his long-time
adviser. Kennedy found Hume strongly supported the
idea:

We had a long evening, I remember at a restaurant, and
talked about this for two or three hours. He talked at great
length and obvious knowledge and with a great sense of
moral purpose, with an eloquence and persuasiveness about
the importance of giving peace a chance. He reiterated something that I believe in, and that it is the people on the ground,
that are risking their lives for peace, bringing a moral dimension to this kind of an issue, who those on the outside should
pay attention to.

Kennedy wrote to the White House, supporting the visa.
O'Dowd's group was by now organising a peace conference, to provide an opportunity to invite Adams to the
US. One of Clinton's senior aides was Nancy Soderberg,
who had previously worked for Kennedy. She recalls the
effect of Kennedy's letter: 'The letter from Ted Kennedy
had an enormous impact on the White House and on
our decision to move things forward. Ted Kennedy has
obviously personally been victimised by violence throughout all of his life. That weighs very heavily on him and
the Irish question. For Ted Kennedy to advocate anything
for Gerry Adams or the IRA was a stunning shift.'

John Hume also had great influence in Washington, as
Soderberg recalled: 'I remember having lunch with John
Hume in the White House mess and I asked him should
I be paying attention to this, and basically he said, "No,
it's not ripe yet." Then, some months later, he was saying,
"You should engage now, this is the time to do it." He

said that with a lot of credibility – having said it wasn't ripe, when he finally said it was ripe, people listened.'

It was not until three days before the conference that the visa application reached Clinton. He remembers the occasion: 'It was a Saturday afternoon. I'd just had this wonderful lunch with Helmut Kohl who loved to eat and so do I. So we had a big time, and I came in and I thought, now I'm going to spoil my meal with indigestion and I was feeling kind of crabby, actually, but anxious to get through this.' Summoning his national security team, which included Tony Lake and Soderberg, he recalled:

Well, we knew we had to make a decision. They all knew I wanted to do it because I wanted to encourage the process. Albert Reynolds wanted me to do it but the State Department was dead against it. The career people in the State Department thought it would be devastating to our special relationship with Great Britain. The Justice Department was against it because they thought it would look like we were coddling terrorism.

But as the time for decision neared, an unexpected development occurred in the most unexpected of places – California. A radio station received a message from someone purporting to speak for the 'South Diego IRA', saying bombs had been planted in British shops there. He warned there would be more, if Adams did not get his visa. The bombs turned out to be hoaxes, but the call shook the White House.

Lake said that he, Soderberg and Clinton 'were thrown through a loop. The President said, "What the hell is this?" and all of us initially thought, this probably puts the kibosh on the whole thing.' Clinton himself remembers: 'I felt I was snake-bit. I thought, my God, how could this happen, and why would they do something so stupid if they did it? Then it turned out they were hoax bombs. But you know somebody did something and said something, so I felt that Gerry Adams had to make some sort of statement condemning it.'

In New York, the organisers of the peace conference were desperate to find out if their star guest would be coming. The link man between the White House and the republicans was Niall O'Dowd, who was urgently telephoned by Soderberg. He recalls:

I just literally was running the shower. I was sitting there stark naked, the phone rings, and I grab a towel. She said to me that people are worried that if we bring Adams into this country, that it will mean that the violence will also be imported with him, and they want a direct statement from him denying this incident. I said, 'It's completely insane. I mean this could not be the IRA – this is obviously British dirty tricks trying to stop this visa.' But as far as Nancy Soderberg was concerned, without some clarification there would be no visa.

O'Dowd rang Adams in Belfast, waking him up: 'So eventually I called him. It was well after midnight his time, and he gets up out of bed, feeling quite grumpy and sleepy. And I say to him, "Gerry, there's one little bit of business." And he said, "What is it?" – very suspiciously.' Adams recalls: 'He went on to say that I would have to condemn what he referred to as the San Diego IRA, and I was a bit taken aback by this.' According to O'Dowd, Adams went on: 'Does this mean that every time an Irish guy gets drunk in America and hits an Englishman that I have to apologise for it?' O'Dowd retorted, 'Probably, but I mean, we need to deal with this one right now.' Adams duly issued a statement condemning the non-existent San Diego IRA.

Adams confirms this account: 'This was quite absurd. My initial response was to be totally dismissive, that I didn't need to be making statements on the back of every little incident or perceived incident or fabricated incident that happened. To tell you the truth, I thought it was ridiculous.'

The following morning, the National Security Council aides put their case to Clinton again. Soderberg explained:

Tony Lake and I presented this as actually a win-win decision. If he issued the visa to Gerry Adams and you had a ceasefire, obviously that was a win for everyone involved. If he issued the visa and the ceasefire didn't materialise, it would give us a very strong platform from which we could isolate Sinn Fein's influence in the United States and crack down on their support for activities related to violence. And that would be a win as well.

Clinton examined Adams's condemnation of the San Diego IRA, then consulted Secretary of State Warren Christopher. He was strongly against the move, as Clinton would recall:

I thought the statement was adequate, so I called Christopher and told him I wanted to do it. He thought it was a terrible mistake, he thought we would do irreparable damage to our relationship with the British. He knew we needed the British, because we were trying even then desperately to get consensus among our allies in Europe to do something in Bosnia, and that in the larger sense the United States would lose for years a relationship without which we cannot conduct the foreign policy of America insofar as Europe is involved. So the stakes were quite high, but I thought it was worth the risk to push the peace process forward. Look, in all these places in the world nobody would ever get anything done if no one ever took a chance.

It occurred to me that it was one of those points when there had to be some tangible evidence that there could be a reward for the renunciation of violence and beginning to walk toward peace. Those kinds of things are always a judgement call. There's no rule book that tells you when this or that or the other thing happens. It was a judgement call. You asked me whether I think I did the right thing? I do.

Soderberg was to spell out just how seminal a move this was:

He listened, he asked questions, he asked about the terrorism issue, about relations with Britain, how would John Major react. He mulled it over for half an hour. He reminded us that he was a President who had been in office for only a year, and he was taking the advice of his White House staff against the very strong recommendation of the Secretary of State, the Attorney-General, the FBI, John Major, the Speaker of the House of Representatives and a number of members in Congress. He was reversing 200 years of American foreign policy, but in the end he said very simply, 'Okay, let's do it.'

By this time the telephone lines were burning between the White House, Downing Street and the British Embassy in Washington. Major recalled: 'We had a phone call from the White House saying that the President had granted a visa to Gerry Adams. I was frankly astonished. It was our clear understanding that there wasn't going to be a visa, and I had no understanding of why that position had been changed,' he said.

My first instinct was to pick up the phone and speak directly to the President and say, 'What on earth's going on? Why has he suddenly got a visa?' Then we decided it might be better, before we had such a discussion, to find out what really had happened. So we summoned the American Ambassador and told him in very clear terms how upset we were. We passed on a message to Washington which I think was one of the strongest messages we ever sent out of Downing Street.

A Dublin source spelt out the opposite viewpoint: 'Our psychology was to give republicans a bit and see if they would deliver. The British psychology was to box them in and then, when they're truly in the box, give a bit. They were using a colonial psychology. Clinton put the whole American weight behind the first model.'

By now, Adams was already on his way for a visit which received almost saturation coverage in the US media, with hundreds of camera crews and reporters covering his every move. On the *Larry King Live* television show he was introduced as 'a man so controversial, his very voice is barred from British television, the political leader of the Irish Republican Army, Gerry Adams.' Adams would remark: 'I don't have cloven hooves or two horns, and when people see that they're pleasantly surprised. So extreme had the British been in the way they had sought to marginalise us that just having a human form was a coup for Sinn Fein.' Peter King gave a flavour of the visit:

Kennedy Airport was packed with reporters – not just regular news reporters, but celebrity type reporters – the type of reporters who would be out if it was reported that Elvis had come back from the dead – mixed in with British and Irish reporters, very serious diplomatic reporters, news reporters, foreign reporters. Every type of media person was there, literally standing on chairs, they were fighting each other for position, pushing each other out of the way. Suddenly this door opens, and Gerry Adams walks in. And you could hear the reaction, almost like some of the oxygen went out of the room when he walked through. He looked the way his pictures had him – he had the glasses, he had the beard, but he didn't have any guns, or he didn't have any grenades, or didn't have any mortar rounds, and I think some of the reporters were surprised by that.

In many ways Gerry Adams is indebted to the British for this, because they had made him out to be this madman, this absolutely horrible human being, and so they had set the expectations bar so low that it was easy for Gerry to show that basically he is a very intelligent guy, and a very thoughtful person.

Adams was the centre of attention at the peace conference in the Waldorf Hotel. Ciaran Staunton, a Sinn Fein representative in the US, described the scene: 'All the cameras came forward, thrust right into Gerry Adams's face. And there was John Hume sitting on his own, no camera bothered with him. They all just focused right in on Gerry – every camera.' O'Dowd remembered:

I looked over at John Hume, the man who had made so much of this possible, and poor John was being totally ignored. They were actually kind of manoeuvring around him to get at Adams, and it must have been a sobering moment for him. I think Gerry was very aware of it, because I know he went over to Hume right afterwards and talked to him. I think for John, maybe the moment meant that the torch had to be shared in America. John had been the face of Irish nationalism in America for so long and, through his work in many ways, Adams was at this conference, and the man who he'd brought over was now replacing him, almost.

Hume had expected such a reaction, commenting of his own temporary eclipse: 'Sitting in the Waldorf with Gerry Adams and others was, of course, quite important because it was evidence that normal politics was starting at last.'

Hundreds of prominent Irish-Americans attended the New York conference, among them Bruce Morrison, who realised that much hard work lay ahead. He commented: 'Those of us who were meeting Gerry there were never allowed to think we'd finished our work. Now it just gets harder, because we actually just raised everything to a new level of commitment. The President has taken a big risk, he's been criticised by some members of the Congress, the British Embassy in Washington is going completely bananas. It can't just have been a one-off trip to New York – now there has to be ceasefire.'

Margaret Thatcher and Garret FitzGerald

John Major

Peter Brooke

Sir Patrick Mayhew

Mo Mowlam

Peter Mandelson

Gerry Adams, Albert Reynolds
and John Hume

Bertie Ahern and Tony Blair

Charles Haughey

John Bruton

Gerry Adams and Martin McGuinness

Seamus Mallon and David Trimble

David Ervine

John Taylor

Gary McMichael

Ken Maginnis

Johnny Adair

Michael Stone

Reverend Ian Paisley

Bill Clinton

Father Alex Reid

George Mitchell

David Trimble, Bono and John Hume

10

Prelude to ceasefire

___

The visit produced international headlines, British anger and Unionist outrage. But the new republican tack caused ominous ripples within republicanism itself, where not everyone believed politics could replace violence. McGuinness recalls: 'I was saying very clearly to people: "This isn't going to be resolved by a benevolent British government standing up some day and saying, we put our hands up, we're going to correct everything that's wrong, we're going to take all the British soldiers out of here, they're going to sail down Belfast Lough and Lough Foyle all the way back to England." That wasn't going to happen, we had to recognise that there had to be political negotiations.'

Republican activist Rory Duggan was one of those worried about such arguments, and who would later split from the mainstream republican movement because of the peace process. He said of McGuinness:

What he was saying was that the armed struggle had gone as far as it would go, and that it was now time to let Sinn Fein pursue the situation. That the IRA couldn't win and the British Army couldn't win, and that virtually they had come to a stalemate, a military stalemate. A lot of us were unhappy. We didn't trust the British for a start. We were worried that they would split us, manipulate us and drive a wedge through us, and the big worry for a lot of us activists on the ground was that the army would split.

The world waited impatiently to see whether the Downing Street Declaration, coupled with pressure from the US and other elements, would have the desired effect of producing an IRA ceasefire. The first half of 1994 brought some encouraging signs, but also more violence. In March, for example, the IRA launched a series of mortar attacks on Heathrow Airport in London. It would later emerge that the devices had been deliberately doctored so that they would not explode: the incident was actually an incredibly elaborate hoax, designed to frighten and pressurise the British government without actually killing anyone. It had, in fact, been more of a threat than an actual attack, an attempt by the IRA to use violence in a finely tuned and almost forensic way to strengthen their political position.

Adams, whose image in America as a man of peace suffered a dent with the Heathrow incident, said in a radio interview: 'The conflict is ongoing. Every so often there will be something spectacular to remind the outside world.' He apparently wished to project that he was speaking more in sorrow than in anger, but his words were taken as a threat. Behind the scenes, the republicans were moving slowly towards a ceasefire, though they felt entirely free to use violence in the run-up to it. As Adams described the process within the republican movement: 'We at leadership level put together what I call the package. And then, if and when we got the package, the IRA had to take its decision.'

McGuinness outlined how republicans were thinking during this period: 'We could create a situation where the Taoiseach, Gerry Adams and John Hume supported by opinion in Irish-America, and ultimately by the White House, could effectively present the British government and the leadership of the Unionist parties with a fait accompli. In other words, that they would have no choice but to engage in inclusive negotiations.'

By July, however, Reynolds was becoming more and more impatient, feeling his credibility was on the line: 'I sent word to the republican leadership that if I didn't have a positive decision about an announcement of a ceasefire before the holidays were out, that I was going away for three weeks' holidays. If I didn't have it by the time I came back, I was going to pull down the shutters on the whole project.'

To deliver this ultimatum to Sinn Fein, Reynolds sent his adviser, Martin Mansergh, to an isolated monastery near the border. Mansergh was, however, highly encouraged by his meeting: 'I found them in a very, very practical-oriented mood, and essentially that the decision had been made. I'm not saying in formal terms, but just mentally the decision had been made, and it was a question of choreographing the next few weeks.'

McGuinness gave a flavour of the discussions:

I told Martin Mansergh that it was absolutely vital that the Irish government pressed for demilitarisation. That this would show people effectively on the ground, at grassroots level, that there was fundamental change going to take place to their lives. We discussed the issue of prisoners and different things which the Irish government could do in relation to improving the atmosphere and creating the very clear impression that, if you like, nationalist Ireland had got its act together.

Sinn Fein then called a special conference, which took place in the summer of 1994 in Letterkenny. It was held in the south, since some IRA activists attending were wanted by the authorities in Northern Ireland. Because of the intense speculation about a possible ceasefire, there was a huge level of expectation and anticipation arising out of the meeting. Pat Doherty accepted that many republican activists were apprehensive, saying: 'Ceasefire talk was very much in the air and was this going to lead to a ceasefire? And I suppose there were concerns and worries and fears amongst republicans about that, and what would that mean, and were the British trying to outmanoeuvre Irish republicans – which of course they were.'

Rory Duggan, who was also present, confirmed: 'People listened. There was a lot of apprehension, a lot of excitement, a lot of wonder, a lot of, "Are we going to be told the ceasefire is on tomorrow night?"' Most of the rhetoric at the Letterkenny meeting was hard-line to reassure the grassroots, causing most observers to believe that the prospects for a ceasefire had suffered a serious setback. Only a few who were intimately involved, including Reynolds and Hume, knew from their private contacts that a ceasefire was on the way. Doherty recalled:

I remember when the conference was over going down to Ramelton, which is just a few miles from Letterkenny, where there are a few restaurants. Gerry said to me we should get a table together, because there's something back here from the Irish government. And he handed me the response, which I read and I thought, that sounds like the stuff we sent to them. And he says, jokingly, well there you are now – they've responded.

Reynolds had responded by moving on all the issues Sinn Fein had raised with him, as he would recall: 'I had succeeded in getting a visa for Adams; I had announced that there would be a parole of prisoners and a total review of their prison sentences; that I would try and convince the British government to do the same; that I had lifted the ban on interviews on radio and television for Sinn Fein. There was very little else left to me to offer – it was make-up-your-mind time.'

No sooner had Reynolds delivered on what he saw as his side of the bargain than republicans were back for more. Instead of a ceasefire, the Taoiseach was faced with a new and difficult demand. Now republicans wanted a US visa for veteran republican Joe Cahill. Then in his 70s, his long IRA career included being sentenced to hang in the 1940s for the murder of a policeman. In the early 1970s he had been arrested on board a boat carrying guns to Ireland for the IRA. The Americans regarded him as an undesirable, twice deporting him after he had entered the country illegally. Cahill's lifelong commitment to the IRA was absolute, and yet, after all his associations with violence, he had come to support the peace process. In the 1940s he had been reprieved but his colleague, Tom Williams, had been executed. He was to remember:

There was no politics then, it was purely and simply IRA then. If Tom Williams were alive today he would be very much in favour of the course we're taking now. I have no doubts that anybody I know who has made the supreme sacrifice would have the same thinking.

I was four-and-a-half weeks in the condemned cell with Tom. I expected to be hanged then, you know, and we talked about life after our death, what we would like to see for the future. To me it's like yesterday we were in the condemned cell, and I can vividly remember the conversations we had. We didn't think we were going to drive the British into the sea, we didn't see that happening. We knew that at some time along the road there would have to be negotiations, that we would have to sit down and talk to the Brits about getting out of the country and all that sort of thing.

The republicans wanted a Cahill visa not for any propaganda purpose, but to allow him to carry out an important task: to tell republican support groups and individuals in the US that the impending ceasefire was not to be regarded as a surrender or a sell-out. The reckoning was that only the old gunrunner had the credentials to convince the hard-line Irish-American opinion that a ceasefire was the way ahead. In the event of an IRA ceasefire, he more than any other republican had the ability to calm the nerves of potential dissidents on either side of the Atlantic.

Reynolds was left in no doubt of how important it was that Joe Cahill gain access to the United States. He recalls the weight Gerry Adams attached to this issue: 'He said this was vital if the ceasefire that we all wanted was going to come about. Vital for the reason that Sinn Fein and the republican movement felt that they should have a credible spokesperson from here over in the United States to explain a change of direction in their policy.'

Reynolds was the principal advocate with the job of persuading the White House to let Cahill in. He had used up much political capital in helping secure the Adams visa earlier in the year, and was well aware that, as months had gone by with no ceasefire, scepticism had grown in Washington. His first problem was a practical one, since it was August, the month when political Washington traditionally all but closes down for the sultriest part of the summer. Eventually, he tracked down presidential aide Nancy Soderberg, who told him Clinton was on holiday at Martha's Vineyard in Massachusetts. He asked her to deliver a message on the importance of the Cahill visa to

Clinton. 'My first reaction was he probably has no idea where Martha's Vineyard is,' she recalled. 'It's an island and somewhat hard to get to but what I did realise was that the message of getting to the President right away was clearly the right one.'

Eventually Clinton got the message, and he and Reynolds spoke on the phone. Reynolds remembers: 'The President said to me, "Did you read this man's CV?" And I said, "No, I didn't, but I don't have to because I don't expect the IRA to be producing saints anyway. And never did." And he said, "You know that this man's CV is such that I wouldn't have any credibility if I was to allow it."'

Clinton recalls the conversation: 'I said, "Albert, what in the hell are you getting me into here?" He says, "You've got to do it, you've got to do it, he'll be fine, he'll come here, he won't do anything wrong, he won't raise money for guns, it'll be fine."' Clinton's message was that he was not prepared to stick his neck out over the Cahill visa until he was convinced that this was the final step to a ceasefire. He said: 'I did require Reynolds to give me some details about exactly what they were going to say, because I didn't want to be in a position of being made to look like a fool.'

Reynolds had an ace up his sleeve: he had secretly already been given the text of the ceasefire statement the IRA intended to deliver. He was thus able to read part of it to Clinton: 'The IRA will announce a complete cessation of military operations effective from midnight on Wednesday night. And I stopped there. And he says, "That seems clear enough to me." I says, "It's very clear, that's what it is, and that's what it means, and that's what'll happen."' Reynolds remembers, with a laugh, how

Clinton responded: 'Okay, we'll take another chance. But I never want to hear from you again if this one doesn't run – goodbye.'

Cahill arrived at New York's JFK Airport to be confronted by a crowd of journalists, while hundreds of republican supporters were assembling in a downtown bar. Congressman Peter King was a witness to the evening's events: 'There was a bar on Second Avenue and we went in a side entrance, and when I looked in there I saw everything from convicted gunrunners to some Wall Street lawyers. Joe Cahill's message to them was that there was now a new phase, and now, just as you trusted us for the last 25 years, we're asking you to trust us as we go into this new phase.'

Even though the IRA ceasefire was imminent, some failed to read the signs correctly. Within the SDLP, Hume came under attack from some of the party's senior figures, who urged him to give up his efforts and his contacts with Adams. As the months passed without a ceasefire, many had concluded the IRA must never have been serious; some assumed Adams was sincere but had not been able to sell a cessation to the hard men; many were simply tired of waiting. Doubts about the wisdom of Hume persevering with the peace process had steadily mounted. Many in the SDLP were accustomed to viewing politics in primarily institutional terms, which is to say their first priority was the well-being of the SDLP as a party. Sinn Fein, viewed from this perspective, were not only supporters of violence but also the SDLP's most direct rival for votes. The sight of their party leader consorting with Adams and helping boost the republican leader on both sides of the Atlantic sowed confusion and unease. The trauma of the many loyalist petrol-bomb attacks on SDLP homes added an extra dimension, for the UDA made it clear these were as a direct result of the Hume–Adams relationship.

Strong criticism of Hume was made at an SDLP meeting, some saying his course was too dangerous and unwise to continue. Hume defended his actions, but it was a highly charged and tense encounter. His aide, Mark Durkan, recalled: 'He was very badly bruised. He was talking about quitting – whatever way it went, he was quitting. He said people were afraid of peace. I told him not to be going on like that. I told him the cessation would take care of a lot of things.'

Tension was also growing in Unionist political circles, with even the normally taciturn Molyneaux accusing Hume of 'supping with the devil' in maintaining his contacts with Adams. In the Protestant paramilitary underworld, meanwhile, powerful voices were arguing against any future loyalist ceasefire. UFF commander Johnny Adair said:

I believe that the time wasn't right, because the loyalists, the Ulster Freedom Fighters, were having great successes against the republican movement. These people had slaughtered our people and got away with it, and here we are, where we're getting it right, where we're just taking the war right to their doorstep, right to their leaders' doorstep, from the top to the bottom, from Sinn Fein to the IRA, scoring big time – why call a ceasefire?

Other loyalists took a more thoughtful approach. Senior loyalist figures in the other main illegal group, the Ulster Volunteer Force, took the step of inviting to Belfast Chris Hudson, a Dublin trade unionist who had been active in various peace movements. He remembered making the journey with some trepidation: 'We travelled through a couple of army checkpoints and police checkpoints, and I knew that as I was passing them I was now going into an area where I was not going to be under anybody's protection, particularly the police or the army.'

Hudson was arriving in the loyalist Shankill Road in Belfast to meet, among others, David Ervine, spokesman for the UVF's political wing, the Progressive Unionist party. Ervine agreed: 'He was as nervous as hell, why wouldn't he be? Here he was being driven to the Shankill Road, the heartland of the empire.' Hudson remembered his surroundings: 'As I came up into the room I'd passed a lot of men sitting downstairs in an ante-room. I have to admit I was very nervous, because nobody knew I was there. There was lots of loyalist paraphernalia and pictures of dead loyalist comrades on the wall. I did notice a bullet hole in one of the windows as well.'

Ervine explained to Hudson that the UVF wanted an avenue of communication with the Irish government and that was why they were interested in meeting him. He added: 'If all we were hearing in the ether was real, that if the IRA were to call a ceasefire, I'd been told to say that a loyalist ceasefire was a serious possibility.'

Hudson recalls: 'So they said to me, "Look, we can offer a big prize." I asked him what was that prize, and David Ervine was the one that responded. He paused before answering and he says, "Peace." I said, "What do you mean by peace?" And he said, "A ceasefire."' But the prospect of peace was accompanied by a threat: that if, as was sometimes rumoured, there was any imposition of joint authority between Dublin and London, the loyalists would orchestrate 'a campaign of violence that had not been seen before which would involve serious attacks into the Republic.'

Yet even as the loyalists edged towards a ceasefire, violence continued on the streets. In June 1994, a meeting of senior loyalists on the Shankill Road was interrupted by the sound of gunfire outside. Ervine remembered: 'I heard a series of muffled cracks. I wasn't sure whether it was gunfire or not, because we were inside. And someone came bursting through the door and said, "Trevor's just been shot."'

Outside, loyalist commander Trevor King and two of his colleagues had been killed in a drive-by shooting by the Irish National Liberation Army, a small republican grouping. Ervine described the scene: 'We listened to the hysteria of the women. It was almost surreal. I don't know that I thought at that time any more – of the brains and the blood, and the grey faces – as the blood drained from those on the ground.'

There were more killings, both by republicans and loyalists, in the run-up to the ceasefire. The UVF exacted revenge for the three Shankill Road killings with an attack on a Catholic pub, very much in the style of the Greysteel incident. Six people were killed as they watched a football match on TV, in the South Down village of Loughinisland. The horror was described by a local man: 'They were obviously all sitting watching the game, and the gunmen obviously just came in, opened fire. The bodies were piled on top of each other, and the people were shot dead as they were watching the game on TV. It's just beneath contempt how people could carry out this type of thing.'

The IRA attacked and killed a number of major loyalist figures. Some were regarded as leading gunmen and bombers, but one was Ray Smallwood, who was emerging as a key thinker within the UDA. Most observers could not understand why Smallwood should have been singled out for assassination, for in the year before his death he had become the most prominent political spokesman for the UDA. It was therefore difficult to comprehend why the republicans, if they were intent on pursuing a political path, should have made a point of killing a loyalist who was apparently thinking along the same lines. In his UDA career Smallwood had been involved both in violence and in dialogue, but in his latter years he had also become interested in political activity. He had been in frequent touch with Father Alex Reid, the Reverend Ken Newell, minister of Fitzroy Presbyterian Church in South Belfast, and other members of cross-community groups, and had introduced them to members of the UDA's ruling inner council.

According to Newell, a strong bond had developed between Smallwood and his group, his commitment to peace impressing the group. Members of the group were most upset when he was killed. Following his death, the group went to a loyalist housing estate where he was being 'waked'. According to Newell: 'Loyalist paramilitary leaders were there, and Father Gerry Reynolds led the entire gathering in prayer. John White, Davy Adams and Joe English (all prominent loyalists) were there. It was quite stunning for me to see a Catholic priest leading everyone in prayer around the table.'

The priests complained bitterly to republicans about the killing. Although Smallwood was interested in politics, it is now known that he was not a straightforward 'dove'. Several of his associates later confirmed that within loyalist circles he had argued strongly against loyalist groups following the IRA on to any ceasefire. One of Smallwood's colleagues said at the time that his killing represented 'a final fling, a final show of strength and a final bloodbath before Sinn Fein go to the talks table.' He was probably correct, though there may have been more to it than that.

It is known that one adviser to the republicans, who favoured a ceasefire, argued that the activities of the loyalist paramilitaries could be turned to the advantage of republicans. Loyalist violence was running at a high level, this argument went, and if the IRA were to call a ceasefire, then loyalists might continue their violence and thus come into direct confrontation with the RUC and British Army. In this circumstance, the IRA could enhance its standing by acting as defenders of the Catholic community, while the loyalists and security forces could be left at each other's throats. If the IRA was indeed following this theory, then the attacks on loyalist targets make more political sense. An identical theory was later advanced independently by a senior security analyst, who said: 'There was an element in republicanism saying, "Let's hit these loyalists so that they have to retaliate, and then we will hit back, then turn off the tap so the government is left only with loyalist violence to deal with."'

David Ervine knew Smallwood well. He said of his death: 'And then the IRA killed Ray Smallwood. And the same question again – what does this mean? Who the fuck are these people, I mean what is it they really want? And I knew that the Provos didn't factor in the loyalists at all, and that Gerry Adams was meant to swan the world stage as a peacemaker.'

II
Cessation

Finally the moment came, on 31 August, when the IRA ceasefire announcement was made. Yet although Reynolds, Hume and some others knew it was on the way, all the intelligence resources of the British government did not. The people whose mission was to work out what the IRA was up to – the RUC Special Branch, military intelligence, MI5, MI6 – did not see it coming. Major was to recall hearing the word from Reynolds: 'I was in the lounge when the phone rang and it was Albert. He said, "I've got some very good news for you, there's going to be a ceasefire and it's a very solid decision and it will be announced very shortly."' But Major was sceptical, Reynolds remembering him replying, 'Wait and see, I hope you're right.'

Then on 31 August two senior journalists in Belfast and one in Dublin were called to meet with a representative of the IRA at prearranged locations. The message they were given was: 'The leadership of Oglaigh na hEireann [the IRA] have decided that as of midnight, Wednesday August 31st, there will be a complete cessation of military operations. All our units have been instructed accordingly.'

In Dublin, Reynolds was attending a meeting of Fianna Fáil deputies. Maire Geoghegan-Quinn recalled the scene:

There was an air of expectancy that something big was about to happen, then word began to filter into the room that the Provos were about to announce a ceasefire. The whole atmosphere was just electric – everything else was forgotten about. Even people who couldn't stand Albert Reynolds were all of a sudden just terribly emotional about the whole thing.

Suddenly there's a knock on the door and a piece of paper with the Taoiseach's name on it was handed in. Albert was on his feet talking. He says 'Excuse me,' puts the glasses on, opens the note, closes the note, puts it down and announces that the Provisional IRA have announced a ceasefire. He then went on to read the text, and he said as he was reading it out, 'I hope to Christ this is what they have released to the papers – this is what they told me they were going to be releasing.'

Everybody jumped to their feet, everybody clapped and screamed and roared, shouted, whistled and everything. I mean it was like a crucial goal in a nail-biting game and there were tears in people's eyes. People were hugging each other, couldn't wait to get to him. He was in a mêlée, just surrounded by people. All of us in that room knew that we had, as a party, grown out of civil war and all that that entailed. You knew that the founder of our party, Eamon de Valera, had played such a crucial role in the civil war himself, had been involved with guns and with war over a period of time, and then had decided that he was putting them to bed and was going to go down the democratic process. All of those kinds of emotions were there – people remembered their fathers having been in that room and having worked on this problem over years and years.

Jean Kennedy Smith was at her Embassy in Dublin: 'I was with two friends and we heard it and we all screamed and yelled. Then I talked to Gerry Adams and I congratulated him. Then the President called and he congratulated me and I congratulated him, and he said we had to make the peace work. That night we had some people for dinner, and we all sang and drank toasts and all that.'

But while Dublin celebrated, the mood in London was much more cautious. Major explained:

When the complete cessation of violence was announced it was a huge step forward, there was no doubt about that, but the lack of the word permanent was a setback for us. There were many people who were quite sceptical about whether this complete cessation would last or whether it would last just for a brief period. We needed to test its permanence for practical reasons – the Unionists were unconvinced, the British House of Commons was unconvinced. We had in our mind a whole series of ways in which we could react but we needed some time to test that this just wasn't a ploy before we began to move too far ahead.

Very shortly after the ceasefire was announced the Irish government began to press us very hard to make all sorts of further moves, but this just wasn't practical politics. They had no conception of the disquiet that there was in the cabinet, in parliament and amongst Unionist opinion. I was very happy to move forward, but I could not have commanded a majority within the government or within Parliament until we were certain that this was genuine, and that necessarily needed a period of time to elapse.

In the north, however, much of the Protestant community was worried and nonplussed. It had grown accustomed over the decades to standing up to IRA violence, but this was something different. Rather than celebration that a protracted cycle of violence might be coming to an end, there was anxiety about what the republicans' real agenda was, and whether the British government had done a treacherous secret deal.

The response of one leading loyalist summed up the difference in approach on the republican and loyalist sides. The republicans had spent years of intricate planning leading up to this moment, years involving interaction with the powers-that-be in London, Dublin and Washington. But David Ervine was to encapsulate the confused and unprepared reaction of many loyalists when he said: 'We nearly shit ourselves. I think that day we did! You know – it was something you wanted, why the hell, here it comes, what are you gonna do about it? What, you know, I'm not sure we knew what we were gonna do about it because we'd never, still hadn't got the answers about what is the British government intent? Are we shafted here? Are we being sold out?'

In an effort to answer some of these questions, leading loyalists, who were themselves generally not at all religious, turned to the head of the Church of Ireland, Archbishop Robin Eames. Organisations such as the UDA and UVF had formed a Combined Loyalist Military Command (CLMC) to debate important issues. Dr Eames remembered: 'They had come as a group, the Loyalist Military Command – these were the godfathers. They referred immediately to the IRA's cessation, they immediately referred to the triumphalism, as they interpreted it. They said, "We have two questions: has a deal been done with the IRA, why are they feeling so triumphant? And secondly, where do we go from here?"'

Dr Eames took the questions straight to Downing Street, where he told Major: 'I am the Archbishop of Armagh. I'm trying to be a spiritual leader in a very difficult situation. You're the prime minister, elected prime minister of Great Britain, including Northern Ireland. I want you to give me a straight answer – have you done a deal with the IRA?'

The prime minister was unambiguous in his response. He said: 'Robin, you can go back and tell them categorically from me, you can say this publicly and privately, there has been no secret deal with the IRA.' Eames agreed to pass on this message to the leaders of underground loyalist groups. He remembered:

They arrived immaculately dressed, and I suppose it was a moment that will live with me for the rest of my life. Here were the godfathers of the loyalist paramilitary organisations, we'd reached a crucial point.

I made two conditions to our conversation. One was that if we were to agree that there was a means of cessation they would express some regret – that they would say there was a depth of sorrow in their hearts for the suffering they had caused. And the second one was that they would not bluff me in any way about their agenda: I said, 'If you do I'll walk away.'

As a result of this and many other conversations with churchmen and others, the CLMC six weeks later announced an end to the loyalist organisations' campaigns of violence. In a community centre in North Belfast, a man called Gusty Spence announced that for the loyalists, too, it was over. It was another electric moment, filled with historic echoes, for Spence had been a one-time icon of violent loyalism, having been jailed for an early sectarian assassination. Like many other loyalists, he had mellowed in prison and become a firm supporter of peace. The loyalist announcement set a new tone by including an unexpected note of apology, Spence offering 'the loved ones of all innocent victims over the past 25 years abject and true remorse.' This new note was confirmation of the existence of a new phenomenon within militant loyalism. This was the emergence, from that violent underworld, of a new political element analogous to Sinn Fein's role in the republican movement, headed by figures such as David Ervine.

Groups such as the UVF and UDA remained in being and retained their capacity for violence, but now they went on ceasefire and sprouted new political wings. The UVF produced the Progressive Unionist party, with articulate new spokesmen such as David Ervine and Billy Hutchinson, while Gary McMichael and the Ulster Democratic party spoke for the UDA. Some of these political loyalists had for months been in close touch with reconciliation workers, such as Father Reid and Father Reynolds.

The loyalist ceasefire announcement took six weeks in coming, but when it came it was not in a spirit of suspicion, but of generosity and goodwill. This was to the astonishment of almost everyone, since only months earlier loyalist violence had been raging at a high level, and the appetite for war seemed high. But many of the new spokesmen were ex-prisoners, who had learned the cost of violence the hard way, and had looked for other ways forward. Some had served life sentences, spending a dozen or more years behind bars, on their release becoming involved in community work. A number had discreet contacts with republicans whom they had met in jail, had come to know individual IRA members, and were convinced the IRA cessation was genuine. This hidden network of relationships helped to break down barriers of mistrust between the two sides.

The sight of the previously violent loyalists embracing the peace process with such unexpected and apparently genuine enthusiasm was as welcome as it was surprising. It gave the process a huge boost, for many had assumed the loyalist groups would pose an active threat. Instead, they became a force for moderation, anxious for talks with the government and others, and presenting a much more open-minded approach than mainstream Unionist politicians.

Ulster Unionist MPs, by contrast, claimed the ceasefire was a ruse, making repeated predictions that it would break down either in January 1995 or at Easter of that year. MP William Ross urged the British government to ignore the calls for concessions to republicans 'from all sorts of do-gooders and fools across the world.'

The Reverend Ian Paisley, meanwhile, declared that Protestants faced 'the worst crisis in Ulster's history since the setting up of the state.' He told his party conference:

Are we going to agree to a partnership with the IRA men of blood who have slain our loved ones, destroyed our country, burned our churches, tortured our people and now demand that we should become slaves in a country fit only for nuns' men and monks' women to live in? We cannot bow the knee to these traitors in Whitehall, nor to those offspring of the Vatican who walk the corrupted corridors of power in Dublin, in Europe and in Washington. In the propaganda war, we must excel, answering the lies with truth, and smoking out from their lairs the media skunks, cleansing their putrid odour from the face of Ulster's earth.

Molyneaux was less histrionic but almost as suspicious, being clearly uncomfortable with the disappearance of the old certainties of violence and apprehensive that the cessation might bring political concessions for the republicans. He summed up his feelings on the day after the ceasefire was announced: 'It's a cessation of hostilities, that's all it is, and that isn't convincing. That's the problem and I think any fair-minded person can recognise that it's inadequate.' He would add: 'It started destabilising the whole population in Northern Ireland. It was not an occasion for celebration, quite the opposite.'

The question of what would follow the ceasefire, and at what pace, now hung in the air. The republicans were eager for negotiations with the British government and other elements as quickly as possible, but Molyneaux and others wanted to proceed with the utmost caution. He recalls: 'When I was asked what my estimate of the time frame would be, I said: "Well, what about three years for a decontamination?"'

There was no hiding the nervousness in the corridors of power at Stormont, and indeed elsewhere, with the emergence of Sinn Fein as fledgeling politicians, demanding full cooperation from the British and Irish governments in the wake of the IRA ceasefire.

For Major, the considerations were military as well as political. He maintained:

Although a ceasefire had been declared, the IRA hadn't started dismantling their weapons, they hadn't stopped their normal activities. They were still setting up mortar positions, they were still conducting surveillance on British army institutions to see when people went in and out, they were still recruiting, they were still active as a body and at any time could have returned to violence. They were still purchasing weapons.

Nothing they did that we learned of privately gave us any

clear-cut assurance that this complete cessation was intended to be permanent. Throughout that period they were putting themselves in a position where they could return to violence, and that for us was a deeply inhibiting factor in moving forward too quickly and taking any further action.

12
Decommissioning

A notable symbolic moment came in December 1994, when a defiantly battered black Falls Road taxi chugged up the half-mile hill to Stormont buildings to deliver Martin McGuinness to the heart of the British establishment. The slightly dilapidated mode of transport projected a different message from the sartorial style of McGuinness and his four republican comrades, for they emerged dressed in their Sunday best. The sartorial style was designed to tell the world that these were confident people striding into talks with every expectation of eventual success. The old taxi, its front number plate slightly askew and a rear hub-cap missing, may have been designed to reassure the folks back home that they had not lost touch with their roots.

It turned out there was a more practical reason for travelling in the taxi, as Sinn Fein's Mitchel McLaughlin revealed: 'People saw it as an expression of our working-class cred. The reason we arrived in the taxi is that it was a bulletproof vehicle and it was the only one that we had at that time.'

Inside, meanwhile, the British civil servants who were due to meet the republicans had their own security concerns. Their approach was recounted by Quentin Thomas, a senior civil servant who had been closely involved in the back-channel from the Northern Ireland Office to the republicans, via Denis Bradley and the link in London-derry. He remembered:

One of the questions which came up when we were preparing for exploratory dialogue was whether we should require the Sinn Fein delegation to pass through metal detectors. I suggested that this was a mistake, and that we should treat Sinn Fein as we would treat the other members of the political parties we were dealing with, and that if Martin McGuinness was to come in and pull out a gun and plug me, I would have to conclude that our analysis was based on a false premise.

No guns were produced at the meeting, however. Instead, McGuinness asked in friendly fashion after Fred, the intelligence officer who had acted as intermediary in the back-channel which had led from McGuinness and his colleagues to Thomas and his colleagues. Thomas replied that he knew who McGuinness was referring to, but didn't in fact know how he was. Thomas was to recall:

We began by some relatively formal opening remarks, but in my own case I tried to dignify the occasion with some sort of appeal to history. I said, in fact, that history was both what we had in common and what divided us. And that to some extent it was like a chain round both our necks, and that one way of characterising the project was that we had to try and escape from the mortal hunger of the martyred past. That was a colourful phrase, but one which I thought had some resonance. I said that I hoped we could look to the future and I said that I hoped we could avoid recrimination. I said that it was not the armed struggle, as they called it, which had brought them to the table, but the ending which had made it possible for us to meet them. I mentioned the need to talk about the consequences of the end of the violence, including arms.

Martin McGuinness responded as I remember by showing

that he'd taken what I said seriously, and asking for a copy of it. They presented their own paper which was a relatively formal piece of republican analysis which I took it they needed to get on the record. We proceeded through the agenda in what I think was on both sides a fairly formal, to some extent stilted, fashion, but with quite a good atmosphere.

According to Thomas, he referred in his opening remarks to decommissioning, the question of what was to be done with the IRA's armoury in the wake of the cessation, an issue which for years to come would remain central to the peace process. The question came under the heading, he said, of 'practical consequences of the ending of the violence', adding: 'I think both sides understood that the expression "practical consequences of the ending of the violence" referred to a number of things. It referred to arms and decommissioning; it probably referred to prisoners and to demilitarisation. And all those subjects subsequently featured quite significantly in the political process leading to the Good Friday Agreement.'

McLaughlin remarked: 'They were, in fact, setting tests for us to pass. They were starting to raise the issue of decommissioning.' McGuinness pressed for early movement to an inclusive negotiating process, 'and that no obstacles be put in the way.' One unexpected matter of disagreement came when Thomas suggested issuing a statement saying there had been a workmanlike discussion. The republicans said they thought 'workmanlike' had sexist overtones, so the word businesslike was used instead.

After the meeting, the republicans deliberately emerged from the front of the building so the cameras would picture them framed against its massive granite columns. Stormont had always been the symbol of Unionist rule, and thus the symbol of nationalist exclusion from power and influence. The republican arrival, however, gave different shades of meaning to the old image. McGuinness would reflect of that occasion, his first trip to the building: 'When I stood on the steps of Stormont, looking down the grand avenue that leads to the Newtownards Road, I felt that we had taken ownership for the first time of the place. I felt we had arrived, that we had arrived politically, and that we could build a new Ireland.'

Republicans placed much store on their working relationship with Albert Reynolds, who shared their view that speed was necessary. He took the opportunity of the first summit after the ceasefire to press Major to move quickly. Major, however, was not going to drop his guard: he wanted more evidence of republican bona fides, and above all he wanted IRA arms decommissioning.

The arms question had, of course, been considered by Reynolds and his advisers. The issue of what should be done with illegal weaponry once violence has been halted is obviously one of the most important issues in conflict resolution. During 1995, however, the peace process virtually stalled on the question of when and how arms decommissioning should take place. The issue of what to do with weapons in the event of an end to violence had cropped up in 1993, during Martin Mansergh's talks with Sinn Fein, but it had not been emphasised. It had been mentioned several times, including in a document sent by Reynolds to Sinn Fein in the spring of that year. But Dublin's conclusion was that talking of the handing over of guns would scare off the IRA and derail the whole peace process.

In the wake of the IRA cessation Major and Mayhew

repeatedly called on the organisation to give up its weapons, and journalists regularly pressed Gerry Adams on this point. Adams delivered what was to become the familiar republican response: 'The whole issue of decommissioning of weapons obviously has to be part of finding a political settlement, and there couldn't be a political settlement without that. But I don't think there's any point in anyone trying to leap ahead on any of these issues. Let's get a political settlement and of course let's get all of the guns out of Irish politics.' In essence, the Reynolds administration took much the same view, regarding decommissioning as an important point to be dealt with during round-table negotiations.

In a Brook Lapping interview, Reynolds would sum up the issue in the most graphic and extraordinarily frank way, saying:

I explained to John Major that my party went into power, went into government and went into Parliament first – and they didn't hand over their guns to anybody. In fact, some of them brought their guns in their hip pockets going into the Parliament. So I couldn't have any credibility in asking the present leadership of Sinn Fein to hand over guns, when our own party didn't hand them over, and all the other parties in government here didn't hand them over either.

At that point, Reynolds's standing had never been higher. Hailed as a hero of the peace process, he was seen as the Taoiseach who had succeeded where all his predecessors had tried and failed. Yet within a few months of his moment of glory, his government became embroiled in a controversy concerning a Catholic priest accused of molesting children in Northern Ireland. Accusations of extraordinary delay in the priest's extradition from south to north grew into a full-scale crisis. When this undermined confidence in the Reynolds administration, the Labour party withdrew from the Reynolds-led coalition, the government fell, and he resigned. Rarely can such a political triumph have been followed so quickly by political oblivion.

The country could scarcely believe it, and nor could Reynolds himself. He would remember his last words in the Dáil as Taoiseach: 'At the end I just let down the script, and finishing off, I looked around and I said, "You know it is amazing that you can cross all the large hurdles, but it's the small ones that trip you up."' There was some initial trepidation that the fall of Reynolds might be destabilising, but the peace process at that point looked so stable that the worry quickly receded. The general view was that peace had come to stay, and that the process was robust enough to survive such domestic political turbulence.

The new Irish government was headed by Fine Gael leader, John Bruton. Fine Gael as a party was much more hostile to republicanism than Fianna Fáil had been, while Bruton himself, having lost a friend and colleague in an IRA attack, was highly suspicious of Sinn Fein and the IRA. He meanwhile continued to work with London on what was known as the Framework Document, which was eventually published in February 1995. This was a booklet, published jointly by the British and Irish governments, and largely written by Dublin diplomat Seán Ó hUiginn, which was to set out a joint vision of the future.

Its genesis was a long and difficult business. Mayhew was to recall: 'Immensely long negotiations took place, and I think I have to admit that on my side we got too much into the detail and stopped seeing the wood. I don't think we sufficiently saw what the wood would look like, and it turned out to be a very green wood indeed.'

Worried about this alleged surfeit of greenery, Major once again invited Molyneaux to Downing Street. As always, he was anxious not to cause too much offence, either to the Unionist population in general, or in particular to the Ulster Unionist MPs, who could be vital to the survival of his government. Once again a delicate little minuet was played out between the Prime Minister and the Unionist leader.

Major remembers: 'I called Jim Molyneaux in – I wished to show him the Framework Document, discuss it with him, but he was plainly very reluctant to see it.' Molyneaux remembers Major attempting to show it to him. He went on: 'So he was pushing his fingertips across the cabinet table, and I put my fingertips to it and stopped it. I said, "Now look, you know more than anybody else that I have been excluded deliberately from running my eye over various drafts of this sort of thing, and excluded at a very high level."' Major said: 'So he pushed it gently across the table. We talked more widely, and his advice as ever was useful; but he did not wish to be in a position where he had seen the Framework Document.'

A crisis developed in February 1995, when a newspaper story threatened to destabilise the process. Word reached Major that there had been a leak to *The Times*:

They had got a story that they were going to run the next day about the Framework Document. And they set out what they were going to say, and it was very pernicious, implying there was going to be a united Ireland. I was absolutely clear that we had to kill that story as much as we could, as speedily as possible. So I asked the whips to summon every Conservative MP they could find around the House at that late hour and bring them to my room.

Mayhew described the moment: 'I was conscious of the high drama of the occasion. Here was this central table – you know how you see in Victorian prints of the cabinet, people always sort of standing up in rather elegant positions – well, nobody was in a particularly elegant position, they were standing up because they had to, it was so crowded.'

Major managed to calm most of his MPs, but the episode stirred up dissension in the ranks, and he looked for other ways of providing reassurance. He recounted how this factor led directly to his stance on decommissioning: 'It was against that backcloth that some token level of decommissioning was necessary in order to reassure opinion – not just the British government, but Unionist and House of Commons opinion – that the IRA were genuine about seeking a permanent peace.'

Major's extreme scepticism about republican motives would lessen in time, but not during his period in office. It was not until 2000 that he would, as an Opposition backbencher, tell the Commons: 'There have been enough signs that there are those in the IRA and Sinn Fein who seek a political path for the future, not a violent path . . . The sensible democrat helps the embryonic democrat to find a way to democracy.'

While Reynolds had made great efforts to welcome republicans into mainstream politics and to maintain momentum, Major took the view that, as prime minister, his attitude was one of challenging and testing Sinn Fein and the IRA, and proceeding with extreme caution. This might be attributed to high-minded democratic principle;

but it was also the approach of a vulnerable prime minister, anxious, as he himself said, not to upset either the Tory right or Unionist opinion.

Major continued to make clear to Washington that he disapproved of American actions such as allowing Sinn Fein to fundraise in the US, and to allow Adams into the White House for the 1995 St Patrick's Day lunch. The fundraising question was discussed between National Security Adviser Tony Lake and Mayhew in Washington in early March 1995. Lake recalled:

The conversation with Mayhew was not a hostile one, but it was certainly a difficult one. His attitude was that we were slow learners, that we still did not understand the issue, that we were offering too many carrots and not enough sticks. I'm not sure that he was getting our argument, that first of all the way to stop terrorism was to resolve the problem in strategic terms, and that tactically any fundraising that we allowed would be under very strict controls – after all, the British allowed fundraising in the United Kingdom for Sinn Fein and it was hard for us to take a different position.

When the White House soon afterwards announced that it would allow the republicans to raise money, John Major was, in his own word, pole-axed. He would explain:

One of the reasons why I was so shocked by it, was that my private secretary had been in the United States and had shown very senior White House officials all sorts of detailed security information as to what the IRA were doing in private. It seemed to me to be absolutely inexplicable, so I was extremely angry about that decision and could not understand how it could possibly have been reached.

I wrote a letter, a very blunt letter, to the President, telling him that I couldn't understand it. After the President had received the letter he set out to phone me. I wasn't, frankly, much in a mood to receive an early phone call. I didn't think there was any proper explanation for what had happened and I was about to go to the Middle East, and in fact we didn't speak for several days. When we did speak, it was the only really frosty conversation I ever had with Bill Clinton on any issue.

Peter King was given an indication of this from Clinton himself. The Congressman recalled:

I was going off to the lunch and I happened to be standing outside the Capitol as the President's car drove up. He was about 50 feet from where I was, and he saw me and he came over. He had a mischievous look in his eye, and he said, 'You fucking Irish, I'm catching more shit because of you guys.' Then he goes, 'Oh, what do I care, it's okay, don't worry about it.' And he laughed, and he went in. It was obvious that he was catching a lot, but it also showed that he had it in perspective.

According to King, the organiser of the lunch, Speaker Newt Gingrich, did not want Adams to meet Clinton there for the first time. This led to arguments involving Gingrich's staff, Jean Kennedy Smith and Irish diplomats. Eventually, King recalled:

Adams said to me, 'I'm just going to walk out.' I said, 'Jeez, Gerry, don't do that, that's all we need.' Eventually Gingrich went to Adams and said, 'Here's what we're going to do. John Hume is going to come down, and he's going to bring Mr Adams up to meet the President.' A few minutes later John Hume comes down to take Gerry Adams. They walk up to the President and they shake hands, and people start to clap.

I walked up there and I heard most, if not all, of their conversation. It was two guys hitting it off right away. First it was small talk, then Clinton was describing how the British wouldn't take his phone calls, they were just giving him a hard time and making life miserable for him. He said, 'Well, these guys can really play tough,' and Gerry Adams just politely interrupted him and said, 'Mr President, now you know what I've had to put up with for the last 47 years.' Clinton just broke into a laugh and the two of them seemed to click right away.

Major left it to Mayhew to spell out the British government's new line on decommissioning. In a speech in the US in March 1995 he specified what came to be known as the Washington Three, three conditions the republicans had to meet before getting into talks, the third of which was 'the actual decommissioning of some arms as a tangible confidence-building measure.'

As Seamus Mallon of the SDLP would relate, nationalist opinion felt this was a grave error:

You could see that here was a man digging a hole that he was never going to get out of. Mayhew dug a really big hole for himself, and it took the rest of us many years to try and get out of it. It almost broke the political process in Northern Ireland, trying to get away from that one mistake. We warned them on a social basis as well as a formal basis. I remember, with Patrick Mayhew and John Major, sitting in the smoking room at the House of Commons, three large whiskeys in front of us, and saying to them: 'For heaven's sake, do you not realise what you are doing here? You have made such an advance and there has been such progress and you are blocking it now with words.'

At first, Washington Three was not generally regarded as being critically important. It was a very clear requirement, yet the government had laid down such conditions before, only to move away from them at a later stage. As the months passed, however, London continued to insist on it: it meant republican entry into talks was directly dependent on the decommissioning of some weapons. Yet Irish nationalist opinion, with some significant exceptions, was practically unanimous in thinking it was impossible to conceive of the IRA giving up guns in advance of talks. Insisting that guns had to be decommissioned before negotiations began was seen as setting them an exam they could not pass.

Adams described the new terms as 'a recipe for complete and absolute disaster.' Bruce Morrison remembered the arguments Adams advanced during a St Patrick's Day trip to Washington: 'Gerry was saying that decommissioning is in the hands of the IRA – "When you tell me in order to do politics I have to get the IRA to do something, you tell me to kick a sleeping dog. Why are you doing that?" In other words, let the dog sleep, and let's do politics, and the better the politics get, the sleepier the dog is.'

It was in the US, nine months after the ceasefire, that the first meeting took place between a Sinn Fein leader and a British minister, in May 1995. It took place in a Washington hotel room, involving Adams and Mayhew, who clearly regarded it as the most distasteful of duties. Mayhew recalls telling Adams:

'Well, we're hung up still on decommissioning, and it is a matter of great importance to the people who we represent and of great importance to the people of Ireland generally.' And they said, 'Well you know very well of course that we have nothing to do with PIRA, the IRA, we're quite separate.' I just looked at them, and waited to see what they were going to say next. And they went on and I made it perfectly clear, without having said so, that in my mind the words 'Pull the other one' were present.

Mayhew's aide, Quentin Thomas, recalled a similar meeting when he too conveyed incredulity about the early Sinn Fein position that arms had nothing to do with them. In reply to this he said: 'I responded that there might be parrots in Peking or poodles in Paris who would believe that, but there was not a dog in the streets of Northern Ireland who would. That produced a bit of laughter and Gerry Kelly – who I think had come to those meetings with the view that his republican integrity should not be compromised by looking other than stern – did smile.'

Adams had set out at the Mayhew meeting not to press home policy points, but to seek some point of personal contact with Mayhew, hoping he might begin the business of building a relationship. He failed, emerging from the encounter with a pessimistic assessment:

We came away with a very distinct view that this government in London wasn't for doing the business. If I'm asked to think back on Patrick Mayhew – and he won't thank me for this – I always felt sorry for him. I always thought that he was just in the wrong place at the wrong time. He is very well known for having an Anglo-Irish, aristocratic, patrician, lofty attitude, which may indeed have belied his true character. Maybe if he had a few drinks he might have been very entertaining, lucid, great crack, a singer, a brilliant conversationalist. But we saw none of that, we saw a rather stuffy, awkward, uncomfortable person acting out a script. He was more a pro-consul than a peacemaker, or even a real politician. He was the end of 20 years of Toryism, the end of all of that.

Mayhew himself thought that Adams and McGuinness were 'very different in character.' He reminisced: 'Adams was really quite easy to see in the role of a university don – interested, taking up ideas, et cetera, capable of rejecting it himself, very agreeably. I thought that this facility had not been granted to Mr McGuinness.'

The sense grew in republicanism that Major and Mayhew were intent on holding them at arm's length, employing a strategy of delay because they doubted republican intentions and sought not to offend Unionists. Mitchel McLaughlin enlarged on this: 'It appeared that the British just didn't seem to be happy with a ceasefire, but they wanted complete and total capitulation of the IRA. That was developing into a huge crisis within the party, because effectively the leadership of the party was being proved wrong.'

The Irish government agreed with this central republican analysis, and tried to change the British government's approach. Irish foreign minister Dick Spring remembered: 'I said to Paddy Mayhew that these guys are under pressure, under extreme pressure, and that we had to be seen to be doing something. But the British government, relying on the Unionists, seemed to be like the rabbit stuck in the middle of the road in front of the headlights.'

Republican tensions may have been building, but attitudes were also hardening on the Unionist side, where the IRA ceasefire was still regarded as a mixed blessing. The drop in violence was clearly highly desirable, but many on the Protestant side felt uneasily that republicans had the wind in their sails and were making significant progress. Some of these worries found expression in the summer of 1995, in what started as a local marching dispute but developed into a major test of strength and will between Unionists and the authorities. It was also to provide the Ulster Unionist party with a new and very different leader.

The confrontation developed in July, when the RUC attempted to reroute an Orange demonstration at Drumcree, near Portadown in County Armagh, away from a Catholic district. The town, ever a sectarian cockpit, had been the scene of a major marching controversy, when Orangemen were refused police permission to parade from a little country church at Drumcree to Portadown centre, via the Catholic Garvaghy Road district. Thousands of Orangemen arrived on the scene to lend weight to the protest. After some days of standoff and confrontation, some Orangemen were eventually allowed through, an event which they regarded as a signal victory. The local Ulster Unionist MP, David Trimble, and Ian Paisley afterwards swaggered through the streets in celebration: the fact that they had clasped hands led to it irreverently being called 'the gay wedding'.

For the rest of the 1990s, the Drumcree dispute was to recur on an annual basis, often leading to large-scale disturbances and violence. The most immediate effect of the episode was to propel Trimble into the leadership of the Ulster Unionist party, most attributing his success to his stand at Portadown. He arrived with a reputation as a hard-liner, partly because of his Drumcree militancy and partly because his career had largely been spent on the uncompromising wing of Unionism. In the years ahead he would, however, surprise many of those who believed they were electing a more militant leader. He would explain his hand-holding with Paisley in defensive terms: 'I was the member for the area, he was there as well, and I did not wish to see myself being upstaged by him.'

The new Ulster Unionist leader immediately brought a new approach to the job. Where Molyneaux had been reluctant to take part in high-profile meetings, Trimble was prepared to sit down with politicians from many parts of the spectrum. Most strikingly, he held a meeting with the new Taoiseach, John Bruton, who, as luck would have it, was not just willing but eager to establish a relationship with Unionism.

Bruton would explain: 'The role that I had to undertake was not just one of keeping the republicans on board and on ceasefire. It was also one of creating conditions in which the Unionists would be willing to sit down with them.' Bruton aspired to broaden the traditional role of Taoiseach, which was that of seeking to represent Irish nationalism, to a new role where he would represent a Unionist viewpoint as well.

An immediate point of potential agreement between Trimble and Bruton quickly emerged on the question of an election. While Unionists were, at that point, refusing to sit down with Sinn Fein, the possibility arose that an election might change that. Trimble recalls suggesting this to Bruton: 'I put it to John, pointing out how the Unionist parties – not just ourselves, but the DUP as well – were clearly on record as saying that they would of course engage with people in the context of an elected body.' Bruton liked the idea: 'David Trimble was suggesting that the mechanism of an election would provide a pretext, after which it would be possible for Unionists to talk to Sinn Fein without decommissioning having previously occurred. That to my mind was quite a creative approach.'

Bruton took an early opportunity of putting the idea to Major during a European summit on the island of Majorca. He recalled:

John Major and I were attending one of the informal EU summits in Formentor, in Majorca. It's a very salubrious resort miles away from anything and anyone, so to have our press conferences with the media we had to travel somewhat downmarket to a distant location. I felt that if a Unionist vehicle, namely elections, could be used to carry nationalist baggage, which was all-party talks without prior decommissioning, that the Unionists would have greater ownership of the talks because it was their vehicle that got everyone there.

Major takes up the story: 'And we sat next to one another on the bus and we were chatting about Northern Ireland, a range of different issues. He saw the possibility of getting Sinn Fein and the Unionists sitting down and talking before there was decommissioning, which was a very attractive proposition from his point of view.' Some months later Major was to take up the idea.

In the meantime, Belfast prepared for a VIP visitor, Bill Clinton. He arrived in the city in late November, not just to switch on the Christmas lights at Belfast City Hall, but to shore up the flagging peace process. As he reached out to thousands of well-wishers on a cold November night in Belfast city centre, he intoned: 'Blessed are the peacemakers, for they shall inherit the Earth. Merry Christmas and God bless you all.' The presidential visit was a huge success from his point of view, as Clinton would remember: 'It was a great moment. Tens of thousands of people were there, both Protestants and Catholics, all come out together to celebrate Christmas.' Soderberg would describe the occasion as 'the most euphoric trip in all my five years in the White House.'

The visit provided a new launching pad to deal with the thorny problem of decommissioning. In a joint approach the British and Irish governments invited a senior American political figure, former Senator George Mitchell, to report on the prospects for decommissioning.

Mitchell recalled that the Clinton visit included ordeals as well as triumphs:

Meetings were arranged that evening between the President and Dr Paisley and then Gerry Adams, among others. Dr Paisley came in with a couple of aides. The President was very tired, he'd been up all night and had a full schedule of events that day. The meeting was scheduled for 20 minutes. The President said good evening, and then he didn't say another word for 30 minutes. Dr Paisley delivered a very passionate description of the history of Northern Ireland, as seen through his eyes. When he finished, the President said, 'Thank you.' That was the end of the meeting.

It was lucky for the President, because he was exhausted and all he had to do was sit there and keep his eyes open. But it was actually quite an interesting and persuasive delivery of a point of view, if you knew nothing else about Northern Ireland. Out walked Paisley, in came Adams. And exactly the same thing occurred, but from a different perspective, the history of Northern Ireland as seen from the republican point of view. Again it was very powerfully delivered; and again the President didn't say anything other than hello and goodbye.

After much spadework and meetings with all sides, Mitchell took his preliminary arms findings to Major. 'It seemed to us that prior decommissioning was not going to work,' Mitchell recalled. 'We'd been told that by almost everyone we talked to.' Mitchell had been particularly impressed by a conversation with RUC Chief Constable, Sir Hugh Annesley: 'I asked the Chief Constable, if Gerry Adams wanted to, could he get prior decommissioning from the IRA? And the Chief Constable said, "No, he couldn't. He doesn't have that much control and they wouldn't do it."'

Mitchell found Major friendly and charming, but tough and with 'a steely candour.' He also found that his assessment that prior decommissioning was not realistic was not at all what Downing Street wanted to hear. On hearing of what Annesley had said, Major's aides had sought a letter on this point from the Chief Constable: it modified and explained what he had told Mitchell, but did not alter his conclusion. Mitchell would later reflect: 'He had been truthful with us, and now, because his opinion didn't fit with the government's policy, it became obvious that his honesty with us had gotten him in trouble with his superiors.'

Mitchell remembers that when he told Major he was thinking of recommending parallel decommissioning, in other words, dealing with the arms issue during political talks, 'he made it clear that he didn't think much of that idea.' In fact, Major said, according to Mitchell, that 'if we recommended parallel decommissioning he would have to reject the report. He didn't want to, but he would have to.' This gave Mitchell pause for much thought, but at the same time he remained convinced that the demand for decommissioning upfront was unworkable. He set out the dilemma: 'The British wanted inclusive negotiations and they wanted prior decommissioning – but clearly they could not have both. How could we help them see that?'

Then Mitchell received an invitation to dinner from Michael Ancram, a Northern Ireland Office minister who would later become Chairman of the Conservative party. Late in the evening, Mitchell remembers Ancram asking softly, 'If you're going to suggest parallel decommissioning, have you thought about putting it in a separate section of your report, not as a recommendation but simply as a suggestion for the governments to consider?' And Mitchell thought: 'Of course.'

Major would explain:

I didn't accept that the IRA couldn't decommission before all-party talks, but I did realise that they wouldn't decommission before all-party talks. I said we were facing two negatives. For the Unionists, there is to be no progress without prior decommissioning, and for the nationalists there's to be no decommissioning without all-party talks. The only route that I can discover through those two incompatible positions was to have an elected assembly in which they would sit down together.

So it was that in the Mitchell Report, parallel decommissioning appeared as a suggestion in a separate section. What was also mentioned in the report was the idea of a pre-talks election, along the lines that had been discussed by Major, Trimble and Bruton. By January 1996 it was the subject of considerable debate, with Trimble championing the idea. Hume was to the fore in opposing it, arguing that it would mean further delay before talks, and that an election campaign would inevitably generate tough rhetoric.

The British were particularly keen to get an election reference into the final report, Mitchell later disclosing that he received numerous suggestions on its wording, 'by letter, by fax, by telephone, in person.' In the end, his report noted with studious neutrality that 'an elective process could contribute to the building of confidence.' The actual production of the report was marked by a last-minute panic, as the computer the Mitchell team was using in London's Churchill Hotel developed a glitch, and printed out garbled versions. His team eventually fixed the problem and delivered the report on time. They could not know that its emergence would be part of a sequence of events which led to an act of extreme violence at London's Canary Wharf.

13
Canary Wharf

———

When the Mitchell Report on arms was published in January 1996, Major chose to focus not on its main findings, but on its passing mention of an election. If illegal groups would not agree to prior decommissioning, he announced, then the road ahead was 'to secure a democratic mandate for all-party negotiations through elections specially for that purpose.'

Major was accused of scrapping the report: Trimble was pleased, but Hume was furious. The SDLP leader rose in the Commons to accuse Major of resorting to a time-wasting device to appease Unionists, declaring pointedly: 'It would be particularly irresponsible for a government to try to buy votes in this House to keep itself in power. Would he now fix a date for all-party talks, rather than the 17 months that he has wasted up till now?' When he was loudly condemned by Tory backbenchers, Hume retorted: 'I live with it – you don't.' He recollected: 'I couldn't understand the slowness of bringing the parties around the table, and I certainly couldn't understand why it was necessary to get an election, because an election would only harden up political attitudes and make negotiations much more difficult.'

Major's aide, John Holmes, recalled: 'John Hume did accuse the Prime Minister of buying votes. John Major was extremely angry about that, because if he'd been in the business of buying votes in Northern Ireland or using

Northern Ireland policy he would not have been where he was at all. He would probably have left the issue on one side, and not spent so much of his time on it.'

A Northern Ireland Office (NIO) source sought to explain the situation at the time, saying:

I think we're in this impossible position, with Number 10 in this business of trying to play a balancing game so the Unionists don't feel the nationalist front is running away with it. The Tory backbenchers and the Unionists still have a key role to play in terms of the balance in Parliament. That's going to be with us this side of a general election, and it's always going to create these sorts of difficulties. You can take it that the NIO and Number 10 do not always see eye to eye. That's a tension that's been there from the start, with in general the NIO being prepared to take more risks than the PM, who has all these other considerations.

By this stage, more and more ominous noises were coming from within republicanism, as a year and a half had gone by without political negotiations. One senior republican remarked at the time: 'There is a big black angry dog out there wanting to be fed.' He meant that the IRA had called a ceasefire in order to facilitate talks, but these had not materialised. Republican activist Rory Duggan caught the mood of the time in the words: 'The euphoria was giving way to despair. People were not only asking, they were counting the days to when the ceasefire was going to end. They weren't saying, if the ceasefire ends – it was, when was it going to end.'

Then, on 9 February 1996, the ceasefire ended. Adams remembered contacting both Dublin and Washington with grim news: 'When it became obvious to me that the process was not just in terminal decline but in fact was all but over, I conveyed that to the Irish government and to the White House.' In Washington Clinton's National Security Adviser Tony Lake remembered the occasion:

My secretary said that I had a call from Gerry Adams. I was intrigued – I hadn't thought there was anything on our agenda particularly at that time. I took the call and it was a very strange call. There was very strong tension in his voice. He was clearly very emotional, very tense and very evasive. He simply said that he had disturbing information, and I pressed him on what that disturbing information might be. He wouldn't tell me, and it was only when we then later got news of Canary Wharf that I understood that was what he was referring to.

We then speculated a great deal as to whether he knew that in fact the bombing was about to take place, or that he knew that something was going to happen, or that he knew that Canary Wharf was going to happen but he didn't know when, etc. We also speculated as to why he had called to tell me this and frankly I still don't know.

O'Dowd was also in touch with the Sinn Fein leader around this time: 'I called Adams and he said things had gone wrong, he'd sent someone to try and sort it out – it hadn't worked out, and now he was afraid that the cease-fire was at an end. And sure enough, an hour later, news of the Canary Wharf bomb came in.'

Shortly afterwards, on that Friday evening, following a confused series of warnings, a huge bomb concealed in a lorry detonated in the City of London, not far from the giant Canary Wharf building in London's Docklands. The explosion claimed two lives, inflicted millions of pounds' worth of damage and apparently wrecked the peace process.

Two men who worked in a newspaper kiosk close to Canary Wharf, Inan Ul-haq Bashir and John Jeffries, were killed by the device, which had been concealed within a specially designed hiding place on a lorry. The two bodies were not found until the following day, after relatives informed police they were missing. It later emerged that preparation for the attack had been under way for some months. The explosives, estimated to weigh in the region of 1,000 lb, had been packed into a specially modified flatbed transporter which bore a tax disc that had been stolen in Northern Ireland some three weeks earlier. The lorry, which had a County Monaghan registration number, was transported across the Irish Sea on a car ferry to Scotland, and driven to London. Police in London raided up to 30 addresses in the wake of the bomb, while a reward of up to one million pounds was offered for information leading to the conviction of the bombers.

In its statement issued shortly before the explosion, the IRA said: 'Instead of embracing the peace process, the British government acted in bad faith, with Mr Major and the Unionist leaders squandering this unprecedented opportunity to resolve the conflict.' It went on to demand an 'inclusive negotiated settlement', adding: 'That is not possible unless and until the British government faces up to its responsibilities. The blame for the failure thus far of the Irish peace process lies squarely with John Major and his government.'

Participants in the process reacted differently. Adams was to say: 'It was a really strange sensation to see the television pictures of Canary Wharf and to have that sense that we had lost something, that the British had just made a complete and absolute mess of it. Obviously the IRA have to take responsibility for its actions, but I remember having an almost out-of-body experience that your worst sort of fears have come true.'

Jean Kennedy Smith recalled that when news of the Canary Wharf bomb came through she was in the US Embassy with John Hume and a group of artists from Donegal. She said:

Television people arrived at the gates wanting to talk to John, and the President called, Gerry Adams called, we were getting phone calls from everywhere. This sort of dancing and singing was going on in the other room so it was very surreal, because of course they didn't know anything had happened, and John went in there and pretended that nothing had happened and was patting everybody on the back. Then he'd come out and take another phone call from the President. It was very sad.

For Major, too, it was a black moment: 'My first thought upon hearing of this news was simply despair. Were we really going to go back to what had happened for so many years? And then as I began to think about it I wondered, Well, are we going back, or is this just yet another occasion when the IRA, misreading the British government, believe they can change the terms of the negotiation by returning to violence?'

Quentin Thomas would look back on the lead-up to the Canary Wharf attack:

We obviously did wonder whether the approach we'd taken had been right, in this period that led to the breakdown of the ceasefire. I guess looking back you can distinguish two different ways of looking at this. Certainly, before the first ceasefire ministers said in a most formal way that if there were a ceasefire, they would want to be imaginative. The question is whether one accentuates the positive and seeks to bring people in when they appear at the door of democracy and want to join talks. Or whether you hold them there and subject them to some examination to see whether their shoes are clean. I think perhaps we, to some extent, fell into the latter when it might have been better to do the former.

More IRA bombs signalled that the IRA had no immediate expectation of getting into talks, and was again concentrating on violence. Faced with this, Major went ahead in May with the election he favoured, setting up a Belfast forum. This would have no powers; the idea was that party delegations for negotiations would be chosen from its ranks. When the election idea was put forward by John Major in January, nationalists denounced it as a tactical concession to Unionists, since both David Trimble and Ian Paisley had pressed for it. John Bruton said it 'would pour petrol on the flames.' But the Irish government changed its stance in the wake of the Canary Wharf bombing, calculating that the attack meant the bomb had made it impossible to remove elections from the agenda.

But the proposed discussions would be multi-party rather than all-party talks, for in the absence of an IRA ceasefire Sinn Fein was to be excluded. The republicans would not take their seats in the forum, saying they were implacably opposed to an election, their candidates standing on an abstentionist ticket. Yet when the ballot boxes were opened, it turned out that they were the main beneficiaries of the exercise. The party surged to an unprecedented 15.5 per cent, surprising everyone, including Sinn Fein itself. The regular republican vote had turned out, but so too had many people who had never bothered voting before, or who had refrained from supporting the party while IRA violence was at its height. The SDLP's vote dropped by a fraction, but John Hume and Gerry Adams both received massive personal endorsements. The message from the republican and nationalist grassroots was one of overwhelming support for a peace process.

What they got was not peace, but more republican violence. This was to be the story of much of 1996: a curious state of limbo, which was not quite war and not quite peace. It was punctuated by occasional bombing attacks, civil disturbances on a large scale and important political developments. Through it all, the thread of debate ran: could and should the peace process be put together again; was the very idea of peace a chimera; were these islands, having had a glimpse of peace, fated to return to the worst of the bad old days?

The long-awaited political talks were finally convened in Belfast on 10 June, but they opened without Sinn Fein. Adams, surrounded by the largest media posse ever seen in Belfast, led a delegation to the gates of the talks. The cameras recorded Adams encountering gates secured with a padlock, and an official informing the Sinn Fein representatives that they would not be allowed in until a new ceasefire was called. The trek to Stormont was a publicity stunt, and a successful one, for the simplistic signal it sent abroad was that republicans were ready for peace but were being denied a place at the table. This, together with the undeniable fact that one voter in seven had supported Sinn Fein, gave the republicans a claim to the moral high ground.

But it proved a momentary phenomenon, for June brought a wave of IRA violence which served as a highly effective reminder why those Stormont gates had remained shut. In that single month, an Irish policeman, Jerry McCabe, was shot dead in the Republic, a large bomb devastated much of Manchester's city centre and a mortar attack was staged on a British army base at Osnabrück in Germany.

Many Sinn Fein sympathisers who had assumed the peace process would be revived within months, were worried and concerned. One woman living in West Belfast, for example, said just after the election result: 'It was a statement of trust in Adams, a vote of confidence in how he handled the peace process. It was also two fingers to the Brits for messing it all up. It was a vote against a return to war. There would be horror if the IRA started up again without a very, very good reason. Something pretty horrendous would have to happen to justify it.'

Just after the Manchester bomb the same woman said: 'People are waiting for an explanation. What the fuck is going on here? They [the IRA] must have decided that this is all a complete waste of time. It makes it harder for Adams to make any progress, and it's given the Unionists all the ammunition they could want on decommissioning. It's difficult to see any game plan emerging. It's quite depressing.' Another sympathiser said: 'This causes enormous difficulties. It's very damaging, but out of loyalty people will bite their tongues and just hope the IRA knows what it's doing.'

The political talks went on, but the question remained of whether there could be a meaningful peace process if Sinn Fein were not involved. The Dublin and general nationalist attitude to this was summed up by Irish official Fergus Finlay, who pronounced that 'without Sinn Fein talks are not worth a penny candle.' But everyone knew that the price of republican admission was another IRA ceasefire: the question was how and when that might come about.

As John Major's government surveyed the ruins of Canary Wharf, and the ruins of the peace process, David Goodall came back into the picture. As a senior Cabinet Office civil servant he had played an important part in putting together the 1985 Anglo–Irish Agreement, but by this stage had retired after a distinguished diplomatic career.

After the London bomb, Goodall was contacted by a nationalist source who told him Sinn Fein were anxious to find an interlocutor who would convey their views accurately to the British government. He stepped into the role, and found himself sitting in Clonard Monastery, in the Falls district in Belfast, opposite Sinn Fein's Gerry Kelly. The two men had very different connections with London: Goodall had served there in the heart of Whitehall, while Kelly had blown up the Old Bailey in 1972, for which he had served a lengthy prison sentence.

Although the former mandarin and the former bomber were both Catholics, their common religion was not to lead to a meeting of minds. Goodall recalled: 'We agreed to meet in the Redemptorist Monastery in West Belfast. Throughout the proceedings, Gerry Kelly sat directly under the great big statue of the Sacred Heart.' Kelly said that the British government had made 'a complete mess of this', further accusing John Major of acting not in the best interests of peace but for party political reasons. He delivered a republican lecture, going through a historical analysis of the British position on Ireland. Goodall's memory is of Kelly saying that 'the British only understood terrorism, the British had used terrorism in Ireland since the year 1167, the British understood perfectly well that there had to be terrorism.'

Goodall recalled: 'I was trying to get them to see that

blowing up people on the mainland actually didn't produce the results they wanted, and that it simply alienated people. I was making the argument that the two governments would decide that they had to go ahead without Sinn Fein being in the negotiating process, and gradually Sinn Fein would become progressively irrelevant. At that point Gerry Kelly broke in very angrily and said, "That would be blackmail." Goodall retorted, "Well, what do you call blowing people up on the mainland if that's not a form of blackmail?" Kelly responded: "All right, I withdraw blackmail."' By this stage it had become obvious that the two men were not on the same wavelength. Kelly summed up: 'I just was thinking to myself, "All the guy is doing here is coming restating the policy, we have already been through this."'

As if to emphasise the gulf between the republicans and the British, the IRA demonstrated, in October 1996, its coolly murderous audacity with an attack on a prestige target: Thiepval barracks in Lisburn, County Antrim, the army's Northern Ireland headquarters. A senior republican later said of the incident: 'It's regarded in republican circles as one of the classic operations of the campaign.'

The base was such an obvious target, and so heavily guarded, that it had long been assumed to be immune from republican assault. At its main gate, which lay at the end of a suburban road, those entering the base are confronted by a formidable system of electrically operated barricades. Soldiers check vehicles entering and leaving, while drivers are required to produce special identification or report to a roadside office. Somehow the IRA got past all the security panoply in three cars, two of them containing 800 lb bombs. Its people produced fake passes and were waved through the entrance without having their vehicles searched. The bombs exploded that afternoon, shattering the base's illusion of security and injuring 31 people.

Planning for the attack had begun months earlier. In June an East Belfast man had sold his red Volvo Estate car for around £5,000 in cash. In July a garage sold another Volvo Estate, this time gold-coloured, again for £5,000 in cash. Then, two weeks before the attack, a Volkswagen Passat was bought at a Belfast auction, a cash sale at £1,800. It was these three vehicles which were driven into army headquarters on 7 October. The two Volvos containing the bombs were left inside the base, the bombers making their exit in the Passat.

The devices were placed so as to inflict maximum casualties. The first went off, without warning, in the motor transport car park at 4.30 p.m. The second exploded 15 minutes later a hundred yards away: it had been placed, with breathtaking wickedness, outside a nearby medical centre. In other words, the intention with the second device was to blow up the injured and those bringing them for medical help. It was, the RUC said, an attempt at mass murder.

There was one fatality, Warrant Officer James Bradwell, a 43-year-old soldier from Gateshead. He was injured in the first explosion and was then caught again in the second blast. The day after the attack his condition was described by a Belfast doctor: 'He has significant soft-tissue injuries to one limb which still need to be addressed. He was too ill last night to have that sorted out. He will be going back to theatre some time today to have that done, but he has significant burns covering about 50 to 60 per cent of his body, in addition to a depressed skull fracture and other minor soft-tissue injuries. The injury to his arm is potentially an amputation, but that I don't know yet.'

Warrant Officer Bradwell died four days later, the first soldier to be killed in Northern Ireland since August 1994. The soldier died on the day John Major addressed the Conservative party's annual conference, and in his speech the prime minister attacked Adams in the most scathingly personal terms. He told the Tories:

For many months, Sinn Fein leaders have mouthed the word peace. Warrant Officer James Bradwell was 43, with a wife and with children, Mr Adams. He joined the army, prepared to lose his life defending the British nation. Soldiers do. But he was murdered in cold blood in the United Kingdom. I sent him there, Mr Adams, so save me any crocodile tears. Don't tell me this has nothing to do with you. I don't believe you, Mr Adams, I don't believe you.

Adams coolly rebuked Major: 'Personalised attacks are no substitute for real politics. It was the absence of real politics and a good-faith engagement by the British government in the peace process which led to its collapse. Mr Major cannot evade his responsibility and he must bear the lion's share of blame for the current difficulties.'

This exchange took place on Friday 11 October. Unknown to practically anyone at the time, Major had the previous day received from Hume the latest version of 'Hume–Adams', which in effect amounted to an offer of a restoration of the ceasefire in exchange for entry into negotiations. Hume was confident that the document could bring about a restoration of the cessation. He said: 'I found John Major friendly, as usual. I told him I was authorised to say that, if he made the October 10th statement, there would be an unequivocal ceasefire announced on the same day. If he made the statement at, say, midday, the ceasefire would come at midnight. I said to Major, "I will give you a guarantee in writing, and if it doesn't happen I will admit I gave you the wrong advice."'

Hume was clearly acting in good faith and was anxious to make progress as quickly as possible. But as the document reached Major's hands the message was unmistakable: the offer of a cessation was accompanied by actual violence and the threat of more of the same.

Major's reply, when it came, angered Hume and Dublin. He made clear that the restoration of the 1994 ceasefire was not enough to guarantee talks. Any ceasefire, he said, would be followed by a period, the length of which he did not specify, during which the government would form a judgement on the IRA's commitment to exclusively peaceful means. In setting out this position, Major specifically mentioned the Lisburn bombing, indicating the government had taken its stance in the light of this and other IRA attacks.

Hume was dismayed not just by the contents of the message but by the manner of its delivery. Having received Major's response on 23 November, Hume had informed the prime minister's staff that he would meet Adams to discuss it. He duly met Adams, together with Father Alex Reid, a few days later for a meeting which he described as very constructive. But before he could report Adams's observations back to Major, the prime minister published his position, making clear that this was the British government's last word on the matter before the general election.

The prime minister's move drew little criticism in Britain, where the Labour party stuck to its approach of not diverging from the government's line on Ireland and the peace process. But Hume and Dublin were angry, taking the view that by introducing new stipulations Major had in effect moved the goalposts. In a statement so cool as to be almost arctic, the Irish government made clear its position that Sinn Fein should be allowed into talks as soon as the 1994 cessation had been restored.

Hume said with some bitterness: 'I believe things were all positively moving in the right direction to an unequivocal restoration of the IRA ceasefire. Westminster doesn't care that much about us, and given our present problems it's quite obvious that the internal politics of Westminster are more important than getting peace on our streets.'

14
Into talks

The general election of May 1997 transformed the peace process, with the departure of John Major and the arrival in Downing Street of Tony Blair. The poll also provided further evidence of the continuing electoral march of Sinn Fein, with McGuinness joining Adams as an MP. Many of the new Sinn Fein votes were said to come from nationalists wishing to encourage the IRA towards another ceasefire.

One of Blair's first and most important tasks as prime minister was to explore whether a second IRA ceasefire was on the cards. He had asked of the republicans in a speech: 'Is participation in the peace process a tactic in an otherwise unbroken armed conflict, or is it a genuine search for a new way forward? If it is the latter, then the door is open – but only if it is the latter.'

Labour's landslide victory changed the political landscape, installing as it did a leader whose large majority had given him great authority both inside and outside Parliament. Labour had traditionally leaned towards an Irish nationalist approach, although nationalists complained that this was more evident in Opposition than while in office. New Labour, however, was to attempt a more balanced approach. It also went for a more modern and informal approach, as personified by the new Northern Ireland Secretary, Dr Marjorie 'Mo' Mowlam. Described variously as blunt, outspoken, given to swearing, intelligent and unpretentious, she supplied a striking contrast to the patrician style of the departing Mayhew, and gave a sense that a new start was being made.

Two weeks after taking office, Blair went to Belfast to deliver a keynote speech which attempted to provide something for both republicans and Unionists. Mowlam remembered: 'We spent a long time trying to find a location that would reassure Unionists. So in the end we went to the heart of Unionism – to the farmers, to the Royal Ulster Agricultural Show, an epitome of the centre of Unionism.' In one part of his speech, specifically designed to please Unionist opinion, Blair declared: 'None of us in this hall today, even the youngest, is likely to see Northern Ireland as anything but a part of the United Kingdom. That is the reality, because the consent principle is now almost universally accepted.' Ulster Unionist party leader David Trimble would say of this: 'The terms that were in that speech were a considerable reassurance to us. We didn't get the same clarity from the Major government – we got greater clarity from Blair.'

Blair's comments on the Union were highly unwelcome to republicans. Adams was to say: 'He made a bad speech here. I told him that; I mean, how can he predict the future, how does he know? I challenged him publicly on that, and I certainly challenged him privately on his remarks. Very, very, very bad start.'

But Sinn Fein leaders essentially got what they wanted to hear when he went on to announce the reopening of direct British government exploratory contacts with them. Not all republicans were happy about this; one who had deep reservations about the Sinn Fein strategy was dissident Rory Duggan. To him the Blair speech was a disaster: 'What he was saying to us was, "You can have everything you want – you can have equality, you can have representation in a government. You can have Catholic policemen smashing your head in as well as Protestant policemen. You can have the Irish language spoken. You can have everything you want within the Union, but you can't have the one thing that the struggle was about."'

Blair explained his aims: 'I wanted first of all to reassure the Unionists that we didn't see it as our mission to push for a united Ireland, and also that I was very comfortable if people choose to remain part of the United Kingdom. I also wanted to say to Sinn Fein, "Look, there is a new government, we are a different type of government, but we can't wait around for ever. The acceptable way is to negotiate, the unacceptable way is to continue violence."'

But IRA violence continued. A month after Blair's speech at Balmoral two members of the Royal Ulster Constabulary were shot dead. These killings posed serious problems for Ulster Unionists, who were discussing whether they should sit down in talks with Sinn Fein. To dissident Ulster Unionist MP Jeffrey Donaldson, the killing of the police officers was an affront. He said: 'This awful news of two young police officers cut down in cold blood, shot in the back, by the Provisional IRA, serves to emphasise yet again the harsh reality, that republicans are wedded to violence, and that violence is their stock in trade.'

However, London and Dublin agreed that IRA decommissioning would not be a precondition for Sinn Fein entry to talks. In what was seen as a calculated gamble by Blair and Mowlam, it was announced that political talks would begin in earnest in September, and that Sinn Fein would be allowed to join six weeks after a new IRA ceasefire. Paisley and other hard-liners had already made it clear that if republicans entered the talks they would immediately leave. Part of the gamble lay in the possibility that, if Sinn Fein were allowed in, Trimble might lead his Ulster Unionists out.

Blair's gamble worked. Much bad feeling was generated among republicans and nationalists when the authorities pushed the Drumcree march through the Catholic Garvaghy Road. Yet even so, the IRA announced a second cessation later in July, this time in a low-key fashion. The general reaction too was low-key, for the Canary Wharf bombing had demonstrated that ceasefires could be broken as easily as they were called. Trimble, after some initial hesitation, decided to stay at the table, though he cloaked the decision in tough rhetoric: 'We are not here to negotiate with Sinn Fein but to confront them – to expose their fascist character. Unionism will not be marginalised.'

It was a big step for republicans too, as they settled into their offices in Castle Buildings within the Stormont estate. They brought with them the trappings of resistance, carrying in Irish tricolours and a portrait of hunger striker Bobby Sands. The building itself was disliked by everyone, and regarded as no help to negotiation. A modified civil service office block within the sprawling Stormont estate in East Belfast, it was described by one who came to know it well as 'the original sick building'. Characterless, cheerless and boxy, delegates complained that its stark '60s design offered no intimate hidey-holes for private politicking. In the canteen most politicians tended not to mix, while the bar was found unappealing. Comparing it to an RUC interrogation centre, Gerry Adams called it 'Castlereagh with coffee'.

It was a difficult moment of adjustment for people on many parts of the spectrum. Quite a few of those at the table could recall the names of friends, colleagues and relatives killed in the troubles; they could also glance round the room and see people whom they held responsible for deaths. Ulster Unionist MP Ken Maginnis, for example, had lost a number of colleagues with whom he had served in the locally recruited Ulster Defence Regiment. He would recall:

I have a deep, deep bitterness about the IRA. I think I have lost almost all my closest friends in the UDR. I lost my company sergeant major; I lost Cormac, who used to come round to the house quite a lot; George Shaw, who took me to my first scout camp; Eric Shiells, who I was very friendly with in the rugby club – all decent, dependable fellows. There are lots more who come to mind. I don't see my presence at Stormont as staying in the talks with Sinn Fein, but rather as refusing to give up political ground. It's not a question of spite, it's a question of disgust. I could never give cognisance to them, not as long as I live.

Gary McMichael, leader of the Ulster Democratic party, suffered even more directly at the hands of the IRA: his father, loyalist paramilitary leader John McMichael, was killed by the republicans. Gary, who was 18 at the time, said:

It's very, very difficult for me, because they not only killed my father but also my best friend, and three years ago they tried to kill me. That obviously makes it more difficult to even be in the room with representatives of those people, never mind engage in any form of negotiation with them. But it's actually that suffering that makes us take the line that we do, and makes us go that extra mile to try and remove the threat against the community for ever. That means that we have to tackle republicanism, because we know that if we walk away from this process there's going to be another stage of conflict, that others will have to go through what we've gone through.

Across the table and across the divide sat Alex Maskey of Sinn Fein, who had been a favourite target for loyalists. In 1986 the UDA shot him: 'I got a sawn-off shotgun blast in the stomach. I lost half a kidney, half my bowel, half my stomach and I still have shrapnel inside me,' he said. 'I also had my house petrol-bombed by loyalists. I had to drag my kids out of bed and down a burning hallway. That was very traumatic for them.' He continued: 'All too often people talk as if only one side has a monopoly on suffering. I'm trying to get on with people who tried to murder me, and that's because I want to make sure others don't have to endure the suffering that we have. We now have an opportunity to break the log-jam.'

Against this background, it was perhaps not surprising that although the negotiations were serious and intense, many of the participants never actually spoke to each other. Talks chairman Senator George Mitchell was to observe: 'There was no discussion directly between the Ulster Unionist delegation and the Sinn Fein delegation. They addressed themselves through me in the chair, when they had any dialogue at all.'

Trimble's deputy, the volatile veteran John Taylor, whose support for Trimble would be crucial in the talks, recalled: 'Gerry Adams was a great operator from his point of view. He knew rightly that we were not prepared to talk to him, so when he would meet people in the corridor he would make some gesture, saying good morning or something like that. But I ignored the man.'

Adams was to recall wryly: 'My best discussions with the Unionists were in the men's room, where they were a captive audience and it was possible to engage in some conversation, sometimes one-sided. But it was obvious that the more rounded human beings there did want to say hello, did want to say, how are you doing, did want to say it's a good day, did want to say you're piddling on my foot.'

Ulster Unionist Dermot Nesbitt would remember: 'I was standing in the toilet relieving myself when suddenly I felt a hand on my shoulder, and realised it was Gerry Adams who was inquiring about my well-being. Lost for words and for want of something better to say I said, "I didn't realise you were so big."'

Some time later this lack of dialogue came as a great surprise to a group, which included both the African National Congress and the National Party, who invited both Unionists and republicans to a conference in South Africa. Because the two sides would not mix, Nelson Mandela ended up making separate addresses to two different – in effect, segregated – audiences. Professor Padraig O'Malley, who helped to organise the conference, said: 'The South Africans didn't understand the intensity of the divisiveness and were astounded and nonplussed by it, saying, "Wow, we thought we had problems – even in our worst days we were never like this."'

Progress in the talks was painfully slow. After three months, Mitchell, as talks chairman, could not even get the parties to agree on what they were negotiating about. He summed up the basic problem: 'People here are very nice and friendly – they're just not friendly to each other. Centuries of conflict have generated hatreds that make it virtually impossible for the two communities to trust each other. Each disbelieves the other. Each assumes the worst about the other.'

Mitchell was much praised for being prepared to listen almost endlessly, his years in the US Senate, with its notoriously leisurely approach to debate, standing him in good stead. But the continuing impasse tried even his patience, so that eventually he almost reached breaking-point: 'I was very, very angry and I considered letting it all out – perhaps an emotional outburst would shock them into action. But I decided against it: it was too late, so I swallowed my disappointment and suppressed my doubts.'

And then, just when Mitchell thought things could hardly get worse, the situation deteriorated alarmingly. A new cycle of violence opened with a killing on 27 December 1997 inside the Maze prison. It was carried out by members of the republican splinter group, the Irish National Liberation Army.

The victim was Billy Wright, one of the foremost figures in the loyalist paramilitary underworld. Wright, a militant who was suspected of involvement in more than a dozen killings, disapproved of the peace process and had broken away from the UVF to form his own group, the Loyalist Volunteer Force. His courting of publicity made him a familiar face, and a figure who inspired fear among the Catholic population, especially in and around the County Armagh town of Portadown, where he lived. His high profile made him a marked man. He said in one interview: 'Personally, I'm a dead man. It would be morally wrong to back off. I have to give my life now. I have kids, but morally I have to lay down my life now. If I was shot dead in the morning, I would laugh in my grave.' Wright, who was serving an eight-year sentence for threatening to kill a woman, was in a prison minibus waiting to be driven to a visit, when INLA gunmen made their way out of another part of the building, crossed a rooftop, opened the door of the van and shot him several times.

Johnny Adair of the UDA, another icon of violence, described the reaction among hard-line Protestants: 'It sickened us all, it sickened all good loyalists, that such a great loyalist could die at the hands of scum in a place where he thought that he was protected by the British authorities – just gutted.' Michael Stone, who had risen to paramilitary fame by attacking the Gibraltar IRA funerals in Milltown cemetery, recalled: 'They had broken an unwritten rule that you don't carry out assassinations within the prison system, because quite honestly they're too easy to carry out.' The Wright assassination had a destabilising effect on the peace process, leading as it did to a spasm of retaliatory killings of Catholic civilians.

Adair and Stone were both in the Maze at the time, with other imprisoned UDA members. The organisation had never been particularly enthusiastic about the peace process, and in the wake of the Wright killing they announced they were withdrawing their support for the process. As Adair said: 'We felt angry and frustrated and felt that we can't support this any more.' Gary McMichael, their political representative, remembered being told by the hard men: 'We had agreed nothing: there was no prospect of us agreeing anything. People were killing loyalists when they [were] incarcerated in prison. Concessions were mainly to republicans. What is there to negotiate about?'

With renewed violence on the streets and death and restlessness in the Maze, there was a clear danger of the peace process unravelling. As part of a series of crisis meetings, Mowlam met Gary McMichael, who warned her that UDA prisoners were highly dissatisfied. As Mowlam remembers it: 'Gary said, "We don't have enough to say to them, we don't have enough to put on the table to convince them that this is a process which is worth holding on to."' UDA commander Jackie MacDonald was blunt in his message to her: 'In no uncertain terms I told her that it is just the bottom line, dead bodies in the street.'

Faced with this, Mowlam took the kind of audacious and unorthodox step that was very much in keeping with her approach and personality. She was to recall: 'I didn't think they were exaggerating, and I didn't think they were playing it to see what they could get. They explained why they were having difficulty with their prisoners and I said to them, "Would it help if I went and talked to them?"' McMichael, slightly thrown by the sudden emergence of such an unprecedented idea, recalled: 'I looked to the other side of her to see her officials, who had their heads down, shaking them, and I asked her if she was serious. And she said, "If this is what it takes, then that's what I'm going to do."' She first ran the idea past the Cabinet Office. Tony Blair was at a European summit and was not immediately contactable, but the go-ahead was given.'

According to Mowlam: 'There was a move by my protection staff and a large number of the entourage from the prison to go in with me, but I said, "No, if this is going to work, I have to talk directly, just me and my private secretary."' Jackie MacDonald remembers: 'She just threw the wig in a corner sort of thing, and says, "Right, how are we going to sort this out?"'

Mowlam had by this stage incorporated her wig as part of her unorthodox political persona. 'Women think I'm ballsy about the wig,' she confided to a friend. The hairpiece was necessary because all her hair had fallen out during radiotherapy for what she has called 'my little tumour.' Her dramatic weight gain at this time was a result of additional steroid treatment. She soon realised that doffing the wig could both startle and impress an audience. 'I don't care about you lot,' she told amazed American correspondents at lunch one day. 'I'm in a mood. I've had a bad start to the day. I'm going to take my hair off.' She used it during some tense moments in Belfast: 'She's a true psychologist,' said one Belfast politician. 'It's very disarming when you're in a strenuous meeting with her and you're about to tackle her hard, and she suddenly takes off the wig. It's extremely difficult to be tough on a lady who is personally bald.'

Her style did not go down well with everyone. One Unionist politician publicly denounced 'the huggy-wuggy lovey-dovey Secretary of State – instead of fighting she's embracing the enemy.' She shrugged: 'There's nothing I can do about being me. The downside is that my style is difficult for some men to handle, but in the end I am what I am. It's me.'

So it was that, in January 1998, a British cabinet minister walked almost alone into those parts of the prison, the most heavily guarded in the UK, which contained men who had ordered, and carried out, scores of killings. She remembers sitting down with Adair, Stone and the others: 'They said, "You must understand how important this is for us. We have to be sure you're gonna be straight, because if it breaks down it isn't gonna be Trimble and his middle-class Unionists that are gonna be hurt. It's gonna be the working people that we represent, and they will get the brunt of the killings. So don't take us lightly."'

Mowlam had one overriding preoccupation, and she conveyed this to the loyalists: 'It was clear that if the ceasefires broke down, we'd all be in trouble. I made it very clear to them that was my view.' When Stone interrupted and asked, 'Is that a threat?' he remembers her reply: 'No, it's a promise, Michael.' He reflected: 'Had she been a man, I would say she's got big cojones.' Adair would recall: 'She was under an amount of pressure, everyone was under pressure. She understood our frustration, she understood why, but her honesty saved the day in my terms.' Flattered by her presence and impressed by her performance, the UDA prisoners shortly afterwards announced that they were once again in support of the peace process.

McMichael recalled:

We met with the UDA prisoners following Mo Mowlam's visit, and they were impressed. They told us that it wasn't what she said, it was the fact that she was there, that's really what it came down to. There were no assurances given, there were no promises made; it was a sign of respect on her part for the contribution that that part of loyalism had to play in the peace process if we were to resolve this conflict. They thought that she commanded respect in return for having taken that risk.

Outside the prison, however, killings by both loyalists and republicans continued. The violence had immediate political implications for the talks, since the RUC said it believed that both the IRA and UDA had been involved in the killings. As a result, the political representatives for each, Sinn Fein and the Ulster Democratic party, were for a time excluded from the negotiations in early 1998. But neither the violence nor the temporary expulsions, though disruptive, deflected the course of the talks.

A particularly poignant incident took place in March in the quiet County Armagh village of Poyntzpass, which had until then largely escaped the worst effects of the troubles. When two members of Wright's LVF machine-gunned a bar they killed a Protestant and a Catholic, Philip Allen and Damien Trainor, who had been best friends. They were having a quiet drink when loyalist gunmen burst in, shouted 'Get down you bastards,' and fired repeatedly into their bodies and those of two other people. Philip, who was 34, had just asked 25-year-old Damien to be best man at his wedding.

The bar owner's son described the scene: 'It was quite simple. There was two men came in through the front door of the bar and they shouted in very rude terms for everybody in the bar to lie down, and everybody just lay down. They did not ask for denominations or anything, they just opened fire on the fellas that were on the ground.' When a priest was summoned to the bar, he found the two fatally injured men. 'I saw Damien and Philip lying on the ground just behind the door,' he said. 'I administered the last rites to Damien and prayed with Philip. They were still conscious at that stage and I tried to console them. I tried to talk to them, to encourage them, give them some hope. They responded for a short time but then we were losing them.'

SDLP deputy leader Seamus Mallon also went to the scene: 'Poyntzpass is in my constituency, I know it very well, used to play football for their football team. I went over immediately. While standing at the corner with I suppose 40, 50 people, everybody deathly still, deathly silent, a senior police officer came over and called me away and he said: "They're both dead, you know."'

The next day Mallon returned to the town on a miserable rainy day: visits to the bereaved have been one of the regular duties of Northern Ireland politicians. There he spotted the car used by David Trimble, whose constituency also included part of the village. Meeting by chance, the two men did something unusual. They decided to visit the stricken families together. Mallon was to remember:

We went down to Mr and Mrs Allen's house, sympathised with them, then we came back up through the village to Mr and Mrs Trainor and spoke to them. Then we went to Mr and Mrs Canavan who owned the bar where the shooting took place. It wasn't pre-organised, couldn't have been, but it just was right. It was right in the sense that we did it together, it was right in the sense that the community expected us and wanted us to do it together.

Trimble was to remark: 'All the killings that took place at the time had an impact on us – reminded us of what it was we were trying to replace.'

By this stage there was as yet little sense of things gelling in the talks. For one thing, republicans and Unionists were not even directly speaking to each other. Yet even so, attacks such as that at Poyntzpass never looked like breaking up the negotiations: in every case, the immediate revulsion at such incidents was followed not by despair, but by a renewed sense of political determination. It had taken the parties years to get round the table together: once there, they refused to be dislodged by whatever violence was played out on the streets.

A similar effect had been visible a few years earlier, several thousand miles away, in the South African peace process. Author Allister Sparks wrote of one violent episode: 'As with all the previous crises, this national trauma strengthened rather than weakened the political centre and spurred the negotiating parties to speed up their work. Perversely, the attacks have had a salutary effect on the negotiation process. The more outrageous the behaviour from the periphery, the more the centre coheres.'

By this stage, even Mitchell's near-legendary patience was wearing thin. He recalled: 'These guys had talked for nearly two years – they could talk for 20 years if given the opportunity. It was at that point I concluded that the only possibility for success required an early fixed and unbreakable deadline, which I thought after looking at the calendar should be Easter weekend.'

15
Deadline

As the pace quickened in the light of this deadline, Tony Blair invited the Ulster Unionists to Chequers to discover whether they were really willing to go into a power-sharing government with Sinn Fein. This was a huge question for Trimble, as leader of a party which for many years had declined to go into government with the SDLP, let alone one of the components of a republican movement which he regularly referred to as 'Sinn Fein-IRA.'

Trimble said that for him the key element was weaponry: 'We were quite comfortable with a rather unusual arrangement for administration that included all the major parties in it. But we felt that wouldn't be viable, there wouldn't be the confidence to operate that system, unless it was clear that people were committed to exclusively peaceful means – and that meant a linkage to decommissioning.'

This line of thought was stressed by the ambitious Unionist MP Jeffrey Donaldson, who accompanied Trimble to Chequers. For Donaldson: 'The most important and key element was the issue of the decommissioning of the illegal terrorist weapons, and the requirement for progress on decommissioning before there could be any question of those politicians, and parties who were linked to terrorist organisations, holding positions in a future assembly.'

Donaldson, however, was to assert that the prime minister gave a firm assurance on guns: 'He said that he understood our concern and that the government would support us in the final round of the negotiations.' Much of the politics of the years that followed would turn on this issue.

Blair would afterwards say that during the conversations he placed decommissioning in the context of a multi-faceted agreement. He has a clear recollection of the meeting:

I remember I was under quite a lot of pressure that day, because it was my wedding anniversary and Cherie and I were going to have dinner together. Therefore, although the meeting was important, it was a Sunday and I wanted to make sure that we didn't go on too long.

I said to Jeffrey and to David that of course decommissioning was an important part of the settlement, and that we had to make sure that there was a process in place that meant that the gun was taken out of politics in Northern Ireland altogether. I was very concerned, and I said this to them at the time, that we didn't want the whole of the agreement collapsing over this hurdle, but that of course it had to be part of the overall settlement.

The Irish government, however, put much less emphasis on decommissioning and much more on what was known as Strand Two, the relationship a new Belfast administration would have with the Irish government. The Irish had agreed in principle to change their constitution to remove their constitutional claim over Northern Ireland, which Unionists found offensive. In return, Dublin wanted a real say in running Northern Ireland, principally through new cross-border bodies. But when Ahern set off for Downing Street nine days before the Easter deadline, he was unhappy with the British proposals. At the time he insisted: 'If we are talking about setting up north-south bodies that have no implementing powers, that are not executive – that are really ad hoc chat-shows – well then, I'm not in the business of negotiating. I'll make my position very clear tonight at Number 10.'

Blair's aide John Holmes appreciated the Irish concerns:

The Irish government were particularly worried that they were going to change their constitution and accept even more clearly than they had before the consent principle, that whether there'd be a united Ireland depended entirely on the wishes of the majority of people in Northern Ireland.

They were going to accept all that, and at the end of the day they would find themselves with a functioning assembly in Northern Ireland, but no need for north-south cooperation. No meaningful north-south implementation bodies to take forward that cooperation. They had memories of previous settlements, as everybody else does, of previous negotiations where these things had apparently been agreed, and then not brought to fruition. They were therefore absolutely determined that this time these things were nailed down in negotiation in such a way that at least some genuine north-south cooperation would take place.

With a week to go before Mitchell's deadline, the two prime ministers had 48 hours to agree a text to settle the north-south structures issue, so that Mitchell could present it to all the parties by the weekend. On Friday afternoon, Mitchell waited and waited for the draft he was expecting, but instead of a paper his telephone rang: 'I picked it up and said hello. A voice came on the line: "Hello George, this is Tony Blair, Bertie's here with me."'

Holmes takes up the story: 'The prime minister started off by explaining the position to George Mitchell, that we'd been negotiating and had made some progress, but we weren't quite there yet.' Mitchell, concerned by this since he had a deadline to meet, asked: 'Well, how much more time?' He hoped the two prime ministers meant a few hours, but instead he was told: 'Well, over the weekend.'

The sense of Mitchell's disappointment was not lost on Ahern's senior adviser, Paddy Teahon, who commented: 'It was clear that despite his renowned patience George Mitchell was becoming somewhat frustrated.' Blair and Ahern were still grappling with the question of the range and powers of the cross-border bodies. Dublin knew that as far as Sinn Fein were concerned this question was critical, since republicans regarded the proposed bodies as a foothold from which they could work for a united Ireland.

Blair knew this too, but was initially apprehensive that making any new north-south arrangements too substantial would alienate the Unionist camp. Holmes described Unionist concerns: 'The most sensitive area was the idea that there could be bodies with some life of their own, which somehow could form the embryo of an all-Ireland government. That's where they feared that they would finish up, with a settlement they couldn't sell to their own people.'

By Sunday, however, the Irish side had essentially won the argument. The draft they eventually produced included long annexes listing more than 50 areas for north-south cooperation. Knowing Unionists would not react favourably, the two governments attempted a certain sleight of hand. The draft was passed to Mitchell with a stipulation and a request. The stipulation was that he must not change as much as a comma; the request was that he should present it as his own document, and not as one worked out by the two governments.

Teahon recalls: 'I said to George Mitchell that if it came

as a document from the two governments, there would have been an immediate perception that this was the Irish government.' Mitchell was unhappy with this request, but in any event he saw a fundamental problem with it: 'I knew instantly that the Ulster Unionists could not, and would not, accept this agreement. The annexes were way too long, way too detailed, and covered far too many areas for them.' But again he went along with what the governments wanted, Teahon saying: 'We convinced him that rather than have a long argument it was worthwhile putting the list on the table and finding out what happened.'

But when the list was released in Belfast, the Unionists hit the roof. Ken Maginnis remembered the arrival of the document: 'The paper finally emerged from George Mitchell's office and a group of us sat round and read it in shocked silence.' Donaldson thought it an Irish government wish-list. Trimble paled as he scanned 'big long lists of areas for cooperation which pretty well appeared to cover everything that was there.' He recalled what he had been told of the status of the document: 'This was an agreement which could not be changed. Now, if the Irish were taking the line that this draft can't be changed, with its big long annexes which were quite unacceptable to Unionists, then that gave us enormous difficulties.' His deputy John Taylor told reporters outside the talks building: 'Clearly this paper is unacceptable to the Ulster Unionists. I personally could not be identified with it – I wouldn't touch it with a 40-foot pole.'

The next morning Trimble headed straight for Mitchell's office to voice his objections. In fact, Mitchell was ahead of him, for he had already told British officials bluntly: 'The prime ministers have to agree to renegotiate, in good faith, the Strand Two section. Otherwise these talks are over. I don't think Trimble is bluffing. He can't live with this.'

In Mitchell's office an obviously upset Trimble, Mitchell remembers, 'took the report and dropped it on the table, and it made a loud thump in the gloomy silence of the room.' Shortly afterwards, Trimble was on the phone to Downing Street. Holmes, who took the call, remembered: 'Trimble said that the document, particularly on Strand Two, was ghastly and hopeless. He didn't think that they could work with it on that basis. He couldn't sell that to his own supporters and there would have to be wholesale change if any negotiation was going to get under way.' Trimble conveyed the same message to Dublin, Teahon recollecting: 'He said that the document had almost wrecked the possibilities of progress, and he wanted the Taoiseach to understand that.'

The Taoiseach was at that moment preoccupied with family affairs, for in Dublin his mother had died. He was accompanying her coffin to the church when his officials told him that Unionists would not accept what he had drafted with Blair.

That evening Blair flew into Northern Ireland, many assuming that his arrival signified that a deal was imminent. He encouraged this belief with his words: 'A day like today is not a day for soundbites, we can leave those at home, but I feel the hand of history upon our shoulder with respect to this, I really do.' In reality, Unionists were on the verge of walking out because of the terms of the Strand Two document.

Ahern's aide, Mansergh, explained the choice facing the Taoiseach: 'Was he going to stick out for a maximalist north-south dimension, in which case the likelihood was that the negotiation would break down and the Irish government principally would be blamed? Or was he going to accept a more realistic position?' Later that night the Taoiseach rang his officials and advised them he was thinking over what Mansergh had put to him, and would give his decision when he arrived in Northern Ireland in the morning.

Ahern asked Teahon to talk to Trimble and reassure him that Dublin wanted an agreement, and that there was a way to resolve this particular issue. Meeting Trimble in a corridor, Teahon told him: 'David, the Taoiseach asked me to have a word with you, to say that he apologises that we're not able to sit down and discuss this document, but you'll appreciate that his mother is dead.'

As Teahon recalled: 'David Trimble very courteously said, "Look, be in no doubt, I appreciate that completely, and please assure the Taoiseach that I fully understand. But this document that you have got George Mitchell to put on the table – it won't do, and why don't you understand?" And he turned and walked away from me, so it was a very quick two-part conversation.'

It quickly emerged that Ahern had agreed to a renegotiation, Donaldson commenting: 'Bertie Ahern made it clear that he wanted to cut a deal with Unionists, and in that sense he was prepared to be pragmatic. He conveyed that he understood the fears of Unionists and their concerns that powerful, all-Ireland structures could be a kind of Trojan horse.' Later that evening, with Tony Blair by his side, Ahern met Trimble's team for a meeting at which, in effect, a renegotiation of the Strand Two document was begun. The Ulster Unionist leader recalled: 'We got into a serious discussion about how Strand Two could be reshaped. The discussion that we had with the Irish government ran through until about one o'clock in the morning.'

In Trimble's analysis, Dublin were afraid of allowing a new assembly to control cross-border bodies: 'The Irish were nervous, very nervous about conceding that authority and accountability should be with Stormont, because they lacked confidence. The reason why the Irish were nervous was that they felt that if they did concede that, then somehow we would double-cross them.' Trimble and Ahern now essentially cut a new deal: this time the number and power of the cross-border bodies were substantially reduced.

But in what was known as Strand One, the form of the assembly and administration which would actually run Northern Ireland, had yet to be finalised. Most favoured an executive which would run government ministries, but for very different reasons Sinn Fein and the Ulster Unionists had voiced opposition to this. Sinn Fein opposed the very idea of an assembly, saying they wanted nothing to do with an essentially partitionist body: this turned out to be a tactical position which they later simply dropped.

Martin McGuinness recalls: 'We would stroll around the grounds of Stormont on our own, and Gerry would say it was a very real prospect that we could be in here.' Adams concurs: 'I remember saying to Martin, "We're going to end up in there if we can get the safeguards sorted out." So we had to face up to that, that was mighty. It's still a building in which I'm not comfortable. It reeks of Afrikaner architecture, it looks down its nose at everybody else, it has an inflated sense of its own importance.'

A number of the Ulster Unionist delegation, however, could not accept that such a deal could be on the cards.

They included some of what were referred to as the 'baby barristers', hard-line young figures, many of whom were lawyers, who had tended to back Trimble in his early days as party leader. By this stage, however, as his own tough stance had softened and it looked as though he was intent on striking a deal, most of his one-time supporters turned into dissenters and critics. Prominent in this faction was Donaldson, who explained: 'I just found it difficult, if not impossible, to envisage a situation where you would have a coalition government, a compulsory coalition government, containing political elements that were diametrically opposed to each other.'

Trimble's party had argued for an administration without an actual cabinet, maintaining that government could be carried out through a system of committees. In this way, they believed they could avoid sitting in a cabinet with Sinn Fein ministers. Most others felt it was decidedly odd to think of constructing a new administration without an executive to control and coordinate the business of government. Hume told the Unionists: 'We are totally committed to a completely inclusive system of government in Northern Ireland where all parties would be included, including Sinn Fein, so that all sections of our people would be represented in government.'

Trimble's deputy, Taylor, made the decisive arguments. He said:

I felt that departments of governments are interconnected, you have to have some body that connects the heads of the departments together, and therefore it would have to be some form of executive or cabinet. Secondly, John Hume had been arguing very strongly that the heads of these departments should be called Ministers, whereas our party at that stage were saying they should just be called chairmen of the committee.

And I remember when we went off privately afterwards, I said to David Trimble, 'Look, I think there's a lot of logic in the idea of an executive or a cabinet, and I certainly agree that these men and women should be called ministers, because no matter where you go in the world if you just say, this is the chairman of the health committee in Northern Ireland, or something, they'll think he's some local councillor.' And then I argued that if you do this, which is only common sense in any case, it will be a gesture towards the SDLP in getting agreement. And when we conveyed this, I remember John Hume jumping with delight and saying, 'Thank you very much, this is great news.' So that set a good tone to get the rest of the agreement on Strand One.

By this stage the outline of a possible deal was taking shape, though it was clear that Donaldson and others in the Ulster Unionist camp were deeply unhappy with the whole business. Donaldson recalls how, at a crucial moment, he was removed from the negotiating team. He would remember:

David Trimble asked me if I would join some of the junior members of the negotiating team who were having discussions with the Irish Attorney-General. I'd never been involved in those discussions before. The meeting with the Irish Attorney-General was a complete waste of time, it was a non-event.

But in the meantime, David Trimble, John Taylor and Reg Empey met the SDLP, so effectively I was excluded from the final round of negotiations on the key issues involving the administration of the government of Northern Ireland. I had a concern that the prime minister was playing the old perfidious

Albion role of divide and conquer – trying to draw out the leader, trying to get some kind of private understanding between the leader of the Unionist party and the government, and that then together they would try and sell something to the Unionist negotiating team and to the Unionist party. That probably was part of the prime minister's strategy, and it was something that we had talked about previously, and indeed, David Trimble had been critical [of] in the past.

The SDLP realised that there were internal Unionist problems. Previous meetings on this topic had involved four representatives from each party, but this time the Ulster Unionists asked for a different arrangement. According to Mallon, Donaldson's absence transformed things: 'Jeffrey Donaldson wasn't at the final meeting. The mood had changed, the temperature had changed considerably.' The meeting unexpectedly produced a series of breakthroughs on important points, as the Unionists dropped their idea of government by committee. Sean Farren of the SDLP was delighted with the progress as Mallon summarised the key points: 'Seamus went through them almost on a checklist approach to make sure what we were agreed on, and Trimble said yes, yes, yes, yes, yes, yes.' Around this time Taylor was heard to remark: 'We're well on our way to reaching an agreement.'

Hume recalled: 'When we finally reached agreement at midnight, myself and my colleagues were absolutely delighted.' Martin Mansergh was to remember: 'John Hume and company erupted into our room and started hugging everyone in sight, because they had achieved an agreement where they had got practically everything they wanted.' Donaldson agreed with this assessment: 'It was pretty clear that, in effect, what we had done was to sign up to the SDLP's concept of a compulsory power-sharing executive,' he said.

By this time a commotion was taking place in the grounds of the Stormont estate. Word reached members of the media assembled in the ill-equipped press hut that Paisley and an entourage were on their way to Castle Buildings. For months, Paisley and his colleagues had found themselves practically ignored by the media after stalking out of the negotiations; now they were determined to make their presence felt. Paisley told an excited gathering of flag-waving loyalists close to the talks: 'You have got the right to come up here tonight and demonstrate that it's No Surrender!' At an impromptu press conference he condemned Trimble, the British and Irish governments and others, but while this was going on other loyalists, who supported the talks, heckled him loudly. One of them called out, 'We should never have listened to you, Paisley. We're not going to prison for you any more.'

The SDLP's Joe Hendron confronted Paisley as he left, imploring him: 'In the name of God, after all these years surely you have enough wit, for the sake of babies unborn – Catholics, Protestants, Unionists, nationalists – I'm asking you, in the latter part of your political career, will you stand up for heaven's sake? You say you're a man of God – well, tonight's the night to prove it.'

Mowlam recalled: 'You could hear the shouts and the chants from the gate outside of Castle Buildings where the talks were taking place.' Inside the talks, the SDLP and the Ulster Unionists had reached a large measure of agreement, but the big question was where Sinn Fein stood. McGuinness emerged to tell the media: 'We in Sinn Fein want an agreement, but as I speak to you now there is no agreement, and the reason for that is because Unionists are blocking an agreement. We have told the British prime minister that he must avoid the temptation to go for the Unionist position.'

This comment caused alarm bells to ring in the Irish government camp, where Bertie Ahern felt he had to attempt to meet republican worries. His aide Teahon remembers Ahern saying: 'Look, what I now want to do is sit down with Sinn Fein, have all the issues that concern them on the table and negotiate this out, however long it takes.'

Everyone was, however, taken aback when Sinn Fein produced their list of concerns: it turned out to contain no fewer than 78 points on which they wanted answers from the two governments. This was doubly unwelcome, both for its unexpected scale and for the fact that exhaustion was setting in. Mowlam would recall: 'Four a.m. on the morning of the Good Friday talks, when we'd been negotiating hard for so long and people were so tired, and I can remember thinking, "This is a standstill, we're not moving."'

Blair prevailed on Mowlam to join Ahern in working towards a resolution of the outstanding Sinn Fein items. McGuinness described the scene in Castle Buildings: 'There were people passing one another in corridors. It was just like people rushing out of the Stock Exchange in New York trying to get to a telephone or pass on information before some other buyer; it was a frenetic negotiation.' To relieve the pressure, Mo Mowlam, who was supposed to be moving people from violence into politics, actually resorted to bringing an element of violence into the political system. She reminisced: 'I can remember going back and forth, back and forth, and the way I kept sane was to punch the security guards at one of the doors in their stomachs. The first time it got them, but the next time they had hardened their muscles and were used to it and were ready for it. That's how I dealt with a lot of the frustration that I had.'

Bertie Ahern would recall:

What did go on that night was that it looked as if Sinn Fein were not going to be part of it. I sat down with Martin McGuinness and Gerry Adams, taking all the questions they raised – there were reams of them about everything and anything. We had the entire Irish team working for hours on end, in the most detailed fashion that we could, with them feeding all those replies back to me as I went back through for hours on end into the night. I painfully went through every single one of those with them, arguing as passionately as I could for the benefits of doing a comprehensive deal. After that long night with them, I believed they would not be obstructionist towards the Agreement, that they would give it a chance. I thought they were on-side to a reasonable extent, I was happy.

By this stage, the people in the corridors included not just Sinn Fein figures but also the highest reaches of the IRA, the organisation's Army Council. British ministers were, as Mowlam confirms, dealing directly with the IRA: 'We sat down with Sinn Fein. We sat at one end and they brought in some people who were obviously members of the Army Council. You don't ask names – you just say hello and you get on with it.' Her disclosure is believed to represent the first time, at least since the 1970s, that a government minister admitted taking part in direct talks with the IRA.

One of the things Sinn Fein and the Army Council

wanted to clarify was the question of when the prisoners could expect to be released. This was one of the most sensitive of all the difficult issues to be covered in any agreement. The two governments had accepted in principle the argument that a major conflict could realistically not be brought to a close while leaving republicans and loyalists in prison: some of them were due to serve ten years or more. But little had been done to prepare the general public that the jails would be emptied. And while there was a tacit understanding between London and the republicans that the prisoners would at some stage be freed, there was no agreement on how long that process should take.

Gerry Kelly, who was an expert on prisons, having been behind bars for lengthy stretches in England, Northern Ireland, the Republic and Holland, posed the question: 'What I want to know is, when is the first prisoner getting out and when is the last prisoner getting out?' John Holmes outlined the government's position: 'We had said that three years was the most we could cope with, because we thought that was going to be very difficult to present as it was.' Martin McGuinness said flatly: 'The British government idea on this, the three-year period, wasn't acceptable.'

Blair was nervous about moving more quickly than the three-year period, as Sean Farren of the SDLP witnessed when he arrived at the prime Minister's room. He remembered: 'Blair, pointing to his aides Jonathan Powell and Alastair Campbell, said: "Well, these people are advising me that the one major issue on which I'm vulnerable in terms of comment on my side of the water is the prisoners' issue. I'm being pressed to agree to releases within a twelve-month period. I don't think that's possible."'

Another Blair aide, John Holmes, was to explain: 'It looked like softness, it looked like a concession to terrorism, we were going to have great difficulties in selling it. But we also knew, though, that if there was not this element there both for the loyalists and the IRA, that probably the Agreement was not going to succeed.'

At this point, the republicans made an unprecedented gambit. They approached their old enemies, the loyalist paramilitary groups, through their political wings, the Ulster Democratic party and Progressive Unionist party. Their idea was that republicans and loyalists could combine to shift Blair on the three-year release timetable, and together might get it down to one year.

A large contingent of loyalists were sitting in their offices when somebody came into the room and said: 'Gerry Kelly's coming down the corridor. He's looking for people.' Gary McMichael of the UDP recalled: 'A rap came to our door. Forty heads turned as I opened the door – and there were two members of Sinn Fein, one of whom was Gerry Kelly, standing at the door. He said: "Could I have a word with you?" I was quite shocked: the IRA killed my father. I didn't think it was a good idea to bring them in and sit them down in front of the other 39 people who were in the room, so we talked in the corridor.'

McMichael and David Ervine listened to Kelly, who recalled: 'I told the loyalists we had got the British down to two years on prisoner release, but if you join forces with us, together we can push them down to one year. If we take the same position, then we will have the prisoners out quite shortly. They said they'd discuss it with other loyalists and get back to me.'

The loyalists considered the approach. They too were

keen to get their imprisoned members out as quickly as possible, but they balked at doing so through cooperating with their traditional enemies. According to McMichael, they had an additional reason: 'We didn't want to push the boat out any further than it had to be, because we knew that that would throw the Ulster Unionist party off board. So we declined.' When Ervine set off for the Sinn Fein offices to convey this decision, he ran into Adams. 'I said, look, Gerry Kelly has just been down and asked me to push and shove the British government,' he recalled. 'I am saying we are not doing it.' Adams told Ervine he was missing a great opportunity.

Blair recalled:

I obviously said to Gerry and his colleagues, 'Look, to release people who have done terrible things, who have murdered policemen, who have killed innocent people, this is a difficult political thing for anyone to do and there will be a lot of people who will be shocked by that.' I think anyone feels a natural repugnance at the idea of allowing out early people who have taken the lives of other people and committed really hideous acts of terrorism against totally innocent people. They may accept it, very reluctantly, as part of a deal which is providing a new future for Northern Ireland – indeed, that was the only basis upon which I could accept it. So I explained fairly forcefully why that was a significant problem.

In the early hours of the morning of Good Friday, Blair called in transatlantic reinforcements. Bill Clinton remembered:

Tony Blair calls me and he says he needs some help with Gerry Adams. It was 12.30, one o'clock in the morning. I had told them they could call me any time and they took me at my word. My long-distance involvement in the Irish peace process was complicated by the time difference. They'd be up in the morning and I'd stay up all night – I felt like a college student pulling an all-nighter.

Tony Blair said they were getting close and George Mitchell was over there hammering away, and he said, 'We're getting close but, we can't get there.' One of the big sticking-points was the prisoner release issue. Tony was willing to do it, but he wanted to wait a couple of years, because he wanted some time for people to see the thing taking hold and both sides doing what they were supposed to do.

Clinton was well-informed on the details of talks since, in addition to Mitchell, he had a senior aide, Jim Steinberg, involved. On the prison issue Steinberg recalls: 'Gerry Adams believed that some of the strongest supporters for the peace process were the prisoners, and so having them out, having them on the street and able to advocate for the Agreement, was something that was gonna be very positive for the process.' When Clinton came on the line, Adams told him 'that the people who were most affected by British rule in this country had to see the prisoners home quickly. I told him basically that we weren't satisfied with the answers that we were getting on demilitarisation, on prisoners.' Steinberg remembers Adams saying to Clinton: 'When the war is over, the prisoners come home. That's why this is so important to me, that's why we need to have this happen quickly.'

According to Clinton's recollection:

I talked to Gerry Adams, he said they were making progress, he said some very nice things about Blair. He seemed to really trust him, which is always a good thing in these kinds of matters. But he said he just couldn't live with the two years, he said it was just too long, he had to show some progress. Gerry said that he needed the prisoners because that would help him to sell it to the IRA, because he still had people in the IRA who really didn't believe in the principle of consent, you know, they wanted to get out of Great Britain.

I joked with him, I told him that I thought he was gonna have to wait for the Catholic birth rate to change the electorate for that to happen. I said: 'Your numbers are getting better all the time.' I said, 'Gerry, you gotta understand this is a nightmare for Blair, because if there's any act of violence after any of these guys get out, he'll be accused of basically being made a dupe for murderers. And so it's hard for him, and the longer it gets to wait, the more he can point to acts of good faith which justify this clemency.'

So we talked about it, and I explained to him what those kind of issues looked like on the other side of the table. It's a very difficult issue if you see people who are in prison as terrorists rather than freedom fighters, this really all depends on what your view is. It's the same exact problem we have in the Middle East every time we have to try to make another incremental step there. So I knew it was tough for him, but I knew it was tough for Gerry too.

Adams was to remark later: 'We decided to sign off, and probably it was my call, in consultation with very, very close colleagues. The British were probably just chancing their arm anyway – you could argue that they could have even been moved further than that.'

16
Good Friday Agreement

By now it was 5 a.m. on Good Friday morning, and the vital arms issue had yet to be finally settled. A draft section dealing with weaponry was unacceptable to Sinn Fein, whose position was that no one should expect prior decommissioning. According to McGuinness: 'We made it clear that it would be a serious blunder for anyone to make a precondition of our participation in the executive an issue that decommissioning must take place.' McLaughlin went further: 'We were prepared to walk away from that negotiation. We made it very clear to them that if the original draft was held to, then Sinn Fein was away. This wouldn't work and we wouldn't be part of it.'

Blair described how the deadlock was broken: 'Gerry Adams had always said that if decommissioning were a precondition to joining the executive, then that was something they couldn't accept. But they accepted the obligation of decommissioning within the context of a process, and that is eventually the position that we came to.'

Adams was to recall:

It was a good conflict resolution, sensible, genuine way of dealing with this matter, that all of the parties would use their influences and their good offices, that all the parties would be committed to peaceful and democratic means. Don't form the impression that in some way the British government came at us with a huge amount of demands around this decommissioning issue and we beat them back. They didn't, they came with sensible suggestions on the issue. I discussed this with Martin McGuinness recently, and both of us had a very distinct recollection that the British government were very sensible about this issue.

Ahern described the Sinn Fein stance:

Sinn Fein had pledged they would do as much as they could to make it work, but they said they couldn't answer for the IRA and they couldn't negotiate for the IRA. They pledged that they would use their efforts to keep guns silent, to keep the ceasefire in place, and to build as much confidence as possible into the process going forward.

If we got an agreement, they would use their very best efforts and their very best persuasive powers to convince others. But they could not sign up for something that they just had no power of delivery over. So it was a question of getting what was available, and it just was not available to get them to sign up to arms that they had no control over. They just could not deliver an agreement that stated that we were going to get decommissioning upfront. They could not put that into an agreement, because it wasn't their call to do it. Equally so, Sinn Fein said that they were connected to these people, they knew these people, they could use their best efforts to convince these people.

Faced with this insistence, the final draft of the Agreement was watered down: it said decommissioning was indispensable, but it did not absolutely commit any group to delivering it; nor did it, crucially, lay down that the IRA must begin to decommission before Sinn Fein could enter a new government. The key section of the text declared:

All participants accordingly reaffirm their commitment to the total disarmament of all paramilitary organisations. They also confirm their intention to continue to work constructively and in good faith with the Independent Commission, and to use any influence they may have, to achieve the decommissioning of all paramilitary arms within two years following endorsement in referendums North and South of the Agreement and in the context of the implementation of the overall settlement.

There was a certain linkage between decommissioning and assuming office, but one was not dependent on the other. This point was vital. Unionists had gone into the talks determined to secure a watertight guarantee that republicans must decommission or face exclusion from the executive. Sinn Fein had gone in with the specific aim of giving no such assurance. The fact that the final outcome was ambiguous would later allow Trimble to argue that decommissioning was implicit in the final text; but it also allowed republicans to retort that no explicit promise was given.

McLaughlin assessed what republicans believed they had achieved by the early hours of Good Friday morning, when he was detailed to go out to the media: 'There was a general conclusion that we had got almost as much as we could reasonably expect, and that we were at a point where our responsibility to the peace process meant that we were having to swallow our spittle on some outstanding issues. Once we agreed on the formulation of what I would say to the cameras, I just went out and got some fresh air, just to get that clear in my head, because I knew that it was going to be a critically important moment.' He made it clear that Sinn Fein had dropped its objections to an assembly, a republican source later explaining privately: 'It was always tactical.' It had always made little sense to envisage any new agreement without a strong component in Belfast, since there had to be some institution to act as anchor for any new arrangements encompassing London and Dublin.

But as republicans were moving towards closure, the Ulster Unionists were continuing to agonise. Trimble returned to Castle Buildings on Good Friday morning, after snatching a few hours' sleep, to find that Sinn Fein had in effect negotiated their way into government without surrendering a single bullet. Furthermore, IRA and loyalist prisoners, many of them jailed for murder, would be walking the streets within two years. An unhappy Ulster Unionist delegation trooped up to see Blair. Donaldson implied that Blair had gone back on his word: 'I said to the prime minister, "You gave us an undertaking at Chequers that you would support us in having a clear requirement for progress on decommissioning to be made before those linked to terrorist organisations could take up office in the Assembly. That's not in the Agreement."'

According to Taylor: 'The prime minister said, "I know what your problems are, but I'm sorry we cannot change. This is the final document and you must either run with it or not." We said, "Well it looks as if we can't run with it." Empey recollected Blair arguing: 'You've got consent, you've got an assembly, you've got north-south institutions that you can live with and have a veto over. In other words, you've got all your principal objectives achieved.'

Trimble weighed in, recalling: 'The point that we were making to the prime minister was that there was a degree of linkage of decommissioning to holding office. But we were concerned about the way in which the linkage was going to operate.' Holmes recalled the scene: 'The prime minister listened to all this, but tried to explain, with some vehemence on his side because obviously he'd invested a huge amount in this process and felt very emotional about it himself, that they should concentrate on the big picture.' The Unionists told Blair they wanted some kind of guarantee in writing, and returned to their rooms to await his response. Holmes recalled: 'We couldn't change the text, but the prime minister nevertheless thought that he would try to devise some kind of side letter which would illustrate that we shared the concerns of the Unionists about decommissioning.'

Ken Maginnis said: 'I remember Tony Blair's officials were furious. I remember in particular Alastair Campbell, who was breathing fire and brimstone. He was literally seething that we had tied the prime minister personally to a guarantee in the form of a letter.' Empey recalled: 'At that point things looked pretty bleak. The atmosphere at the meeting was not good, and as we were leaving officials were shaking their heads, they looked very down. Alastair Campbell and people like that were lying slumped in chairs in despair at that stage – I think they probably felt after that meeting that things were going to crash.'

As Blair remembers that meeting:

The Unionists were in a lot of difficulties as to whether they were going to accept this or not. I said very strongly to them, 'Understand what this Agreement gives you, because it is so important to realise that you are Unionists, you are fighting for the Union, you are fighting for the principle of consent. It gives you this, it gives you an Assembly, it gives you the ability, for the first time in years, to look forward to some

sort of sensible and solid relationship within the United Kingdom that has the consent of all parts of the community in
Northern Ireland. Of course decommissioning is a part of
this process, but it is going to happen as part of the process
– to take it out and isolate it as the only issue I don't think
is sensible.'

We had been going at it for days, everyone was very tired,
most of us had had about two, three hours sleep in the last few
days and no sleep whatever the night before. I do remember at
a certain point in the meeting when I really thought they
were at the point of leaving – I really was concerned at one
point that they would just get up and walk out – I remember
actually getting up and saying to them, 'For goodness sake,
calm down, we will sort this out, there is a way through –
there has got to be, we haven't come this far to fail now.'

In the course of the meeting, it was suggested that I should
write them a letter that made it clear that if people did go
back to violence, if they were part of the Assembly and went
back to violence, and there were insufficient ways of getting
rid of people in those circumstances from the democratic
process once they had shown that they were not prepared to
abide by the democratic process, then we would review the
rules for that. So I gave them that assurance. Then we dictated
the letter, basically giving them the assurance that they
needed, and perfectly justifiably needed.

John Holmes recalled: 'We quickly devised a side letter,
which one of the secretaries hastily typed with the prime
minister standing over her shoulder, hastily signed it, gave
it to Jonathan Powell, who'd been operating as a link with
the Ulster Unionists, to take downstairs. All this was done
in such haste, I may say, that we don't have a proper copy
of that signed letter on our files, even now. It seems to

have helped to give David Trimble renewed heart to persuade his colleagues.'

Blair also rang Clinton and asked him to talk to Trimble. When the call came through, Ken Maginnis recalled people saying to Trimble, 'Tell him to put pressure on the Irish government, tell him that he must put pressure on the Irish government to give greater reassurances.'

Clinton remembered: 'I guess it was about mid-morning I called David Trimble, because Tony Blair had asked me to call him, and I encouraged him to support the deal.' Trimble would recall the phone call:

When he started to speak to me, I immediately broke into the conversation with him to say, 'Look, let me tell you what the up-to-date position is.' I told him what the problem was. I told him that there was a possible solution in terms of what the prime minister was planning to do. I said that if that solution is delivered, then we've got an agreement, but if it is to be delivered we need the Irish government and the SDLP to give us space for it to happen.

Clinton realised how high the stakes were for the Ulster Unionist leader:

I remember him telling me that he wouldn't be able to maintain his leadership position if it looked to his people as if he were being played for a fool on this decommissioning. He needed to be able to tell them that they could pull out of the process if it became a fraud in their eyes. I tried to give him enough reassurance so that he knew that we wouldn't just all cut his legs out from under him, without saying something that might later have an adverse impact on the peace process. And I think I threaded the needle about as well as I could.

US aide Steinberg remembered Trimble's concern: 'Trimble wanted the President's assurance that, if progress was not being made on decommissioning, or if there was a return to violence, the parties associated with that would not be able to sit in the government. So it would have the practical effect of giving Trimble the provision which he wasn't able to achieve in the formal Agreement itself.'

In the bleary-eyed early hours, many of those involved were experiencing physical as well as political discomfort, since the building had run out of food, drink and cigarettes. Seamus Mallon recalled snatching a few hours of sleep stretched out on a table, and then going to the canteen: 'I went down to get my breakfast – nothing left, couldn't get anything. Coffee machines were turned off, everything was cleared out of the canteen. I said at least I'll have a smoke: I went to the cigarette machine, empty, that was it.'

By this stage everyone was waiting for the Unionists, and growing aware that something close to a crisis was taking place in their offices. Martin McGuinness recalled: 'I ran into Martin Mansergh some time towards the middle of the day. There were intense debates and discussions taking place within the Ulster Unionist negotiating team. I said to Martin, "What's wrong now, what's the problem?" Mansergh told McGuinness: 'It's you, Martin – the fact that you're going to be in government.'

Ken Maginnis recalled the occasion: 'Everybody was terribly much on edge, everybody was very excited. I can remember Lord Alderdice of the Alliance party virtually – not quite, but virtually – ready to strike David Trimble. In the corridor, he was so viciously angry that we were, as he saw it, nit-picking, that we were delaying the process. I think he saw the possibility, we all did, that things could crumble. That's a huge difficulty for everyone, after years of negotiation.'

Trimble relived the moment when Powell arrived at the Unionist offices with the letter: 'Jonathan gave me the letter. I was standing there, starting to open it, when I saw John Taylor was coming up beside me, so I held it so that John could read at the same time as me. As we reached the end of the letter together John said: "Well, that's fine, we can run with that."'

The support of John Taylor for this position was a boost for David Trimble. The question was, however, whether it was enough to carry the day with the others, many of whom were extremely nervous. By this stage it was four o'clock in the afternoon of Good Friday. Maginnis had no doubt about the next move: 'I remember pointing out that if we walked away from the Agreement we couldn't come back tomorrow morning – we were actually turning our back at a defining moment in history.' The contrary view was put by Donaldson: 'I just felt that the discussions were going nowhere, that we were not going to get the kind of safeguards and the changes to the text of the Agreement,' he said.

Trimble remembered the different opinions in his party: 'From the discussion, it was clear that there was a consensus, but that it wasn't unanimous. What wasn't clear to me at that stage was that the reservations were of such a radical nature that they would lead people to walk out.'

Maginnis remembered:

People knew that we hadn't got as much of our wish-list as we would want. They knew that if we walked away we would be surrendering things that we did want. And so there was this balancing act. Eventually we took a quiet moment again, we looked through it, and I remember saying to David: 'Well, David, I'll accept it.' And he looked round and he said: 'I'm going to accept it.' And there was comparative silence; one or two people nodded, and then Jeffrey Donaldson said he wouldn't accept it. It was difficult, I remember we were all emotionally drained at that moment, there were people who were close to tears.

Maginnis, who had had many colleagues killed by the IRA and had himself been the target of several assassination attempts, was able to contemplate a new beginning. He said:

I remember going out and pleading with Jeffrey that we could build on this, we'd got the basis, we'd tied terrorists to a democratic process and he had to think of his two little children. I didn't succeed. There were none of us who were totally convinced we'd done the right thing. Yet we could not, after all that time, find an alternative.

If you are in a negotiating process there are no absolutes, and one of Jeffrey's difficulties has been with the literal translation. That's my biggest frustration in politics – that Unionism believes in absolutes, that Unionism believes its own propaganda and hence weakens its negotiating position. Being based on a fairly strict Protestant ethos, everything that you do that brings you close to what is seen as the evil in society, is a minus, it's a negative force.

Empey explained his motivation in accepting the Agreement:

We had been dying death by a thousand cuts for 30 years. Unionism had been excluded from the decision-making process since 1972. Throughout that period, direct rule had worked against Unionism. Terrorism had gone on. Policy decisions had been taken on a whole range of issues that were not in the interests of Unionism.

My argument was simple. If this all collapses, do we not prove that Northern Ireland is a failed political entity? How do you put together circumstances again when Unionism can negotiate from any strength? Instability works against Unionism. It drives people out. It sends our students away. It weakens our economy and therefore weakens the Union. However difficult it is with emotional issues such as prisoners, my argument was that we had to look at the bigger picture issues in the long term.

Trimble rang Blair, John Holmes recalling: 'David Trimble phoned the prime minister and said that the way was clear now for the Agreement to go ahead, that he'd managed to persuade his colleagues, with some difficulty. The plenary session – which George Mitchell had been itching to call for about ten hours at that stage – quickly convened. All the other parties were mightily relieved, as were we.'

Elsewhere in the building, Mitchell waited to hear from Trimble that his party was prepared to join the others in signing-off the document. Then came the call he had hoped for: 'At 4.45 the phone rang. It was David Trimble. He said to me, "We're ready to do the business."'

Unknown to many of the other delegates in the building, four of David Trimble's advisory team had left the complex before Mitchell convened the final session. They included Donaldson and some of the 'baby barristers'. They did not, however, stage a dramatic exit, Donaldson remembering: 'I informed the leader that I was returning to my constituency. It wasn't a walkout, in the sense that the negotiations had been concluded anyway. I just felt that the terms of this Agreement were unacceptable. I was devastated,' he said.

At 5 p.m. that day, 10 April 1998, Good Friday, George Mitchell was able to say: 'I'm pleased to announce that the two governments and the political parties of Northern Ireland have reached agreement. The Agreement proposes changes in the Irish Constitution and in British constitutional law to enshrine the principle that it is the people of Northern Ireland who will decide, democratically, their own future.'

Martin McGuinness noticed a small but significant piece of behaviour by Trimble when the parties gathered together. He said:

At the table he had a pencil in his hand. We all had these intercom systems in front of us, and when we had to speak we had to press a button and a red light would come on. David was uneasy, and rather than push the button with his finger he hit it with the pencil. From that stage on I knew that we had problems. He said yes, but it was a very conditional yes, and I could sense that we were gonna have great difficulty up the road implementing the Agreement that we had just agreed.

It was a historic moment: during seven months of negotiations, Sinn Fein and the Ulster Unionists had not directly spoken to each other. Dialogue had been confined to the occasional brief exchange in the toilets: now they had agreed to go into government together. The sense of breakthrough was tempered by feelings of relief and exhaustion. Blair lost no time in departing, as Holmes recalled: 'The plenary actually went on while everybody thanked George Mitchell and all the officials for their help. But we'd left by that stage. The final statements were gone, and we jumped into our helicopter and fled.'

Mallon had a reminder of how much was at stake when he went outside the building to meet the media: 'The first person I was interviewed by is actually from Northern Ireland. I could see the tears in his eyes as he was doing the interview – it was quite remarkable to see a hard-bitten, very experienced journalist actually with tears in his eyes, and I suppose it was only then that we began to realise the enormity of what had happened in the hours beforehand.'

17
Guns and government

This historic Agreement was a lengthy document, which attempted nothing less than the creation of a whole new political dispensation. The idea was to convince everyone that a level playing field was being provided as the basis on which Northern Ireland politics and Anglo–Irish relations would be conducted in the future. The document was full of ingenious formulations, which together provided a closely interlocking system designed to take account of all the political relationships within Northern Ireland, between north and south and between Britain and Ireland.

The accord defined consent as requiring that the people of Northern Ireland would decide whether Northern Ireland stayed with Britain or joined a united Ireland. It provided for a rewriting of the Irish Constitution to remove the southern claim to the territory of Northern Ireland. It provided for a new 108-member Belfast Assembly, to which Westminster would devolve full power over areas such as education, health and agriculture, including the right to make new laws. London would retain responsibility for matters such as defence and law and order, though it promised to consider devolving security powers at a later stage.

There would be a Unionist First Minister, and a Deputy First Minister who would be a nationalist, with up to ten departmental ministers. The ten ministries would be allocated in proportion to party strengths, on an agreed mathematical formula. A battery of safeguards was built into the Assembly's rules to ensure that important decisions needed the support of both Unionist and nationalist members. A powerful committee system would shadow each government department, with committee chairs and membership again in proportion to party strengths.

The Assembly was to be linked with London, Dublin, Scotland and Wales by a new constitutional architecture. A British–Irish council would be established, consisting of representatives of both governments and of the new devolved institutions in Northern Ireland, Scotland and Wales. There was to be a new British–Irish agreement and a north-south ministerial council, with associated implementation bodies, to develop cooperation on an all-Ireland basis. Major new commissions would review policing and emergency legislation. New bodies would safeguard human rights and equality.

The nationalist and republican community did not take long to give its general endorsement, but the Agreement produced deep divisions within the Ulster Unionist party and, unsurprisingly, outright hostility from Paisley. Trimble secured his party's support, but some important party figures such as Donaldson strongly opposed it.

The next step came with the holding of simultaneous referendums, north and south, in May 1998, to give approval to the Agreement. Catholics were well over 90 per cent in favour, north and south, but there was much agonising within the Protestant community. In the end it split down the middle, with around half of Unionists voting Yes in the referendum and around half voting No. The final outcome was an overwhelming endorsement in the south, and a 71 per cent Yes vote in the north. This was more than many of the Agreement's supporters had dared hope for, and amounted to a solid vote for the accord. Yet at the same time the outcome contained an imbalance, in that the 71 per cent was made up of virtually 100 per cent nationalist voters but only half of Unionists. The stage was thus set for yet another chapter in the familiar running battle between Unionist moderates and hard-liners.

The frankest account which David Trimble has ever given publicly of his own analysis of both the republican and Unionist positions was in a speech he delivered to a conference of Young Unionists in late 1998. It gives a unique insight into his thoughts and his actions:

The event that has caused the greatest problems to Unionists in recent years is the adoption by the republican movement of a different political approach. When the republican movement was wholly involved in terrorism, it was simple enough: we knew what we were dealing with, we had lived with it year in, year out, and our response was straightforward and simple. But then they changed their approach. Now we can discuss it, analyse it and argue about the nature of that change. Was it just as republicans would now represent it? Or was it a series of changes as they adjusted to events as they happened?

It was a shock to many Unionists who were accustomed to the ongoing terrorist campaign and had categorised Sinn Fein and the republican movement simply as mindless terrorists. But we ought to bear in mind that the campaign of violence was not going to go on for ever – it was always going to end at some point. Now, we would have liked to see it end in the unambiguous defeat of terrorism, but the ending has not, so far, been clear-cut.

Indeed, there is reason to believe that the reason for the change of approach by the republican movement was precisely because its leadership could see that their campaign was failing. Undoubtedly, the IRA were not winning. They could do damage, but they could not 'drive the British out.'

The republican movement thought that their war of attrition would eventually bring about disengagement of the British government. Behind the change in policy or tactics by the republican movement in the early '90s was a realisation that their campaign was failing, and that if the campaign continued, then their only future was the slow decline and extinction of that campaign. I think that they decided that, while the campaign still had some life in it, they would try and cash it in for political advantage – some political concession or developments. That, basically, is the origin of the so-called peace process, the Hume–Adams process, call it what you will.

A number of responses were possible to the changed situation. I remember a parliamentary colleague saying at the time that we should simply adopt a particular position and then present 'a stone face' to the opposition. In effect, he was saying we should not try to achieve anything, and revert to saying No all the time. I can remember when it was believed in this party that, if we closed down the avenues that government was trying to explore, they would then be driven back to what we believed to be the only valid position that could be adopted, to the particular outcome we wanted, because there would be no other way they could go.

The important point that I draw from this, generally speaking, is that it is not good enough to be passive, to adopt a tactic or approach that consciously or deliberately leaves the decision in the hands of other people. At the end of the day, the more sensible thing to do is to be seriously engaged. You cannot be a spectator, you cannot be someone who deals purely with an idealised situation or a situation as you would want it. You have to engage with it as it is. It is not always the way you like, and you can never be certain exactly how it is going to work out, but you have to engage.

Even with such cynicism around, however, the sense of a new era was in the air, many feeling that nothing would ever be quite the same again. The Agreement and the referendum vote did not defeat traditional tribalism, but the 71 per cent vote represented, potentially at least, the emergence of a new majority in favour of making a deal.

Elections to the new Assembly in June produced a solid pro-Agreement majority. There were strong showings for the SDLP and Sinn Fein, but the vote again revealed a divided Ulster Unionist party. The party won the largest number of seats, but its lowest ever share of the vote, with Paisley and other anti-Agreement elements only two per cent behind Trimble. When the assembly met, Trimble was elected as First Minister designate in readiness for the devolution of power, with Seamus Mallon of the SDLP elected Deputy First Minister designate.

July brought yet more confrontation when the annual Drumcree march was banned and loyalist protests broke out across Northern Ireland. Several days of roadblocks and riots came to a head when one of many petrol-bombing incidents led to tragedy, three young boys dying in a fire started by a loyalist petrol bomb thrown into their house. The protesters were chastened and the disturbances quickly petered out. The lull did not last long, due to the actions of a small republican splinter group. Although most nationalists supported the Agreement, a small number of republicans held that Sinn Fein, and indeed the

IRA, were selling out on their traditional positions. Some of these people went on to form political groups, such as the 32 County Sovereignty Movement, while others formed a violent group calling itself 'the Real IRA'.

One of those active in these circles was Bernadette Sands-McKevitt, sister of hunger striker Bobby Sands. She spelt out her opposition to the Agreement:

It's not addressing the core issue, which is the British claim of jurisdiction over the six north-eastern counties. Until Britain relinquishes that claim, I feel that we're not ever going to see a peace process that is going to actually work. There was nothing in the Agreement to suggest that there was a stepping-stone approach to a united Ireland. The Agreement was very explicit, there were numerous sections spelling out very clearly that, in its words, Northern Ireland was an inextricable part of the United Kingdom until the majority decided otherwise. Which in layman's terms was the Unionist veto.

While she and others denied that the 32 County Sovereignty Movement had anything to do with the Real IRA, the authorities on both sides of the border believed it was the political wing of the new organisation. The Real IRA was small in number, but it included some seasoned republican activists in its ranks. The most prominent of these was its chief of staff, who as quartermaster general of the mainstream IRA had led a few members in a walkout in protest against the peace process.

The Real IRA, though small, was to prove particularly dangerous. It launched a series of bombing attacks on towns across Northern Ireland, culminating in August 1998 in the incident which is regarded as one of the most tragic of the troubles. Following misleading warnings, a car bomb exploded in the County Tyrone town of Omagh on a busy Saturday afternoon, killing 29 people. Its impact was all the greater since it came so unexpectedly, at a time when most presumed that violence was tailing off. The dead were all civilians, among them Protestants, Catholics and two Spanish visitors, and included young, old and middle-aged, fathers, mothers, sons, daughters and grand-mothers. Unborn twins also died.

Although at first there was speculation that the attack might spell the end of the peace process, it became evident within days that it had made most politicians more, rather than less, determined to go on. In its aftermath the British and Irish governments hurried through tough new security measures, with Westminster and the Dáil recalled from summer recess to pass the necessary legislation. A fortnight after the explosion Clinton and Blair visited Omagh, meeting around 700 of the injured and relatives of the dead and injured.

Sinn Fein had long declared that it did not take part in what it called the politics of condemnation, but in the wake of Omagh, Adams broke new ground in what he said: 'This action was wrong. I hope that the people involved will reflect on the enormity of what they have done. I would like whoever is responsible to accept that responsibility in a public statement and I want them to cease. I want them to stop.' The Omagh incident did not spell the end of the Real IRA, but it did the organisation much damage. Attacks which cause military casualties can impress potential republican recruits, but the fact that all those killed in Omagh were civilians did nothing to increase the group's reputation. An IRA source said: 'Had these people connected and taken out five or six soldiers or police in some of their attacks, we could not have stopped our young people from joining them.'

September brought renewed political activity, with Trimble agreeing to his first-ever direct contact with Adams. They met behind closed doors, the fact that they spoke, but did not shake hands, pointedly indicating that although new relationships were emerging they were accompanied by neither friendship nor trust. The hopes of the international community that a lasting settlement was on the way were symbolised by the Nobel Peace Prize conferred jointly on Hume and Trimble.

In 1999 the peace process stayed on track, but everything moved much more slowly than most of its supporters had hoped. Decommissioning remained an unresolved issue, with Unionists insisting on its centrality, while nationalists and republicans argued it was being given too high a priority. Various parts of the Good Friday Agreement were implemented, including the setting up of cross-border bodies and a new Human Rights Commission. Yet the devolution of power from Westminster to the Assembly did not take place, being held up throughout the year by the decommissioning issue. Several intensive negotiating sessions attended by Blair and Ahern failed to make a breakthrough.

The Ulster Unionists refused to go into government with Sinn Fein because the IRA had not given up any weapons. Trimble encapsulated the policy when he declared: 'The position of the Ulster Unionist party is and will remain – simple little phrase, you've heard it before today – no guns, no government.' The Sinn Fein position was that republicans were prepared to talk about decommissioning, but would not contemplate delivering up guns, certainly not in advance of the formation of an administration.

The summer of 1999 brought renewed questioning of whether republicans were genuine about peace when the

IRA was blamed for the killing of a West Belfast man, and for an attempt to smuggle in guns from America. These incidents gave rise to a formal government judgement in August, by Mowlam, on the state of the IRA cessation. She said she had 'come very close to judging that the IRA's ceasefire is no longer for real' but added: 'I do not believe that there is a sufficient basis to conclude that the IRA ceasefire has broken down. Nor do I believe that it is disintegrating, or that these recent events represent a decision by the organisation to return to violence. The peace we have now is imperfect, but better than none.'

Blair said with some frustration: 'We've got everything there ready to go, we've decided the principle of consent, the changes to the Irish constitution, the Assembly is there, the north-south bodies are there ready to run – we've got everything there, ready to go.' Clinton, too, was impatient and irritated. During a visit to Canada he told an audience: 'I spend an enormous amount of time trying to help the people in the land of my forebears in Northern Ireland to get over 600 years of religious fights. And every time they make an agreement to do it, they're like a couple of drunks walking out of a bar for the last time. When they reach the swinging doors they turn right round and go back in and say – "I just can't quite get there."'

To break the impasse, the British and Irish governments turned to ex-Senator George Mitchell and asked him to return to Belfast to conduct a review in the autumn of 1999. He reassembled the political parties at Castle Buildings, to look for a way of ending the stalemate and getting them into government. Mitchell was to recall: 'The first meetings were disastrous – angry, harsh recrimination – "You're a liar" – "Don't call me a liar."' One close observer said: 'At the start it was almost like *In the Psychiatrist's Chair*, with people offloading their grievances about the summer and how they felt they'd been hurt by the other side.'

Trimble remembers: 'There was just a lot of argument about who had done what to whom at one time or another.' His colleague, Sir Reg Empey, also pitched in: 'We argued that we hadn't engaged in a 30-year war – we hadn't caused people to disappear, we hadn't buried bodies in the beaches. We said privately to George Mitchell that really, if we went on with any more of these the review would collapse.' Mitchel McLaughlin of Sinn Fein summed it up: 'No discussion, no dialogue and no trust.'

Mitchell then experimented to see whether a change of scenery might bring about an improvement in the atmosphere. He moved some sessions to London, to a US-owned mansion there, Winfield House, residence of the American Ambassador to Britain. In the Regent's Park grandeur of the house the delegates could meet in its ornate splendour and could walk in its eleven-acre grounds.

Things did not all go smoothly at Winfield House, and at one point Mitchell was on the point of admitting defeat. Mallon recalled: 'He asked to see me and I went into his office. He said, "I'm writing my failure speech." It was as serious as that – there he was writing it.' McGuinness recalled another occasion: 'I could see that George, who normally was very sensible and commonsense about his approach, was showing signs of frustration. On one memorable occasion he said to Gerry Adams and myself, "You guys have a life and this is it. I have a life and this is not it."'

But the switch to Winfield House began to pay dividends, as an element of social mixing took place. Mitchell remembered: 'I insisted that there not be any discussion of issues at the meals, that we just talk about other things. So they could come to view each other not as adversaries but as human beings, and as people living in the same place and the same society and wanting the same thing.'

Ken Maginnis recalled:

George Mitchell would work with intensive discussions until dinner time, and then he would have us in to dinner, so really for the first time some of us were sitting down, socially, inverted commas, with Sinn Fein-IRA. It was a strange experience. Once George looked at Martin McGuinness, and then he looked at me and he'd say, 'You two must be related – Maginnis, McGuinness – there must be a relationship?' And I remember saying to him, 'I know mine's the Celtic name – Martin's is the Anglo–Irish.'

Martin McGuinness laughed, and maybe for the first time I saw him ever really laugh. Let me put it like this, it probably didn't change Martin McGuinness's attitude to me: he sees me as part of the establishment. It doesn't change my attitude to him: I see him as the active IRA man. What it probably does is demonstrate that if we hadn't been such poles apart, we might actually have been able to laugh together, to talk together. It didn't make a personal change for us, but I think it could perhaps have given us a vision for the future. Our children, or our children's children, perhaps won't have this animosity and distrust.

McGuinness, recalling the same exchange, commented: 'Ken trying to claim that he was more Irish than I was – I thought it was grand, it was great. Eventually, as the conversations moved on, Ken brought in photographs of his grandchildren and showed them to me, and talked to me about his family and about his son. That was probably the first real sensible conversation that I had had with Ken Maginnis, even though I'd heard about him and known about him for many years. So that was progress.'

Adams related a semi-comic moment when, tongue-in-cheek, he suggested: 'Look, I think what we should all do is just stand up, forget about this and give each other a great big hug. Which shocked the Unionists – and Martin McGuinness, who immediately made it clear that I wasn't speaking on his behalf.'

But the new atmosphere at Winfield House gradually thawed the relationships, and Mitchell put his 'failure speech' to one side. At first, Trimble, ever nervous about carrying his divided party with him, brought large delegations along, trooping in with teams of seven or more Unionists. Mitchell intervened, however, to suggest that give-and-take would only realistically occur with much smaller numbers.

In the end Mitchell got what he wanted, talks involving only two from each side. The main discussions were therefore contracted to Trimble and Empey, with the republican side represented by Adams and McGuinness. As the weeks went by, Mitchell was encouraged by what he witnessed: 'There developed not a sense of trust – one delegate later said that trust crept in, but I think that was probably overstating it – but a sense of realistic understanding that they were in this together. Gerry Adams said to David Trimble: "We know you're our best chance; and we want you to know that we're your best chance."'

A government source commented: 'The body language changed after Winfield. Before that it was always stiff and stilted, but afterwards they no longer seemed instinctively uncomfortable in each other's presence. Winfield was the psychological breakthrough.' But increasing familiarity played a large part too. Over the ten weeks of the talks the two sides had close to 300 hours of face-to-face meetings. This statistic is rendered all the more remarkable by the fact that Trimble and Adams spoke together for the first time only in September of the previous year.

The exercise worked, producing an agreed sequence of moves by the two sides and the two governments. Trimble reached a decision that he needed a variation on his party's familiar mantra of 'no guns, no government', arriving at the conclusion that the IRA was simply not going to decommission weapons simultaneously with the formation of a new executive. He was to say: 'It's the syndrome of whether the bottle is half-full or half-empty, and a question of whether you actually want things to proceed, or at the end of the day your basic preference is not to make progress.' Instead of guns upfront, he settled instead for the idea of statements from the IRA and Sinn Fein, reiterating the republican commitment to the peace process and confirming that the IRA would appoint a go-between to meet the international disarmament commission headed by Canadian General John de Chastelain.

Though this fell well short of a formal guarantee of IRA decommissioning, the calculation was that republicans would be universally censured if they pocketed Trimble's concessions while simply stonewalling on the arms issue. The republicans gave no actual promise on decommissioning, but those who dealt with them felt they realised it was necessary for Trimble's survival. Mitchell recalled: 'I told Sinn Fein that I felt that there had to be progress on decommissioning at an early date. Otherwise Trimble would not be able to sustain his position within the Ulster Unionist party, that he was stretching himself to go this far, and without some reciprocal action he would not be able to continue.'

October had brought a new player to the scene with the arrival of Peter Mandelson, as a Northern Ireland Secretary who was known to be a close friend and confidant of Blair. Unionists were glad to see the departure of Mowlam, whom they accused of being pro-nationalist, and looked for a more sympathetic ear from the new man. Mandelson spent much time with Trimble's deputy, John Taylor. He recalled Taylor's concerns:

One was the familiar one, which was, 'If it all goes wrong, we'll be locked into this executive without any progress on decommissioning.' The big question for them was, if they do this, and it gives a chance, what happens if it goes wrong? Are they going to be left to carry the can by themselves? And I was able to give them a very firm assurance that if a political crisis was sparked by the absence of decommissioning by the IRA, and the institutions were threatened, then we in the British government would step in and assume our responsibilities.

Taylor recalls receiving an assurance: 'Peter said, "Look, I would not run away from the necessity of the suspension of the Agreement."'

To put Mandelson's assurances to an early test, Trimble turned to a stratagem. Taylor remembers Trimble outlining it to him: 'He explained to me that he was going to try out his idea of a post-dated letter, whereby he and therefore all the Ulster Unionist ministers would automatically resign by the end of January 2000 if there had not been progress in the Assembly, and especially by IRA-Sinn Fein, on the issue of decommissioning.' Many in the party were sceptical, with Jeffrey Donaldson as usual numbered among the sceptics: 'I asked David Trimble if he had received any private assurances from republicans about decommissioning; he told me he hadn't. I asked him about the timetable for decommissioning, when he anticipated that it would actually begin, and he indicated to me that he expected the republicans would mark the new millennium with a start to decommissioning. I told David that I didn't think this was enough.'

Nonetheless, in November 1999 Trimble convinced his party's ruling council to go into government without prior decommissioning. This was a momentous turning-point, though the fact that he won the vote by 480 votes to 349, with 42 per cent of the party opposed to him, underlined yet again that he headed a deeply divided party which harboured serious doubts about his chosen course. Trimble also built in the post-dated letter of resignation, both as a fail-safe device and as a device to persuade the many waverers in his party's ranks. Peter Mandelson said of the letter: 'I didn't know David Trimble was going to do that. It came as a surprise to me on that morning, but I understood in a sense why he was doing it, with a party that was reluctant to jump. What he was doing, in effect, was putting in a safety net.'

On 1 December devolution was restored at midnight to Northern Ireland. One year and seven months after the Good Friday Agreement was signed, it could be at last implemented. In Dublin the Irish government altered their constitution, replacing the territorial claim over Northern Ireland. Mandelson described the very different moods in Dublin and Belfast:

We were all gathered in the great hall of the Department of Foreign Affairs in Dublin and there was champagne flowing, and crowds of people and children. It was a grand occasion – it was as if we were re-signing the Treaty of Versailles all over again, and it was very exciting.

Then I went back straight to Belfast, just to make sure everything was running smoothly there. The contrast couldn't have been more stark – I mean, there was a sort of nervousness, people were afraid to smile, as if they were holding their breath – pleased that it was happening but just waiting for it to collapse at any moment.

Most attention was concentrated on Sinn Fein chief negotiator Martin McGuinness, whose appointment as education minister generated political shock waves. The elevation of a one-time street fighter who left school at the age of 15 was greeted with gasps in the Assembly chamber, and caused a general stir.

To the surprise of many, McGuinness and the other ministers seemed to settle in well to the working of their departments, though for many the most important question remained whether, and when, decommissioning might begin. In December, de Chastelain's International Decommissioning Body issued an upbeat report. In the same month Mandelson met Adams, remembering: 'We talked about how things were going, and I said that we needed progress on decommissioning if we were going to keep the whole thing in the air.' Adams's reply was not upbeat: 'I certainly told Peter Mandelson it was nonsense to think that after 18 months of an impasse, 18 months of no institutions, that they're put together in December, there's a break for Christmas and it's to be sorted out by January and February.' Mandelson said: 'He was rather discouraging to me, and said that he really didn't think that we were going to get any substantive shift on decommissioning by the end of January. In fact, he said it would be rather lucky if we had anything by the end of May.'

In January 2000 de Chastelain reported that the IRA had done nothing about getting rid of their weapons. The next day Mandelson met the new Irish foreign minister, Brian Cowen, to tell him he might have to suspend the Northern Ireland institutions. Cowen was dead against this:

I said to Peter Mandelson, 'Look, let's not pull the curtains down here immediately, because if you decide you are going to suspend the institutions that the nationalists have been waiting for for 30 years, what impact does one think that's going to have in the nationalist community? Let's recognise that the potential within the de Chastelain report, that it's not all black, it's not all gloom. There are ongoing negotiations, and let's see can we firm up a declaration of intent by the paramilitaries.'

According to Mandelson, Cowen was buying time: 'He had just been appointed foreign minister, it was his first job and it was a major crisis, with the whole peace process possibly blowing up in front of us. So he asked me for more time. He took more time, he got his officials talking to Sinn Fein. I spent the next two weeks just piling on the pressure for him, that they had actually to deliver something.'

On the night before the deadline of 11 February, Sinn Fein leaders met a number of Irish officials at a West Belfast house. Martin McGuinness says: 'We presented them with an advanced position which would give General de Chastelain an opportunity to come out with a positive report.' Paddy Teahon, who represented Taoiseach Bertie Ahern, regarded this as a major advance: 'What was now on the table was, for the first time, a clear-cut commitment from the IRA to put their arms beyond use.'

But there was a context, which might well be a catch. The arms would be put beyond use only when the parties to the Agreement had removed the causes of conflict. That could mean many things: indeed, it could be interpreted as signifying that the causes of conflict primarily sprang from the British presence. According to Adams, the Irish civil servants had a goal: 'What the officials tried to do was to get the IRA to accept that the Good Friday Agreement would remove the cause of conflict.' Gerry Kelly recalled: 'It came down to the Irish government pushing the boat on it and Sinn Fein saying, "Look, this is what the IRA have decided, we don't have the leeway to negotiate."' McGuinness concurs: 'It was made clear to the Irish government officials that this was the most advanced position we could achieve and what they now had to do was talk to the British.'

In the early hours, Teahon judged he had pushed things as far as they would go, recalling: 'At half past three in the morning we came to the view that, yes, this was so significant, in terms of the IRA saying they would put their arms beyond use, that we really should give it every opportunity, even though it's not the full agenda as far as we were concerned.'

Some hours later Ahern telephoned Blair to convey that in his judgement this was the furthest the IRA had ever moved and they should regard it as a major opportunity. On the morning of 11 February there was frantic telephone trafficking between London and Dublin.

In Washington, in the weeks leading up to suspension, the American administration had been trying to help. Clinton remembers:

We were all working like crazy to get everybody to do what had to be done to avoid the suspension. I thought we'd gone to all this trouble, they stood up to this government, they're working along – I even had a couple of the people in the Unionist community tell me that Martin McGuinness was doing a good job as the Education Minister.

And I had McGuinness bragging to me that he'd given the schools with the Protestant kids in them at least as much, if not more, money per cápita than he'd done with the Catholic kids, and how fair he was being. They were all so proud of themselves, that they were showing up and acting like normal people and doing their real jobs. So I saw it working, and I was frustrated and worried and a little bit angry that anybody would not do whatever it took to keep the process going.

Mandelson recalls: 'The fax came in that morning at 10.45 from Number 10, and I spoke to the prime minister immediately. We both agreed that it was a good sign, it was encouraging. It represented some progress in the right direction – but it was David Trimble and his colleagues who needed to be satisfied, they needed to be convinced by it.' Mandelson claims his hands were tied by the IRA's insistence that a wording they had put forward should not be disclosed to Trimble. Mandelson had the IRA wording but, he recalls: 'I couldn't give it to him, I couldn't even describe it to him, I couldn't read it out over the phone to him. I just had to offer a description of its sort of shape rather than its precise content.'

All the time, however, the Trimble letter of resignation was poised to be delivered. Trimble remembered: 'Round about lunch there'd been a phone call from the Secretary of State in which he was saying in very general terms that he hoped something was happening. But he was not at that stage in a position to tell me what was happening.' Mandelson recalls the First Minister's response: 'David said, "Well, what am I getting here? This is a sort of pig in a poke. I have got to see something in writing. I have got to see the text, and I have got to know from the horse's mouth what it is exactly they now think that they are proposing to do."'

The First Minister then heard that McGuinness wanted to see him. He said: 'I wasn't then surprised when Martin McGuinness requested a meeting, and I immediately facilitated him.' On his arrival, McGuinness said the IRA would not allow him to disclose their new position. But, according to Trimble, McGuinness made demands: 'He needed more time, no question of resignation and no question of Unionist Council meetings. Now, particularly the last one was not something that was in the real world at all.' McGuinness remembered:

I explained the position that in my view very shortly there was going to be – imminently, that day – a report from General de Chastelain that I believed was a report that he could live with. I also told him that the sword of Damocles that the Ulster Unionist Council held over the process had to be removed, that it was absolutely vital that we got away from this continual sense of crisis these meetings had imposed on the process. He certainly listened very carefully to what I had to say, but because he didn't speak that much that clearly told me plenty – that he wasn't in any way enthused by what he had heard.

Trimble's position was that he had heard nothing concrete from McGuinness: 'He didn't tell me anything other than saying that they were working on it. They thought they could sort it out, but they needed a few more weeks.'

Adams argued that the IRA was inhibited because the organisation's members had not yet been briefed on what was being put on offer. He said: 'For the IRA's position to have been released or made public without its grassroots having had the opportunity to engage in the issue, and certainly without there being some sense of quid pro quo from others, would have been a total disaster.'

The Irish government was exasperated, Brian Cowen contending: 'The idea that we could get a decisive final outcome on this issue that evening, on the basis of a deadline set by the Unionist party, was simply not going to happen.' As the day wore on, tensions mounted. Trimble had lodged his letter of resignation with his party chairman, Sir Josias Cunningham, and the impression was given that he was about to deliver it to Mandelson at any moment. Adams recalled the mood: 'This letter took on a life of its own. This letter which David had given to Josias Cunningham was making its way towards Stormont, and as every hour went past we would get a phone call from somewhere saying Josias was approaching.'

Trimble's position was that suspension should be done in time for news of the move to be broadcast on the Friday evening six o'clock news. He explained: 'We had delegates who would be travelling early on the Saturday morning, and news bulletins on Saturday are few and far between. There was the very real fact that, unless there was something clearly in the public domain on Friday afternoon or evening which people would hear then, there would be a very serious management problem for us on Saturday morning.'

During the afternoon of 11 February Tony Blair called the Sinn Fein president and warned him that suspension was inevitable. Adams immediately phoned Ahern's office.

Paddy Teahon recalls that moment, which he felt was a dramatic turning-point: 'Gerry Adams had phoned to say that the IRA were at last prepared to put their position to John de Chastelain without conditions.' Ahern contacted Blair, according to Irish foreign minister Brian Cowen: 'The Taoiseach rang Tony Blair to indicate this further improvement in the position, and stating: "Look, there's an unencumbered, unconditional statement here which we have been trying to obtain during the course of today. It's happened – let's not press the button." But the button unfortunately had been pressed.'

After five o'clock, Mandelson took the action of suspending the executive, indicating that he found this regrettable but inevitable. Mandelson spent the evening dashing round television studios explaining and defending his action. From then on he was viewed by nationalists and republicans as, in effect, a villain who had aligned himself with Unionism and brought down valuable institutions.

The sense of frustration was sharp in Dublin, where Ahern's aide Teahon became involved in an angry conversation with Blair. He said:

There was a real sense of upset on the Irish side at what had happened by way of suspension. We were disappointed in the way it was presented by Peter Mandelson that evening, especially on BBC *Newsnight*. When the Taoiseach was speaking to Tony Blair that evening he passed the phone to me. I have to say I was in a moment of real frustration at all the efforts we had made, and I feel that I expressed that frustration very strongly to the prime minister.

I said, 'Prime Minister, look, we have spent days, virtually 24 hours a day, negotiating with the republicans. We have a really significant shift in the IRA position, and if we're not careful this position is going to get lost, and I would appeal to you not to lose this opportunity and not to throw away what we have got now from the IRA.'

Blair remembers his conversation with Ahern:

The difficulty was, as I explained, that it had come so late and that David Trimble had taken quite a risk going through that Mitchell process a few months before. It was not five to twelve, but five past twelve, by the time the Irish statement came through, and it was then impossible really for David Trimble to draw back from where he was.

I explained that I thought the choice really, very simply, was letting David Trimble go, which I thought would be disastrous for the process, or just understanding we were going to have to suspend and then try and revisit the situation. Now of course Bertie didn't want the suspension, perfectly understandably from his point of view, but we agreed we would just have to find a way through, which indeed we did.

The following week, Sinn Fein leaders met Mandelson. McGuinness recalled: 'We told Peter Mandelson that he had made a huge mistake, and we believed that he would live to regret that mistake.' Pat Doherty remembered: 'He had this arrogant air of, "Oh well, the natives are coming in to give me a telling-off – let's get it over with and we will move on." He was right about the natives giving him a telling-off.'

Mandelson vividly remembers the encounter:

They were absolutely unrelenting. They were pointing their finger at me and saying, 'This is the biggest mistake you have ever made, this is an historic moment for Ireland which you have destroyed single-handedly, you will live to regret this, you will not be able to live with yourself.' It got worse and worse, only pausing with Adams turning to me in the meeting and saying, 'By the way we are really going to vilify you as an individual publicly, but you know you needn't take it personally.' I didn't feel any better for that.

Republican posters appeared all over Belfast accusing the government, and Mandelson in particular, of wrecking the Good Friday Agreement. The IRA condemned Mandelson and announced they were breaking off all contact with de Chastelain. The Assembly was in cold storage, and few could work out how it could be revived again. The general mood was one of pessimism that the executive could be revived. In March 2000 most elements of the Belfast political scene as usual flew to Washington for the annual St Patrick's Day celebrations. But with no breakthrough in sight, Bill Clinton found it initially a depressing experience. 'God, what an awful St Patrick's Day it was,' he remembered. 'Here it was, my last St Patrick's Day in the White House. I thought it was going to be an occasion of joy, I looked forward to those St Patrick's Days so much, but I was frustrated and a little bit angry that anybody would not do whatever it took to get the government up and going again.'

But David Trimble had a surprise for everyone, showing an unexpectedly flexible approach. The man who had brought about the suspension because of the lack of IRA decommissioning, suddenly gave the plainest of indications that he was prepared to go back into government without prior decommissioning. He told a Washington news conference: 'We are prepared to be involved in a fresh sequence, which probably will not involve arms upfront, but it has to involve the issue being dealt with, it has to involve the issue working.' He would explain: 'I said that so that the White House would be able to put the issue up to republicans and say, "Right, they're prepared to have another sequence – what are you prepared to do?"'

Clinton, who met Trimble shortly after his remarks, was delighted: 'I was thrilled by what he said, so he came in and I thanked him for what he said. I remember him telling me that he wouldn't be able to maintain his leadership position if it looked to his people as if he were played for a fool on this decommissioning.'

As Trimble had hoped, Clinton then pressed Adams to make a move in response to the Unionist leader's initiative. Steinberg recalled Clinton telling Adams: 'Look, what David has done today is very significant. He's really shown that he's prepared to move forward on this process. I think it's critical that you too engage and show that you're prepared to move forward as well.' Clinton himself remembered: 'I really tried to get to the bottom of why we couldn't get more movement on decommissioning.' He has a memory of Adams telling him:

Look, these guys have been fighting the struggle for 30 years and are being asked to give up their arms. It has to look like they're giving up their own arms, because the people they've been fighting for chose a particular path to peace, and it's been fully implemented. But if they give up their arms before it's clear that this is going to happen, subject to British pressure, then it will look like everything they did for 30 years was for nothing.

Behind the scenes, however, the republicans were thinking about their next step. According to Adams:

The only people involved in it from our end were myself and

Martin McGuinness at this point. We actually stripped it right back, because the thing was just so delicate. This was either going to succeed in getting the institutions put in place, or it was going to be our last throw of the dice. We had a job of work then trying to figure out how this could be sorted. The Sinn Fein negotiating team had submitted a document on the whole issue of weapons to Senator Mitchell way back. So we started then to tease out if there was any possibility of getting the IRA to even start approaching this issue, on its own terms. And we came up with this idea – could the IRA open up arms dumps?

Mandelson recalled: 'We asked some experts in the Ministry of Defence what experience, what practice did they know of. The Balkans, somebody suggested, might be a good set of circumstances.'

The Americans were also involved in this exploratory exercise, as Clinton's senior aide Jim Steinberg was to recall: 'The idea was to look at the model that had been used for disarming the KLA, the Kosovo Liberation Army, in Kosovo, where they voluntarily agreed to have their arms sealed under international supervision. This was so that they would give confidence that the armed part of their struggle was over, but in a way that they felt preserved their dignity.'

Back in Belfast, the idea of an inspection of arms dumps was developed. Mandelson remembered: 'Everyone was so keen to get the thing restarted and get some sort of breakthrough, that they were sincerely prepared to consider anything. And this sort of Balkans model was put to Adams, and he said, "Well okay" – he didn't turn it down flat.' Martin McGuinness says of the inspection idea:

There were quite a number of meetings which saw myself and Gerry Adams meeting privately with Tony Blair, and in fact I went to Chequers to meet with him and to discuss the possibilities. One possibility that was raising its head was the prospect that you could see the IRA deal with the whole issue of arms dumps in the context of having trusted international inspectors who would come and symbolically, at the beginning, inspect a number of IRA dumps. We wished to explore with the British government whether or not there was any potential in that, providing a way out of the difficulty that we were all facing.

If the IRA were to buy into the emerging arms inspection approach, then the government would have to pay a price. A mere reversal of suspension would not be enough: the republicans sought a wider context, including movement on what they termed demilitarisation. McGuinness says he put it to Blair:

South Armagh, Tony, is one of the most beautiful parts of Ireland. And all along every hilltop there is a hilltop fort. There are military encampments linked all over the place. There are at least three, four, five, six helicopters in the area at any given time, and the people of the area deserve better than that. And the people of the area deserve better than that, Tony – the best defenders of the Good Friday Agreement in South Armagh are the people of South Armagh, they are more effective than a million of these soldiers. And he said, 'I agree with you,' which I thought was progress, important progress.

Blair himself remembered:

Martin McGuinness said to me, 'Look, the very best guarantee of trying to deal with the extremists and these splinter groups from the IRA is for local people in the areas that they are trying to recruit being up for the peace agreement, and against them.' I accept that entirely, that is the best guarantee – that local people say, 'This is unacceptable, we want the peace deal, we do not want violence and terrorism.'

I explained to him, however, that if I took a measure against security advice and dismantled some of the security apparatus, being advised that this was a mistake, and a Real IRA bomb gets through and kills people, then people are going to ask some pretty serious questions of me. What I said to Martin very simply was, 'We can deal with this issue, but it has got to be in the context of a genuinely changed situation in which not merely is there a ceasefire from the IRA, but there is no possible threat.'

Dublin agreed on the importance of demilitarisation, Brian Cowen recalling: 'Failure to change the status quo on the ground in those areas is the best prospect of recruitment for the Real IRA. That's a fact. We are getting into a very normalised situation for many people, and they need to see the signs of militarisation recede. It's important in getting the substantive changes we need on the other side of the argument – which is disarmament by paramilitary groups.'

Bertie Ahern observed:

To make progress on any issue there has to be a balancing issue on the other side, and of course decommissioning has always been linked to demilitarisation. It's not linked so far as the British government will say, 'You give the decommissioning and we'll give demilitarisation,' but they're unlikely to do it unless there's something happening on the IRA side. So while the issues are not negotiated back-to-back, there is a clear link – reduce the security threat and then you're likely to deal with the demilitarisation. Reduce the risk of IRA guns, and you're likely to get progress on that side. That's the way that this has progressed endlessly for the last number of years.

Hundreds, if not thousands, of conversations were held by Sinn Fein leaders as the republicans engaged ever more deeply in politics. By this stage they had taken part in innumerable meetings with major players on both sides of the Atlantic. In Washington, for example, Tony Lake found that he enjoyed speaking to Adams: 'I always remembered that there were things from the past that should limit my enthusiasm here in personal terms, but he was engaging, he had a nice sense of humour. We developed conversations about sports – he sent me a tape of hurling which convinced me that American football is not the most violent sport in the world.'

McGuinness, meanwhile, found himself actively enjoying some of his many encounters, even with those whom he had grown up regarding as the old enemy. He spoke fondly of one meeting with Blair at Chequers: 'I remember it very clearly, mostly because we spent most of the time sitting outside on garden chairs, very close to the rose garden at the back of the building. It was a nice day, there was no rain and Chequers is a fairly amazing place. It's a very old building, the scenery around it is absolutely beautiful, it just stretches for miles and miles and miles, and so it was a very relaxed atmosphere.'

Adams recalls becoming even more relaxed during one long-drawn-out set of talks in Downing Street: 'Others thought there was something going on, but there wasn't – I was asleep on the carpet in the room up the stairs. At one point, because the room was too noisy, there are very large broad window ledges, and I sat on the window ledge and pulled the curtains and dozed off while looking at a couple of workmen in the garden of Downing Street.'

It was the same garden which had been damaged by the IRA mortar attack on Downing Street, but republicans and ministers seemed prepared to let bygones be bygones, and to behave in a friendly way.

McGuinness remembers such an occasion during negotiations at Hillsborough Castle:

We would come in the back door of Hillsborough, we were away from the glare of publicity. We were meeting in a very small sitting room, one where we had become accustomed to meeting both the Taoiseach and the British prime minister. I remember being at one meeting, and normally I don't bring my mobile telephone into the meeting, but I did on this occasion because my daughter was about to have a baby.

The four of us are sitting there talking about hugely important issues in relation to the peace process in Ireland, and suddenly my mobile goes off. And it's my wife, and you would have thought that she'd won the lottery, and at that stage I became a grandfather. So the meeting just more or less collapsed for about ten or fifteen minutes for all of us to fully absorb the great event, and both the British prime minister and the Taoiseach wrote messages of support for my daughter, which I appreciated.

By early May 2000 the two governments believed they had a package. The vital question was: if the political institutions could be restored, and dates could be confirmed for fulfilling all outstanding parts of the Agreement, would the IRA open arms dumps to inspection, and begin the process of putting their weapons beyond use? As soon as they could, they called a summit meeting at

Hillsborough Castle, involving Tony Blair, Bertie Ahern, David Trimble, Gerry Adams and John Hume.

The Sinn Fein team arrived straight from negotiations with the IRA. McGuinness recalled: 'Gerry Adams and I had been up effectively all night, and we arrived very early on the morning, and we effectively presented the two prime ministers with a very forward position from the IRA.' This statement agreed to allow international figures to inspect a number of arms dumps, and said it would initiate a process which would 'completely and verifiably put IRA arms beyond use.' This last, however, was subject to a veritable thicket of undefined conditions, namely, 'the full implementation, on a progressive and irreversible basis by the two governments, especially the British government, of what they have agreed will provide a political context, in an enduring political process, with the potential to remove the causes of conflict and in which Irish republicans and Unionists can, as equals, pursue our respective political objectives peacefully.'

Peter Mandelson was delighted: 'Martin McGuinness and Gerry Adams brought in what they described as the one and only final offer of what the IRA would say – take it or leave it. It was a huge step forward. In particular, it had a commitment, really for the first time, that weapons would be put beyond use.'

Everything, however, hinged on the Unionist response but, as Empey pointed out, they had reservations: 'These negotiations and meetings about IRA statements are always very coy. They're always held in this mythology of, "Well, we don't know whether the IRA's going to be able to do this or not." So we go through this charade every time we have this sort of discussion.' Mandelson remembered: 'I took the statement up to David Trimble, in the upper conference hall room at Hillsborough Castle, where he and all his colleagues were gathered. He read it and, I have to say, he reacted with deep scepticism. His reaction was quite adverse, quite negative, which took me aback and made me worried, obviously.'

This was, however, not to be Trimble's final judgement on the IRA move. He explained: 'You've got to bear in mind that we don't like being bounced into things. We will exercise our own judgement rather than accept someone else's judgement at face value.' He pored over the statement, Taylor recalling: 'I pointed out one or two weaknesses in it, and David said, "Well, we can change that."'

Because of the 'take-it-or-leave-it' nature of the statement, Mandelson was concerned at what he witnessed when he later returned to the Unionist quarters to get their response. 'I came back 40 minutes later,' he recalled, 'and David was busy, just with John Taylor, there with his portable laptop, doing things – very frenetic activity. I said, "What are you doing, David? You're not rewriting the IRA statement are you?" And he said, "No, no, no, but we can get improvements here."'

Trimble was seeking certainty on the intentions of the IRA regarding the inspection of arms dumps. He remembered: 'We asked whether any obstacles would be put in the way of the international observers in terms of the conduct of their inspections, and in whatever mechanisms or measures they wanted to take to assure themselves that things would remain secure. We were assured that no obstacle would be put, that the inspectors would be free to come and go and install any mechanism they wished.'

Both governments had a tense wait while Trimble weighed the value of the scheme and the accompanying reassurances. Paddy Teahon remembered: 'We spent some significant anxious moments before they came back and said, "Look, if the IRA are really genuine that they will deliver on that, then we believe we could be in a position to persuade our people to go along."'

Delivering the Ulster Unionist party was by no means a formality, since many in its ranks did not want to revive an administration which featured Martin McGuinness as its education minister. It was a close-run thing, but Trimble just squeezed through his party's ruling council by a margin of 53 per cent to 47. While it was clear his party was deeply divided, he would say philosophically: 'No point getting over-excited about these things, and at least we do get a result. There's no need to rush off and hire lots of lawyers to challenge the result – it's there and it's clear.'

McGuinness was to say that the IRA move was momentous:

No one had ever heard the likes of this before – the annals of republican history don't contain anything of this nature. Now, the difficulty with dealing with the Unionists is that no matter how big a thing is, the Unionists are inclined to say, 'Well, that really is nothing.' That can be very dispiriting for people like myself within the process, who know the resonances of this type of development. I think that there were those within the British establishment who did understand the importance of these moves.

The re-established administration went back to work, most reckoning that it functioned surprisingly well in the months that followed. It was buffeted by a series of events, such as an internal loyalist feud which claimed more than a dozen lives in Belfast and elsewhere, yet it appeared to withstand such pressures well. Much of the feuding calmed down after Shankill UDA leader, Johnny 'Mad Dog' Adair, who had been freed from prison under the Good Friday Agreement's early release scheme, was sent back behind bars.

Early in January 2000 Peter Mandelson hosted a reception at Hillsborough Castle for members of the media and their spouses, appearing highly pleased with his position and delivering a speech of welcome to the gathering. Before the end of January, however, he had been catapulted from Cabinet office for the second time, leaving the government in the wake of a scandal unconnected with Northern Ireland.

The government's new man was surprised to find himself in Belfast. Mandelson's replacement was the Scottish Secretary of State, Dr John Reid, an ardent supporter of the Celtic football team, who was the first Catholic Northern Ireland Secretary. A fluent television performer often described as a safe pair of hands, Reid first found himself trotted out to defend Mandelson and then suddenly delegated to take over from him.

Reid recalled the changeover:

It was more like a whirlwind than anything else. I had been asked if I would front up on the Mandelson crisis as it were. It wasn't unusual for that to happen because I had been asked to do it on a number of occasions when we had pretty tough things like the fuel crisis, Mo's resignation, et cetera. Anyway, by midday that day it looked as though Peter was going to go. He resigned about one o'clock and at approximately ten past six I got a phone call asking if I could meet the prime minister urgently.

I met the prime minister: it was a very brief discussion

because he had a million things on, and when I came out I already had police protection, which had miraculously appeared. When I came out there was a new car, the armour-plated Jag.

The new Northern Ireland Secretary was faced with a number of daunting problems, not least that of how to stabilise the political situation in the wake of Mandelson's departure. Reid set himself a number of goals:

It seemed to be that the short- to medium-term priorities were to get the Assembly up and running, to try and make some movement on cross-community policing support and to get movement on decommissioning. In the midst of all the other myriad of things that had to be done those seemed to me to be the three priorities.

I was very well aware that Peter Mandelson had been a master of the press and profile, and that Mo had also gone for a very high-profile presence in the euphoria that surrounded the original Agreement. I decided therefore not to try and emulate them but to be more workmanlike, and to go for the substance if you like rather than the profile – just get involved in the details and negotiations and see if we could move the three main topics forward.

It had been virtually standard practice for Unionists to attempt to drive a wedge between the prime minister of the day and his Northern Ireland Secretary. This was regarded as a favourite tactic of David Trimble. Knowing this, Reid sought assurances from Blair, recalling:

I was aware that problems had arisen in the past about the closeness with which Downing Street and the Secretary of State needed to work, and about the constant potential for others to try and use the prime minister's involvement as a lever against the Secretary of State. We had a relatively short but extremely good discussion on that and I'm pleased to say that – as of now, touch wood – no one has been able to drive a wedge or put a cigarette paper between the prime minister and myself.

Two inspections of IRA arms dumps took place, but as the months passed it became obvious that Protestant opinion increasingly regarded this as inadequate movement on the guns issue. Largely as a result of this, Unionist support for the Agreement steadily ebbed away, Protestants in general increasingly feeling that republicans had got the better of the deal. This feeling was heightened when the government accepted much of the report of a commission, established at the time of the Agreement, on future polic-ing. The hundreds of changes recommended by the com-mission were a blueprint for a policing transformation, but the measure that stimulated most Unionist ire was its recommendation, accepted by the government, for chang-ing the name of the force from the Royal Ulster Constabu-lary to the Police Service of Northern Ireland.

As First Minister, Trimble sought to reflect Unionist disaffection by preventing the administration's two Sinn Fein ministers from attending north-south meetings. As the Westminster general election of June 2001 approached, Trimble also announced that he would resign in the fol-lowing month unless the IRA had begun to put its arms beyond use.

The election itself represented a significant setback for the more centrist elements, with Trimble losing West-minster seats and important gains being made by both Paisley's Democratic Unionists and Sinn Fein. For the first time ever Sinn Fein gained more votes than the SDLP, so that the overall result was seen as a clear sign of growing alienation between the two communities. Not long afterwards John Hume, who had been ill for some time, announced his decision to step down as party leader; he was to be followed in the job by his long-time aide, Mark Durkan. With no sign of IRA movement on arms, Trimble resigned as First Minister in early July. This plunged the future of the Assembly and executive into doubt, since in effect it meant that unless he was reinstated the institutions seemed headed for collapse.

It was thus in an atmosphere of high pressure and some desperation that the two governments and major parties gathered in the sedate surroundings of Weston Park, a secluded English country estate, for yet another attempt to achieve a breakthrough and save the Assembly.

In the talks the government was primarily concerned to produce a decommissioning move, while in return Sinn Fein pushed hard for concessions on other fronts. The government made some moves on policing, demilitarisation and the question of inquiries into controversial troubles killings, but the talks ended with no republican advance on decommissioning.

Sinn Fein was meanwhile severely embarrassed, in the summer of 2001, when three Irish republicans were arrested in guerrilla-held territory in the South American state of Colombia. This brought allegations from many quarters about an IRA connection with narco-terrorists, but although Sinn Fein and the IRA issued assurances that the peace process was not threatened, no detailed explanation was offered. Washington in particular was not amused by the episode.

In Belfast the atmosphere was not helped by the fact that on the streets of the city disturbances and rioting continued at a high level. In particular many ugly scenes resulted in north Belfast when loyalist protesters sought to prevent Catholic girls reaching their primary school in a Protestant area of Ardoyne.

With the Assembly apparently close to collapse, Reid resorted to an unexpected move which some denounced as sleight of hand but others welcomed as an ingenious tactic. Instead of mothballing the Assembly he suspended it for a weekend, to create a further six-week breathing space for negotiations. It was not a particularly graceful device, but it worked and was repeated a second time when more time was needed.

Reid explained: 'In terms of getting the Assembly and the executive up and running again that was a pretty arduous task. It took a long period and a number of technical suspensions. The key thing was to find a mechanism which people would understand was not a slight to the Assembly by prolonged suspension, which could have been interpreted as a disregard for devolution. It was clearly a mechanism to buy a bit more time in order to allow for movement on decommissioning.'

The temporary suspensions of the Assembly and its institutions provoked criticism from republicans, nationalists and to a lesser extent the Irish government. Reid remembered:

The mechanism for a technical suspension first of all surprised some people – they had not conceived of it previously. Then whatever the various politicians said, including the republicans, to any reasonable person it clearly appeared as a positive action to buy time to find a resolution, rather than as a negative action to put aside the new democratic institutions. That was crucial.

There was at one stage an attempt by the republicans to demonise what I had done, in the same way that they had demonised Mandelson when he suspended. But the fact that it was a short suspension, and that it was clearly intended for good reasons and positive reasons rather than negative ones, was apparent to everyone. I think also that the relationship that I had been lucky enough to establish with the Irish government helped, because they remained very muted and actually quite supportive behind the scenes.

The extra time proved invaluable in finally bringing about decisive republican movement on decommissioning, the issue that had dogged the political process since at least 1994. It had resulted in a number of breaks in the workings of the Assembly as the IRA refused to deliver or destroy guns. The blunt phrase 'Not an ounce – not a bullet' appeared on more than one wall in republican areas, yet eventually, in October 2001, the IRA moved.

It did so in strict secrecy, letting it be known that some arms had been put beyond use but not specifying how or where it had happened or how much armament was involved. It simply said it had implemented a scheme which had been agreed with de Chastelain, adding: 'This unprecedented move is to save the peace process and to persuade others of our genuine intentions.' De Chastelain himself confirmed that an act of decommissioning had been carried out to his satisfaction.

While many hailed it as a historic breakthrough, a number of Unionists, especially in the anti-Agreement camp, expressed scepticism and suspicion about the exercise. Peter Robinson of the Democratic Unionists dismissively declared: 'Smoke and mirrors and sleight of hand and fudge and haziness simply won't cut it.' It was, however, enough to allow Trimble to convince his party to return to government, and within days ministers were back at their desks.

The move touched some of the deepest nerves within republicanism, some senior activists later saying they had wept when they heard the news. Tremors of disapproval were evident within both the IRA and Sinn Fein, as it emerged that their normally infinitely careful leaders had not fully prepared the ground for such a development.

In the view of one former IRA activist the organisation had worked too hard to convince its constituency that decommissioning would never happen. He said:

We had done a powerful job in saying it would never happen. We said it was one sacred cow that would not be touched, so when it happened it could have been viewed as the IRA rolling over. Activists have to worry – are they doing the right thing? In this case few of the activists were involved in the decision. There was no convention. The decision to put arms beyond use was taken by the leadership. People kept saying to us, 'You are doing this to keep David Trimble in office.' We told them to forget about David Trimble, that no matter what happens we have to deal with Unionism.

He in effect confirmed the theory that the IRA moved only because the Unionist leader had brought the process to the verge of meltdown. The irony was that Trimble the politician brought the political process to the brink of collapse, only to have it rescued at the last moment by an armed group. The fact that the IRA had decommissioned in order to preserve the process was a telling sign that republicans placed great value on the new institutions.

The ex-IRA member continued: 'For the whole peace process to go forward it had to happen. What was of paramount importance to us was to build on the process, and the process was on the way down. If we had wanted a battle to bring David Trimble down we would have won that battle hands down. We could have hung David Trimble out to dry, but we would still have to deal with Unionism. The process is what is important – saving that was more important than anything.'

Reid and his advisers had their own assessment of why the IRA decided to put arms beyond use. He believed the terrorist attacks on New York and Washington on 11 September played a part in the decision, but only as one of a range of reasons. Reid recalled:

I think there were a number of factors. The first was that there was an inherent logic in what Sinn Fein had embarked upon that required at some stage that there be an act of decommissioning. Secondly, in terms of negotiations, despite continual pressure and warnings that they would have to decommission before we could give stability to the Assembly, they naturally thought in terms of squeezing as much as they could out of it.

They tried to get away with an agreement simply on the method of decommissioning. When they did that, which was four days before one of the deadlines, they assumed that four days would be regarded as an unreasonable period to move from agreeing which was in itself an historic move, agreeing a method to the act of decommissioning. I think what they didn't calculate was that it was possible for me to have a very, very short suspension which appeared to everybody as a perfectly reasonable move to give more time for them to decommission. They found themselves for the first time in a long time behind the game. I think it was a misjudgement on their part.

They then found themselves isolated over the question of

policing, and then the Colombian adventure meant they had to show even more good faith on that question. And as a result of that the international pressure on them, from the United States and elsewhere, and of course the eleventh of September, I think all of those played a part in the timing of what they did.

My own view was that pressure and persuasion behind the scenes was more important than a public demand from the British Secretary of State. One thing that people should recognise is that the British Secretary of State and the British government demanding things of the republican movement publicly isn't always the best way to get the objective you desire.

Nevertheless it was a very historic move. I thought in February or March of that year that they would have moved by the end of the year. I even internally had in my own mind November, I thought before Christmas in the run-up to the 2002 Dublin elections. The events of the eleventh of September and so on brought it forward a bit but I think it would have happened anyway.

The move by the IRA was widely acclaimed in nationalist Ireland and abroad in America and Europe, though the Colombian adventure, and the lack of explanation for it, took some of the shine off the image of a violent group turning its back on the gun.

In the wake of decommissioning many assumed Trimble's re-election as First Minister would be something of a formality, but in the event it turned into something of a fiasco. This was because a few of his party's Assembly members rebelled and refused to vote for him, leaving him short of the support he required under the Assembly's convoluted rules.

It all turned into a fraught exercise which resulted in much vexation within the government and most of the political parties as a scramble took place to scrape up the votes Trimble needed. John Reid paints a picture of a frenetic weekend at Hillsborough Castle as he tried to square the political circle: 'Well, it was as frantic as you would imagine. Normally when you would conduct such discussions you would have everybody in the same place. What made this quite intense was the fact that no one was in the same place, none of the parties were here in Hillsborough so all of this was done by telephone, or by fax on occasion, and that made the conducting of discussions rather difficult.'

With Trimble lacking Unionist support, attention focused on the middle-of-the-road Alliance party, since it was open to some or all of its members to change their Assembly designation to that of Unionist. It meant in effect becoming Unionists for a day. This the party was loath to do, since it prided itself on representing middle-ground elements and regarded itself as neither Unionist nor nationalist.

Reid remembered:

The Alliance said they wouldn't redesignate. The SDLP said they were against redesignation, and Sinn Fein were supposed to be for fresh elections. When I started out it didn't look as though it would be possible but I always believed it would be possible. There is a public posture from the various parties but there is one thing that I hoped all of them recognise: that when people say what is the sanction on this group or that group, the sanction for all of those committed to the Good Friday Agreement is that it falls.

That's the ultimate sanction because that means that,

whatever qualifications they may have had about how the process is continuing, their commitment to that process is being shown to be a failure. So ultimately we were staring in the face the fact that if the Assembly was indefinitely suspended everyone was likely to lose, that if it went to general elections there was likely to be a further polarisation.

That was helpful in concentrating the minds. What we had to convince people was that, although all of them were asked to move over that weekend, it was as of nothing compared to the problems they would face if the thing fell.

Eventually the Alliance party reluctantly agreed to re-designate and Trimble's re-election was secured. When Assembly members flooded out of the Stormont chamber and into its central hall, where the television cameras were massed, tempers frayed and undignified and ugly scenes resulted in what was called 'the brawl in the hall'.

Partly because of this, the act of decommissioning and the reinstatement of full devolved government produced no feelings of elation or celebration. The administration did, however, go back to work, with many hoping it would experience a helpful period of stability. Sporadic rioting continued in north Belfast, however, accompanied by occasional killings. During 2001 loyalists killed fourteen people, while two died at the hands of the IRA and three others were killed by other republicans.

At the end of the year the area of policing, already a contentious issue, provided a fresh jet of controversy in relation to the Omagh bombing which had claimed twenty-nine lives in 1998. Chief Constable Sir Ronnie Flanagan became embroiled in intense controversy with the Police Ombudsman, Mrs Nuala O'Loan, who, after an investigation, accused his force of essentially bungling the investigation into the bombing. Very public disagreements followed, to the dismay of those who hoped a fresh start in policing could be achieved.

The issue became one of the first major tests of the new Policing Board. Many expected it to divide along party lines, since it contained politicians from the Unionist party, the DUP and the SDLP. Unexpectedly, however, it came up with an acceptable compromise approach, reaching agreement that a senior officer from another force should oversee the continuing Omagh investigation.

Reports in early 2002 that the results of the previous year's census would show a significant drop in Protestant numbers, and a continuing rise in the Catholic population, provided yet another signal that Northern Ireland could not hope for a tranquil future. Unionists complained that Northern Ireland had become 'a cold place' for them, with nationalists benefiting inordinately from the peace process. Trimble's people worried that they would lose seats in the 2003 Assembly elections.

Yet almost everyone had a sense that, whether the Agreement survived or not, the worst of the troubles was over: after all the years of full-scale conflict the troubles had indeed entered their endgame. This sense was best caught by former Senator George Mitchell when he summed up: 'I've been involved in Northern Ireland long enough to know that every step forward is followed by a step backward. That it's good not to get too high at the good moments, nor to get too low at the bad moments. That you build on this process, you do what you can under the circumstances that exist at the time, and then you proceed from there.

'But this has been centuries in the making; it will be years in the changing.'

Chronology

1980

October   Republican prisoners began a hunger strike to demand the return of special category status. It was called off in December.

1981

March   A second hunger strike began with IRA prison leader Bobby Sands the first to refuse food.

April   Sands won the Fermanagh–South Tyrone Westminster by-election.

May   Sands died on the 66th day of hunger strike.

October   Hunger strike called off after ten republican deaths.

1982

December   17 people died in an INLA bomb in Ballykelly, Co. Londonderry.

1983

March   The Irish government announced the setting up of the New Ireland Forum to discuss nationalist aims.

1984

May   New Ireland Forum Report was published.

July   Northern Ireland Secretary, James Prior, rejects the main recommendations of the report.

October   An IRA bomb at the Conservative party conference hotel in Brighton killed five people.

November   At the end of a summit with the Irish government
Margaret Thatcher forcefully ruled out the three
main Forum options.

1985

February–   John Hume met members of the IRA's Army Council
June   but walked out within minutes when the IRA insisted
on making a video recording of the occasion.

November   Prime ministers Margaret Thatcher and Garret
FitzGerald signed the Anglo–Irish Agreement on
November 15. An estimated 100,000 Unionists
gathered in Belfast to voice their anger at the
Agreement.

December   First meeting of the Anglo–Irish Inter-governmental
Conference set up under the Agreement.

1986

March   Unionist protest 'Day of Action' disrupted public
services and halted most of industry amid widespread
violence and intimidation.

April   The Ulster Unionist party announced it was ending
its last links with the Conservative party.

November   Sinn Fein decided to permit successful candidates to
take their seats in the Irish Parliament in Dublin,
ending decades of abstentionism.
Huge Unionist protest rally against the Anglo–Irish
Agreement took place at Belfast City Hall.

1987

May   Sinn Fein published a document entitled *Scenario for
Peace*, demanding British withdrawal and an
all-Ireland constitutional conference.

November   An IRA bomb in Enniskillen killed 11 Protestants
during a Remembrance Day ceremony.

1988

January SDLP leader John Hume and Sinn Fein President
         Gerry Adams met at the request of a third person
         'interested in creating political dialogue'.

March   Three unarmed IRA volunteers were shot dead by the
         SAS in Gibraltar.
         In Milltown cemetery, Belfast, UDA member Michael
         Stone attacked the funerals of the IRA members
         killed in Gibraltar. He killed three men and injured
         others.
         Two soldiers in plain clothes were attacked by a
         crowd and then shot dead at an IRA funeral in West
         Belfast.

June   Gerry Adams called for a national consensus on Irish
         reunification.

August   John Hume rejected criticism of talks with Sinn Fein
         and called on republicans to abandon violence in
         favour of political methods.
         Eight soldiers travelling on a bus were killed by an
         IRA bomb at Ballygawley, Co. Tyrone. Thatcher
         ordered a security review.
         Three IRA volunteers were killed by the SAS in Co.
         Tyrone.

September End of Sinn Fein–SDLP talks announced, though
         John Hume and Gerry Adams continued to meet
         privately.

1989

September IRA bomb at Deal in Kent killed eleven military
         bandsmen.

November Northern Ireland Secretary, Peter Brooke, said the
         IRA could not be militarily defeated and that
         the government would have to be imaginative
         and flexible in its response if there was a
         ceasefire.

1990

February   Martin McGuinness said Peter Brooke was the first Northern Ireland Secretary 'with some understanding of Irish history'.

March   Sinn Fein dismissed speculation about an IRA ceasefire.

April   Gerry Adams said an unannounced IRA ceasefire could be effected if Britain entered into talks with Sinn Fein about eventual disengagement from Northern Ireland.

July   IRA bomb at London Stock Exchange.
Tory MP Ian Gow was killed at his home in Sussex by an IRA boobytrap bomb.

September   An IRA spokesman said the only debate within the republican movement was how to 'prosecute the war'.

November   Peter Brooke, in what became known as his 'neutrality speech', said Britain had 'no selfish strategic or economic interest' in the Union.
Resignation of Margaret Thatcher as prime minister.

December   For the first time in 15 years the IRA declared a three-day Christmas ceasefire.

1991

February   Gerry Adams described as 'fictitious' reports that he was preparing proposals for a ceasefire but said Sinn Fein was ready to 'take political risks'.
The IRA fired three mortars at 10 Downing Street.

September   Gerry Adams said he was prepared to engage in 'open dialogue' and wanted to see an end to all acts of violence.

December   IRA announced a three-day Christmas ceasefire.

1992

January   Peter Brooke said Sinn Fein could only become involved in talks if there was a cessation of violence, not 'temporary ceasefires'.

	Eight Protestant workers who had been repairing a police station were killed by an IRA bomb at Teebane, Co. Tyrone.
February	An IRA spokesman said its campaign would cease only when it had secured a British 'declaration of intent' to withdraw.
March	Gerry Adams said the slogan of republicans having a ballot box in one hand and an Armalite rifle in the other was 'outdated'.
April	Presidential candidate Bill Clinton said that if elected he would lift the visa ban on Gerry Adams.
	A massive IRA bomb wrecked Baltic Exchange area of City of London, killing three people and causing hundreds of millions of pounds' worth of damage.
October	IRA planted a series of bombs in London.
December	Further bomb attacks on London.
	NI Secretary Sir Patrick Mayhew said in speech at Coleraine that there were welcome signs of fresh thinking in some republican circles.
	IRA announced 72-hour Christmas ceasefire.

1993

March	Two young boys were killed in an IRA explosion in Warrington.
April	It was revealed that Hume–Adams talks had been going on in secret when Gerry Adams was spotted entering John Hume's home.
	Taoiseach, Albert Reynolds, said he was willing to talk to Sinn Fein if IRA ended its violence.
	In a joint statement John Hume and Gerry Adams rejected any internal solution to the conflict in the north. They also said they accepted that the Irish people as a whole 'have the right to national self-determination' but added, 'We both recognise that such a new agreement is only achievable and viable if it can earn and enjoy the allegiance of the different traditions on this island, by accommodating

diversity and providing for national reconciliation.'
IRA lorry bomb at Bishopsgate caused many millions
of pounds' worth of damage to City of London
financial district. A journalist was killed while trying
to photograph the lorry.

May	The IRA planted a series of bombs in Northern Irish towns. John Hume said he would have further talks with Gerry Adams despite IRA bombs.
June	Irish President, Mary Robinson, visited West Belfast and shook hands with Gerry Adams.
July	John Hume said he believed IRA wanted to end its campaign.
September	IRA observed undeclared ceasefire for one week to coincide with trip to NI by prominent Irish-Americans. John Hume and Gerry Adams announced they had reached agreement in their talks and would submit their ideas for the governments to consider.
October	Sir Patrick Mayhew demanded an unconditional end to IRA violence and ruled out the notion of Britain 'persuading' Unionists to accept Irish unity. IRA attempt to bomb Ulster Defence Association HQ on Shankill Road killed nine Protestant civilians and IRA bomber. Gerry Adams was criticised for shouldering the coffin of Thomas Begley, the IRA member killed in the explosion. Gerry Adams said that he would be able to persuade the IRA to end its campaign if the British responded positively to Hume–Adams. The UDA killed seven people in the Greysteel pub massacre, bringing to 13 the number killed by loyalists since the Shankill bomb. In a joint communiqué, the British and Irish governments appeared to reject the Hume–Adams initiative and renewed their support for the three-strand inter-party talks.

November   John Major ruled out the Hume–Adams initiative.
He told John Hume it was 'not the right way to
proceed'.
Despite denials, details emerged revealing extensive
secret contacts between the British government and
the IRA.
At a Stormont press conference Sir Patrick Mayhew
denied official contact and claimed that intermediaries
'in a chain of communication' had been activated
because IRA had sent a message saying that the
'conflict is over' and they needed British advice on
how to bring it to a close.

December   Albert Reynolds said he was not seeking
self-determination 'in Ireland as a whole collected in
a single entity. There will be no change in Northern
Ireland without a change of opinions there,' he
added.
Adams said, 'The Six Counties cannot have a right to
self-determination. That is a matter for the Irish
people as a whole, to be exercised without
impediment.'
Downing Street Declaration released in London by
John Major and Albert Reynolds.
Sir Patrick Mayhew said any post-cessation talks with
Sinn Fein would have to address the surrender of IRA
arms.
Gerry Adams called for 'clarification' of Declaration
from London. John Major turned this down.
Bill Clinton welcomed Declaration and said the
question of a visa for Gerry Adams was being kept
under review.
IRA announced three-day ceasefire.

1994

January   Albert Reynolds said he would clarify Declaration for
Sinn Fein.
Republic lifted the long-standing broadcasting ban on
Sinn Fein.

	Gerry Adams said he would not accept a ceasefire as precondition of involvement in talks.
	Bill Clinton granted visa to Gerry Adams, resulting in condemnation from John Major.
	Gerry Adams visited New York on three-day visa.
February	Vice-President Al Gore urged Gerry Adams to accept Declaration and reject violence.
	John Major repeated Peter Brooke's British neutrality formula on Northern Ireland.
March	IRA mortar attack on Heathrow Airport – none of the devices exploded.
	IRA called three-day ceasefire. Gerry Adams said ceasefire 'did not come easily'.
June	Irish foreign minister Dick Spring said there would have to be a handover of IRA guns to verify ceasefire.
	Six Catholics killed in a loyalist attack on a pub in Loughinisland, Co. Down.
July	Sir Patrick Mayhew called for clear abandonment of Articles 2 and 3 of the Irish constitution, which Unionists found offensive.
	IRA killed three loyalists and bombed three Protestant pubs in Belfast.
August	IRA called a 'complete cessation' of its campaign. John Major called for evidence that it was permanent. Albert Reynolds said the campaign was over 'for good' and said he would swiftly recognise Sinn Fein's mandate.
September	Albert Reynolds, John Hume and Gerry Adams met in Dublin and shook hands in public.
	John Major said the IRA had to say it had abandoned violence 'for good'.
	Bill Clinton lifted White House ban on contact with Sinn Fein.
	John Major said exploratory talks with Sinn Fein could begin around Christmas if republicans indicated they intended to give up violence for good. Sir Patrick Mayhew said IRA arms would feature in the discussion.

Chronology

October   Declaring the Union to be safe, loyalist paramilitary
            groups announced a ceasefire.
            Speaking in Belfast, Major said it was now his
            government's 'working assumption' that the IRA
            intended the ceasefire to be permanent.

November   Bill Clinton administration announced an aid package
            for Northern Ireland.
            Newry post office worker Frank Kerr killed by IRA
            during armed robbery. The IRA said its statement of
            31 August stood, with Gerry Adams expressing
            'shock and regret'.
            Reynolds resigned as Taoisach and leader of Fianna
            Fáil.
            Bertie Ahern was elected as new leader of Fianna
            Fáil.

December   Government announced that exploratory dialogue
            with Sinn Fein would begin on 7 December.
            Bill Clinton appointed George Mitchell as his
            economic envoy to Northern Ireland.
            Gerry Adams said it was 'unlikely' that weapons
            would be decommissioned 'short of a political
            settlement'.
            First official meeting between government officials
            and Sinn Fein. Decommissioning was identified as a
            stumbling block.
            Albert Reynolds said it was not 'a sensible
            precondition' to require the IRA to hand in weapons
            before multilateral talks.
            Fine Gael leader, John Bruton, elected Taoiseach in a
            coalition government. Bruton said it was important
            not to get into a stand-off over IRA arms.
            Second meeting at Stormont between Sinn Fein and
            British officials. Sinn Fein said question of IRA
            weapons was best addressed at all-party talks.
            John Major said a Sinn Fein promise on arms would
            not be enough: there had to be 'significant progress'
            before the British and other parties would join Sinn
            Fein at the table.

1995

January   Northern Ireland Office announced end of ban on
             ministers meeting Sinn Fein and political
             representatives of loyalist paramilitary groups.

February   The document *Frameworks for the Future* was
             released by the two governments.

March   Sir Patrick Mayhew outlined conditions for Sinn Fein
             joining all-party talks, including 'actual
             decommissioning of some arms'.

May   Sir Patrick Mayhew met Gerry Adams in
             Washington, the first encounter between a republican
             representative and a government minister.

August   Gerry Adams said republicans were ready to make
             'critical compromises' to achieve peace.
             James Molyneaux announced his resignation as
             leader of the Ulster Unionist party. David Trimble,
             regarded as a hard-liner, was elected to succeed him.

October   Mayhew told the Conservative party conference that
             the governments were considering inviting an
             international commission to help resolve the
             decommissioning dispute.

November   The government published a paper *Building Blocks*. It
             proposed all-party preparatory talks and an
             international body to consider decommissioning.
             Bill Clinton shook hands with Gerry Adams during a
             visit to Belfast.

1996

January   British and Irish ministers met Sinn Fein leaders at
             Stormont.
             The international commission on guns, headed by
             George Mitchell, recommended that talks and
             decommissioning should occur in parallel. John
             Major announced plans for elections in Northern
             Ireland.

February   IRA ceasefire ended after 18 months with the
             bombing of London's Canary Wharf district, killing

two men and causing enormous damage.
John Major and John Bruton announced 10 June as start of talks to decide format of elections. Sinn Fein would be excluded in absence of an IRA ceasefire.

May   Forum elections were held.
An IRA statement said there would be no decommissioning in advance of an overall political settlement.

June   John Major and John Bruton opened preliminary talks at Stormont chaired by George Mitchell but without Sinn Fein.

October   An IRA bomb attack on army headquarters in Lisburn, Co. Antrim, fatally injured a soldier. It was the first IRA bomb in Northern Ireland since 1994.

1997

February   Bombardier Stephen Restorick was killed by the IRA in Newry, Co. Down.

May   Labour won a general election and Tony Blair became prime minister.
Blair named Mo Mowlam as Northern Ireland Secretary and gave go-ahead for exploratory contacts between government officials and Sinn Fein.

June   Sinn Fein was barred from entering the resumed inter-party talks at Stormont.

July   IRA announced new ceasefire.
The Rev. Ian Paisley's Democratic Unionist party withdrew from talks.

August   Mo Mowlam met a Sinn Fein delegation.
Establishment of Independent Commission on Decommissioning, headed by Canadian General John de Chastelain, to oversee the weapons issue.
Mo Mowlam pronounced the IRA ceasefire sufficient to allow Sinn Fein to join talks.

September   Sinn Fein signed up to the Mitchell Principles of non-violence and entered all-party talks. Two days

later the IRA announced that it had 'problems' with
the Principles.

David Trimble led the Ulster Unionist party into
talks, walking in alongside representatives of loyalist
paramilitary groups.

The governments agreed on the composition of the
International Decommissioning Body to be chaired by
John de Chastelain.

October	Martin McGuinness said Sinn Fein was 'going to the negotiating table to smash the Union'.
	Substantive negotiations began at Stormont with the participation of eight parties and the two governments.
	Sinn Fein leaders Gerry Adams and Martin McGuinness met Tony Blair for the first time at Stormont.
December	Gerry Adams and Martin McGuinness made their first visit to Downing Street.
	The Stormont talks adjourned for Christmas, the parties having failed to reach agreement even on an agenda.
	Ulster Unionist MP Jeffrey Donaldson said he was advising party leader David Trimble to withdraw from the talks because of the 'concessions train'.
	Loyalist paramilitary leader Billy Wright was shot dead within the Maze prison by members of a republican group, the Irish National Liberation Army.

1998

January	Mo Mowlam visited Maze prison to persuade loyalist inmates to back the peace process following an upsurge of extreme Protestant violence in the wake of the Wright killing.
February	As the peace talks moved to Dublin Sinn Fein was suspended from the process because of IRA involvement in recent killings.
March	Joint government paper on British–Irish relations released to parties.

Tony Blair met Gerry Adams at Downing Street in an attempt to get the peace process back on track. Tony Blair said agreement was 'agonisingly close'.
David Trimble and Gerry Adams attended British Embassy lunch in Washington.
Gerry Adams said a deal was possible within three weeks and that he wanted Sinn Fein to be part of it.
George Mitchell released paper on north-south relations. Talks resumed and Sinn Fein returned. Mitchell set deadline of 9 April for agreement.

April	Taoiseach, Bertie Ahern, said there were 'large disagreements' with London over the powers of cross-border bodies.

Gerry Adams said in a newspaper article that history could be made but the deal would be 'transitional'.
On 7 April the UUP rejected as 'too green', a draft presented by George Mitchell, plunging the talks into crisis only 72 hours before a settlement was due.
Tony Blair flew to Belfast to help rescue the deal. He said: 'I feel the hand of history upon our shoulders.'
Throughout the night of 9 April, Bill Clinton telephoned the participants at regular intervals.
At about 2 a.m. on 10 April the UUP and SDLP resolved their differences.
A letter was provided by Tony Blair to reassure Unionist representatives on arms decommissioning, as requested by David Trimble.
4.45 p.m. David Trimble telephoned Tony Blair and George Mitchell to inform them his party would join up.
Unionist MP Jeffrey Donaldson withdrew, leaving Stormont before the final speeches.

April 11	David Trimble received the support of his party executive.
April 18	The Unionist party's ruling council supported the Agreement.
April 27	Chris Patten was named as chairman of Independent Commission on Policing set up under the Agreement.

April 30	The IRA said it had no plans to decommission.
May	A special Sinn Fein conference voted overwhelmingly to support the Agreement and allow members to take seats in the proposed new Assembly.
	Strong support for the deal was expressed in referendums on both sides of border.
June	Elections to new Northern Ireland Assembly. Supporters of the deal won 80 seats and opponents 28.
July	Assembly met for first time. David Trimble elected First Minister designate with SDLP's Seamus Mallon as Deputy First Minister designate.
August	Real IRA car bomb in Omagh killed 29 in the single deadliest attack of the troubles.
September	Sinn Fein said it considered violence to be a thing of the past.
	Tony Blair and Bill Clinton visited Northern Ireland and travelled to Omagh to view the scene of the explosion and meet some of the relatives. They also travelled to Stormont to meet Assembly members. David Trimble promised to create a 'pluralist parliament for a pluralist people'.
October	David Trimble told his party conference that Sinn Fein could not join an executive without IRA decommissioning.
November	John Hume said that decommissioning was not a precondition of the Agreement but that it was the will of the people that it should take place.
December	John Hume and David Trimble jointly received the Nobel Peace Prize in Oslo.
	Agreement was reached on the structure of the executive and cross-border bodies.

1999

| February | Assembly voted to confirm the new government departments and cross-border bodies. |
| March | Tony Blair called for IRA decommissioning to begin |

if Sinn Fein were to join the executive.

The two governments signed treaties establishing the new north-south, British-Irish and inter-governmental arrangements.

April   Decommissioning talks ended in stalemate, but the governments produced a declaration calling for a collective act of reconciliation and the putting beyond use of some weapons on a voluntary basis.

June   Tony Blair's deadline passed without agreement on decommissioning.

July   Tony Blair and Bertie Ahern set out a plan entitled *The Way Forward* under which devolution would begin on 15 July. Within days decommissioning would begin, to be completed by May 2000.

UUP rejected Tony Blair's urging to join devolved government before IRA started decommissioning. Mo Mowlam called on the Assembly to meet on 15 July to nominate an executive.

UUP members boycotted Stormont as the executive was nominated, causing it to be declared invalid since it lacked sufficient cross-community membership. Seamus Mallon then resigned as Deputy First Minister, calling on David Trimble to step down. Tony Blair and Bertie Ahern started review of peace process, with George Mitchell recalled in September as a facilitator.

September   Unionists reacted angrily to publication of the Patten Report which proposed far-reaching changes to policing and changing the name of the Royal Ulster Constabulary.

October   Peter Mandelson replaced Mo Mowlam as Northern Ireland Secretary.

November   Ulster Unionists and Sinn Fein expressed mutual desire to set up inclusive executive. Pressure mounted on Trimble from anti-Agreement Unionists.

IRA said it was ready to discuss decommissioning and would appoint a representative to the decommissioning body.

George Mitchell concluded his review saying that the basis existed for decommissioning and coalition government.

Peter Mandelson told the Commons that he would freeze the workings of the Agreement if the IRA did not deliver on arms decommissioning.

The UUP ruling council voted to accept a leadership compromise, paving the way for Assembly and executive to operate.

David Trimble promised he would return to seek the support of the party council in February 2000. He revealed he had given a senior party official a post-dated letter of resignation as First Minister, to come into effect in the event of inadequate movement on arms.

The executive was formed, with David Trimble at its head and Seamus Mallon as his deputy. Ten departmental ministers were appointed, two of them from Sinn Fein. Rev. Ian Paisley's Democratic Unionists said they would function as ministers but would not attend executive meetings.

December 1 Devolution was restored at midnight.

December 2 Irish government signed away Articles 2 and 3 of the Irish constitution laying claim to Northern Ireland.

IRA appointed an interlocutor to Decommissioning Body.

General de Chastelain issued an upbeat report saying that recent events and meetings 'provide the basis for an assessment that decommissioning will occur.'

The Irish cabinet met members of the Northern Ireland executive in the first meeting of the north-south ministerial council.

2000

January   General de Chastelain met the governments to deliver a report on progress on decommissioning. It was not immediately published: Tony Blair reported to the Commons that insufficient progress had been made.

David Trimble made clear his intention to resign in the absence of progress on decommissioning in advance of his party council's meeting on 12 February.

February   Peter Mandelson announced the suspension of devolution and a return to direct rule. This led to major controversy and many recriminations from nationalists and republicans. Sinn Fein claimed a major advance on decommissioning had been outlined in a new IRA statement, later withdrawn.
The government welcomed the new IRA statement as a significant development.

March   In Washington for St Patrick's Day, David Trimble told a press conference that the executive might be re-formed without prior IRA decommissioning as long as there were firm guarantees that decommissioning would take place.
David Trimble was re-elected UUP leader defeating a challenger, the Reverend Martin Smyth, by a narrower margin than expected.

May   Tony Blair and Bertie Ahern spent two days at Hillsborough Castle meeting local parties. The two governments then announced the target date of 22 May for the return to devolution.
The IRA issued a statement saying that if the Good Friday Agreement was fully implemented they would 'completely and verifiably put IRA weapons beyond use.' They also agreed to a number of arms dumps being inspected by international figures.
Cyril Ramaphosa, former Secretary-General of the South African National Congress, and former Finnish President Martti Ahtisaari, were named as the monitors of the IRA arms dumps.
The Ulster Unionist Council approved the party rejoining the executive on the basis of the IRA arms offer.
At midnight on 29 May devolution returned.

June   A number of IRA arms dumps were inspected by the international monitors.

July   The final prisoner releases were made under the Good Friday Agreement.

August   For the first time in two years troops returned to the streets of Belfast as a loyalist feud claimed more than a dozen lives.

Loyalist leader Johnny Adair was returned to prison by Northern Ireland Secretary Peter Mandelson on security force advice in an attempt to calm the feud.

October   There was a second inspection of IRA arms dumps by the international monitors.

The UUP's ruling council narrowly supported David Trimble after he announced a plan to exclude Sinn Fein ministers from north-south ministerial meetings unless significant progress was made on decommissioning IRA arms.

November   More loyalist feud killings took place.

December   President Bill Clinton visited both parts of Ireland for the third time.

The loyalist feud was declared to be at an end.

The two Sinn Fein ministers initiated a legal challenge to their exclusion from north-south meetings.

General de Chastelain issued a pessimistic report on the decommissioning process.

2001

January   John Reid became Northern Ireland Secretary after the resignation of Peter Mandelson.

April   A further loyalist death brought the feud toll to 16 in 17 months.

May   For the second time David Trimble wrote a letter of resignation. The resignation was to take effect on 1 July if there had not been significant progress on the decommissioning of IRA weapons.

Bill Clinton, now no longer President, made a fourth visit to Ireland.

The IRA announced that it had established regular contacts with General de Chastelain.

June In the general election and local elections Sinn Fein and the UDP made significant gains at the expense of the SDLP and the UUP.

In the aftermath of the election the UUP's ruling council met and re-elected David Trimble as leader, though there were doubts about his continued survival.

July David Trimble carried out his threat to resign as First Minister.

August Intensive negotiations produced government movement on policing, followed by an announcement that the IRA had suggested an acceptable method for disposing of arms. David Trimble said this was not enough and actual decommissioning was needed.

The government announced a one-day suspension of the Good Friday Agreement, in effect creating another six-week interval for further negotiations.

Sinn Fein and the IRA were pressed to explain what three Irish republicans were doing in the South American country of Colombia.

September Worldwide publicity was given to a loyalist protest in the Ardoyne area of north Belfast aimed at preventing Catholic schoolgirls from attending school.

John Hume announced his decision to stand down as SDLP leader on health grounds.

A second one-day suspension was announced to allow another six-week extension for talks. Trimble threatened to withdraw the UUP ministers from the executive.

The UUP and DUP nominated members to the new Policing Board.

Martin O'Hagan became the first journalist to be killed in the troubles when he was shot by loyalists.

October Northern Ireland Secretary John Reid declared that

the UDA, UFF and LVF ceasefires were over.

The three Unionist Party ministers in the executive resigned to put more pressure on the IRA on decommissioning.

In an event which was hailed as a major breakthrough, Unionist ministers resumed their positions after General de Chastelain announced that the IRA had carried out 'a significant act of decommissioning.' David Trimble announced that he was prepared to resume office.

November   The RUC badge was removed from police stations as the force became the Police Service of Northern Ireland.

David Trimble was re-elected first minister, relying on the votes of some non-Unionist assembly members.

Mark Durkan of the SDLP, who succeeded John Hume as party leader, was elected deputy first minister. The election was followed by scuffles involving assembly members.

The GAA voted to abolish Rule 21 which banned members of the Northern Ireland security forces.

December   Police Ombudsman Nuala O'Loan published a highly critical report on the police investigation of the Omagh bombing, which was in turn strongly criticised by Chief Constable Sir Ronnie Flanagan.

William Stobie, the only person to stand trial in connection with the 1989 killing of lawyer Pat Finucane, was killed by loyalist associates.

The new Policing Board agreed a new badge for the force.

Amid much criticism, particularly from American allies, Gerry Adams visited Cuba and met President Fidel Castro.

2002

January   Thousands attended a march in Londonderry marking the 30th anniversary of Bloody Sunday.

Index

Index

Index